GREAT HUNTING RIFLES

Also by Terry Wieland:

Dangerous-Game Rifles

A View From A Tall Hill: Robert Ruark in Africa
Spiral-Horn Dreams
The Magic of Big Game

Spanish Best: The Fine Shotguns of Spain
Vintage British Shotguns
A Shooter's Guide to Shotguns

GREAT HUNTING RIFLES

RIFLES

Victorian to the Present

TERRY WIELAND

Foreword by Jim Carmichel

Skyhorse Publishing

Skyhorse Publishing books may be purchased in bulk at special discounts for sales promotion, corporate gifts, fund-raising, or educational purposes. Special editions can also be created to specifications. For details, contact the Special Sales Department, Skyhorse Publishing, 307 West 36th Street, 11th Floor, New York, NY 10018 or info@skyhorsepublishing.com.

Skyhorse® and Skyhorse Publishing® are registered trademarks of Skyhorse Publishing, Inc.®, a Delaware corporation.

Visit our website at www.skyhorsepublishing.com.

10 9 8 7 6 5 4 3

Library of Congress Cataloging-in-Publication Data

Names: Wieland, Terry, author. | Carmichel, Jim, author of introduction, etc.
Title: Great hunting rifles : Victorian to the present / Terry Wieland ;
   foreword by Jim Carmichel.
Description: New York, NY : Skyhorse Publishing, 2018. | Includes
   bibliographical references and index.
Identifiers: LCCN 2018020513| ISBN 9781510731691 (hardcover : alk. paper) |
   ISBN 9781510731714 (ebook)
Subjects: LCSH: Hunting rifles--History.
Classification: LCC SK274.2 .W543 2018 | DDC 799.2028/32--dc23
LC record available at https://lccn.loc.gov/2018020513

Cover design by Tom Lau
Cover photo credit: Terry Wieland

Print ISBN: 978-1-5107-3169-1
Ebook ISBN: 978-1-5107-3171-4

Printed in China

For

Clare Irwin and his old Winchester 94

He owed me nothing and gave me everything.

Rifle by Al Biesen, a .270 Winchester built on an FN Deluxe Mauser action, sometime in the 1980s.

TABLE OF CONTENTS

Reading Terry Wieland on guns is like sitting in on a lecture by a popular college professor: After the first few words, you soon begin to share his fascination with the subject and appreciate the way he conveys his enthusiasm. It may be a subject that you at first felt would be of little interest (Ross rifles, for example) but soon find yourself completely absorbed and delighted with what you have discovered. Ross himself is revealed as ambitious, but the possessor of an unlovable personality. And the man with a name and career straight out of a Charles Dickens novel, Arthur Savage, maker of one of the author's favorite rifles, we also discover to be a Barnumesque promoter of the cartridge that cracked the 3,000 feet per second barrier. And on custom guns, a topic obviously dear to his heart, we could just as well be hearing a great art historian compare and contrast Turner with Whistler.

I came to know Terry at some time, almost past remembering, when the major gun makers put on what were known as "New Product Seminars." They would invite a gaggle of writers to some fancy place that offered comfortable hunting and shooting venues, and there we were able to do hands-on testing of whatever new wares the company would be introducing for the coming season. Some such seminars are most memorable as Falstaffian revelries, but some of us seriously wanted to learn what the makers and designers of sporting firearms had to offer. Which is when I became aware of Terry's studious interest in guns and his perceptive way

of reporting what he had learned. A well-earned reputation that was recognized when he became one of the very first writers to receive Leupold's Jack Slack Shooting Sports Writer Of The Year award, which was justly considered the Nobel Prize of Gun Writing.

Terry is one of the very few left standing of the *old school* of professional gun writers. I can think of no greater accolade to offer, and can say it with authority because of my own half-century involvement in the gun-writing trade, including nearly forty years as Shooting Editor of *Outdoor Life*. I came to know nearly all the men whose stories had enchanted me when a boy. Askins Sr., Brown, Keith, Nonte, O'Connor, Page, and Whelen were giants that strode the plains of my boyhood imaginings. In time, I even hunted with some. Guns or hunting, they knew what they were talking about and had the experience to back it up. It was wise to listen to them and not argue. All gone now, bequeathing a legacy of unforgettable bylines. Then, into the decades of the '70s and '80s, came Wieland and other newcomers like me, searching for space in the exalted firmament to pitch our tents: Boddington, Brister, Gresham, Petzal, plus a small fistful of similar souls. Each had new stories and fresh ways of telling them and perhaps a special talent or know-how setting us apart from our fellows. A few of us had the good fortune to be encouraged (abetted) by editors like John Amber (*Gun Digest*), George Martin (*Petersen's Hunting*), and Dave Wolfe (*Handloader, Rifle,*) who could tell by reading half of the first paragraph if the writer had anything to say that would interest their readers.

Those were pretty lush times for gun writers, especially those of us who had regular salaries from magazines like the "Big Three," plus expense accounts that let us more or less hunt whatever, wherever, and (usually) whenever we wanted. We were further enabled by makers of guns, ammo, and everything that went with them, who were invariably eager to supply whatever equipment we deemed essential to the success of our expeditions, home or abroad. Great hunting opportunities were available in those heady times, and worldwide transportation was affordable. Most of us drank deeply from those ever-flowing wells and picked the sweetest of the low-hanging fruit. With such abundances of experience to provide foundations to our opinions, and spice to our writings, we became like those legends of generations past who trod similar trails before us.

The reason those easy times are important to describe is because, in the context of today's shooting and hunting environment, such opportunities scarcely exist—except perhaps for the privileged few who wing the oceans in their private jets. And the makers of guns, who once prided themselves on making a better gun than their competitors, have largely been gobbled up by vast consortia that take comfort only from an ability to make a gun cheaper than their competitors. The bottom line of which is that so few of us are left from the Old School, who, like Terry Wieland, were there when great guns were being made to write about, and great hunting adventures to tell.

There is a whiff of sadness when coming to the last chapter, not just because you wish there were more chapters, but with the realization that writers of such story-telling talent and know-how to back it up are a vanishing breed. Theirs was a golden era, the *belle époque* of gun writing, but it spanned barely a century and Terry Wieland is one of the remaining few.

Jim Carmichel
November 2017

The old-time London gunmakers had an expression they used when a rifle was finished and ready to be delivered. They did not say it was shipped to the client. Instead, it was "sent home," like a newly weaned setter or any other addition to the family. The rifles that left the shops of James Woodward or Holland & Holland were living things and recognized as such.

Great hunting rifles are individuals. They have personalities. Some, I am convinced, have souls. Like a man who has led a long and adventurous life, a rifle's personality is a mix of the skill of the gunmaker's hands, the places it's been, and the owners it's had. Since a fine rifle can last almost indefinitely, it may have outlived four or five hunters, been carried on several continents, or been used for poaching or trophy hunting. It may have traversed the Khyber Pass, strapped to somebody's back, protecting a caravan. It may have lain in wait by a waterhole in Arizona for an old desert ram, or sat in a machan as a tiger growled.

There is an indefinable something in a rifle that was fashioned by skilled, human hands. For years, I have pondered this question, and wondered exactly what it is that makes a rifle from the Edwardian era more interesting to me than even the best of modern products, produced of exotic alloys on CNC machines. My best guess is that older rifles are made from materials that, in their own way, are alive. Carbon steel is a most wondrous material and can be shaped into almost anything by a skilled man with a file. It also rusts,

gets pitted and scratched, yet it can be annealed and hardened, restored and reblued. The same is true of walnut, which blackens with oil and hard use. Walnut can be scratched to a fare-thee-well, and yet be restored to its original glory. A good rifle has more lives than a cat.

You can also tell a lot about a hunter by his rifle, for no piece of hunting equipment is more personal. At its best, the rifle is an extension of the hunter himself and he feels naked without it. There are many examples from history. J. A. Hunter, the famous East African professional, was rarely seen without his .500 Nitro double, riding on his shoulder like a parrot. Jim Corbett, the hunter of man-eating tigers, carried a .275 Rigby the way other men carry a walking stick. Who can imagine David Crockett without Ol' Betsy, or any mountain man without a Hawken?

These are men of legend, but the legends are incomplete without the rifles. As a teenager, more than half a century ago, I fell under their spell and have never emerged. My mentors on the subject, found in books and magazines, were Jack O'Connor, first and foremost, in *Outdoor Life*. Then there was Clyde Ormond, an Idaho writer who is almost forgotten today, and Larry Koller. John T. Amber, the editor of *Gun Digest*, showed me, by publishing a wide-ranging and eclectic selection of articles every year, that every aspect of rifles could be fascinating. Old rifles, new rifles, big ones, little ones—all fascinating, and all part of a grand, captivating, historical picture.

It was Amber who published an article on double rifles by Elmer Keith, and caused me to fall hopelessly and forever in love with his Westley Richards doubles. This was reinforced when I acquired, more or less by accident, John Taylor's *Big Game and Big Game Rifles*. That book is exclusively Africa, big doubles, and dangerous game. In addition to reinforcing my double-rifle lust, it introduced me, on paper at least, to the Cape buffalo.

Above all, however, my guiding light on hunting rifles was Jack O'Connor. I read *Outdoor Life,* joined the Outdoor Life Book Club, and bought all the O'Connor books I could afford. Although my first big-game rifle, acquired secretly at the age of fifteen and smuggled into the house, was a Marlin 336 in .35 Remington, O'Connor turned me into a bolt-action man, and I've remained one to this day. In my teens, the idea of owning one of Al Biesen's custom masterpieces was about as plausible as a date with Kim Novak, but our teenage years consist mostly of dreams anyway. This, however, was a dream I never let go of (a Biesen rifle, not Miss Novak.)

As John Amber unwittingly guided my education, like the fictional Strickland with Kipling's Kim, I made forays into the world of varmint cartridges, military-match target rifles, benchrest shooting, *Schützen* rifles, and black-powder single-shots. Lucian Cary's masterpiece from the 1930s, "The Madman of Gaylord's Corner," reprinted in *Gun Digest*, displayed yet another side of rifles—rifles as science—and really awakened me to the many facets of ballistics. At the age of sixteen, I became a handloader, cobbling together ammunition for my first proper bolt action, a semi-sporterized Enfield P-17.

Through it all, however, big-game hunting—or the possibility, at least—was my real passion, and big-game rifles became my lasting love. Stray as I might, I always returned to them. Although I never thought of it exactly this way, the next fifty years consisted of a never-ending search for the "perfect" hunting rifle.

For me, the perfect rifle must have all the obvious qualities: enough power and range for the job at hand, and sufficient accuracy to make it dependable. It must have everything I need, but not be encumbered with anything I don't. Beyond the obvious, it should not sacrifice a critical quality, such as reliability, for a slight gain in accuracy that might not be of any real value. It must carry comfortably, in one hand or two, handle like a fine bird gun, and be graceful of line, because that translates into effortless handling. Finally, it must be attractive to the eye—a thing of beauty that is always rewarding to look at.

A man's hunting rifle is the direct descendant of the knight's sword of centuries ago—a vital tool of protection and attack, but also a badge that bears his personal seal. In medieval times, such implements were handed down from one generation to the next. Ancestral swords were placed on castle walls alongside shields, blood-stained banners, and trophies of the chase.

Anything so intensely personal is bound to cause arguments, and everyone who has ever killed a big-game animal has firm opinions on rifles. Many of us, like knights of old, learned from fathers, uncles, and grandfathers. Such is the cult of family in America that, if we heard it from Granddad, it must be God's own truth. Unfortunately, the majority of fathers and grandfathers, no matter how well-meaning, often know little or nothing beyond what they heard from *their* forebears. My old and dear friend, Michael McIntosh, who was, until his death in 2010, the acknowledged expert among American writers on the subject of double shotguns, retained throughout his life a bias against Damascus barrels that bordered on obsession. In the face of all evidence—the testimony of

English barrelmakers, European proof houses, and American gunsmiths—Michael railed in print against Damascus as mortally dangerous. His father had drummed this into him, and he was never able to let go of it.

In thirty years in the business of gun writing, I have found that it is unwise, when confronted with such hand-me-down knowledge, to state bluntly that the father in question was wrong, or that his advice was pure hogwash. It's also largely pointless. These firm opinions, right or wrong, are the cause of countless arguments (and not a few fistfights) in which facts are discounted or ignored entirely.

All of this is leading up to a mammoth disclaimer: The hunting rifles included in the pages that follow are, in my opinion, very close to perfect for their intended purposes. This is based on fifty years of reading, shooting, trial, and error. *Lots* of error. Of having custom rifles made from scratch, of existing rifles altered and modified; of experiencing one disappointment after another, only to find exactly what I was looking for, when least expected, sitting forlornly on a dusty gun rack somewhere. Like great horses that come out of nowhere to win the Derby, winners are where you find them. Bloodlines can be an indication, but that's where it ends.

Earlier, I tried to explain what a perfect hunting rifle consists of, but those are just technical aspects: power, accuracy, reliability, and so on. Any rifle can have all of the above, and still fall short. Great hunting rifles, like great racehorses, have spirit and heart. You can feel it when you pick them up. It's agility and fluidity of motion as if, like Pinocchio, they were touched with a wand and given a life of their own.

If this is too esoteric, then you may be one of those poor souls who has not yet been imbued with a love—a real, serious, hopeless love—for fine hunting rifles. But then, since you're holding this book, I suspect you are already one of the Brotherhood of the Afflicted.

* * *

This being a book about rifles for hunting big game, a note is in order as to what, exactly, constitutes hunting. As I write this, there is a fashion for so-called "sniping" of game animals at impossible ranges, using equipment worthy of the space program. Based on everything I have read and been taught, this is unequivocally unethical. It's not illegal, and I'm not saying it should be. There are too many laws and restrictions as it is, most of them written by non- or even anti-hunters.

That does not change the fundamental tenet of ethical, fair-chase hunting, which is that any game animal deserves the utmost respect. Integral to that respect is doing everything you can to ensure a quick and painless death, insofar as that is possible. That means getting yourself to within a reasonable range where a mortal shot is as certain as you can make it. If forced to name a distance beyond which the vast majority of hunters should never attempt a shot, I would say 350 yards, and even that is probably overly generous.

The other trend in modern hunting, especially for white-tailed deer, which is the most popular big-game animal in North America, is shooting from stands, sometimes over feeders or food plots. In this case, ranges are rarely more than one hundred yards, although the odd longer shot occasionally presents itself. For this type of shooting, almost any rifle will do, provided it has enough power and accuracy. You could use a fourteen-pound benchrest rifle if you wanted to.

To me, big-game hunting involves a lot of walking, climbing, and carrying—or at least, the possibility thereof. The most traditional way of hunting in North America is what the English call "stalking" and we call "still hunting." The word "still" is derived from stealth, and that is exactly what it is: stealing through forest and glen, as silently as possible, moving slowly, pausing often, being always ready to take a quick shot at a bounding deer, or settle in for a longer shot if it presents itself. This kind of hunting demands the classic stalking or woods rifle.

Then there is wilderness mountain hunting. This could be backpacking or horseback, with ranges from very short to quite long. Hunting on the plains, for pronghorns for example, you might cruise in a vehicle but carry out the final stalk on foot. Such a stalk often turns into a long-distance game of cat-and-mouse that stretches into hours, with miles of crawling and walking.

In some parts of the East, where the woods are thick, deer hunting is often done by driving or pushing deer with dogs. Hunters set up along a deer trail and hope an animal happens along, but they walk to get there and, with luck, walking back they'll be dragging a fat buck. Again, a job for a stalking or woods rifle.

In Alaska, hunting brown bears, the cover may be impossibly thick, or you might get a long shot across a tidal flat. In Africa, chasing elephant or Cape buffalo, ranges are sure to be relatively short or, in the case of a charge, measured in feet. The dangerous-game rifle, for use in such circumstances, is as specialized a hunting rifle as you are likely to find. Its specific requirements are not unlike those of a woods rifle for deer, but it's much more powerful and brings with it a whole different set of problems.

In these pages, you will find deer rifles, mountain rifles, and antelope rifles; there is one rifle that was India's favorite for tigers, and another tailor-made for chamois in the Austrian Alps. Some will have riflescopes, some not; in age, they range from one made circa 1878 to the most recent, put together in the 1980s. We do not claim that these are the *only* great hunting rifles ever made. Far from it. But they are representative, and the one quality they all share is that indefinable something that sets a gilt-edged hunting rifle apart from a mere firearm.

Also, these are specific rifles, not representatives of a class or particular make. We don't say "the Savage 99 was a great hunting rifle," we say "this Savage 99 E, a .250-3000 made in 1922, is a great hunting rifle." Many 99s were good and some were not so good, but only a few were great. That, really, is the point of this book: Like the hunters who use them, great hunting rifles are individuals.

Terry Wieland
Fenton, Missouri
November 1, 2017

ACKNOWLEDGMENTS

The education of a rifleman takes many years and wanders down many paths. Mine began with an old deer hunter named Clare Irwin, who owned a well-worn Winchester 94. Clare was a sophisticate. I knew that because he had fitted out his 94 with a Lyman tang sight. He introduced me to his rifle, took me deer hunting the first time, and we stayed good friends until his death, thirty years later.

Books played a major part in my education—books by men like Jack O'Connor and John Taylor, and the annual *Gun Digest*, when it was edited by John T. Amber.

Later came conversations with fellow riflemen and hunters: Tony Henley and Robin Hurt, in Africa; Jack Carter in Texas; Tom Turpin, Dave Petzal, John Barsness, Dave Scovill, and John Sundra in America. Jim Carmichel, with his *Book of the Rifle*, changed some of my ideas as I began writing for magazines, and they stayed changed. Older writers, like O'Connor, were forbidding characters to me, dwelling on some rifle-making Olympus, discussing cartridges with Zeus. When I met Jim Carmichel the first time, I half-expected thunderbolts to spring from his fingertips; instead, I found him to be a gentleman of the old school, and that is the best kind.

Riflemakers contributed a lot, both those I knew personally and those I only read about, or whose creations I had the good fortune to see, handle, and sometimes shoot. There was Siegfried Trillus and Edwin von Atzigen, the former of German extraction, the other Swiss, and both as dedicated to rifles and riflemaking as it is possible to be. Through O'Connor, I learned about Al Biesen, and later owned one of Biesen's rifles. And a lovely thing it is, too, but the .450 Ackley that Siegfried built for me after my first safari in Africa is every bit as fine as my Biesen, and that is a compliment to both.

As for the rest, well, James Woodward, Henry Holland, and John Rigby, of course I never knew. Nor Paul Mauser, Ferdinand von Mannlicher, John Browning, or Arthur Savage. Would that I had. Not sure about Sir Charles Ross, though.

My education as a rifleman aside, Clare Irwin taught me something invaluable about hunting: One November day, it was blowing and snowing outside, as I recall, and the boat was bumping up against the dock. We were in by the fire, thawing out after a long walk back, and the coffee was just starting to bubble. Clare turned to me and said, "You know, I don't really care if I get a deer. I just like to be up here, hunting them."

Clare Irwin had killed a lot of deer out of that cabin over forty years, whereas I had yet to get my first, and so I didn't really understand what he was talking about. But that was then.

Cape buffalo in Tanzania, with .450 Ackley built by Siegfried Trillus on an FN Supreme Mauser action.

INTRODUCTION: THE PERFECT HUNTING RIFLE

Shooting writers are fond of blanket statements such as "the Winchester 94 is a great hunting rifle." Or the Model 70, or the Remington 700. What the writer usually means is that *some* 94s, Model 70s, and 700s are great hunting rifles, depending on the caliber, barrel length, and stock shape. There are many factors to consider in the making of a great hunting rifle, and getting any one of them wrong can result in a gun that just isn't very good.

There are many examples of this in the history of the modern big-game rifle. We will briefly look at a couple. One that is often singled out is the Savage 99 lever action, a rifle that was born in 1895 and stayed in production for almost a century. During this time, it was made in a bewildering variety of models, calibers, barrel lengths, and configurations. Cataloging them all has defied the efforts of firearms historians for years, and even now no one knows exactly how many of which model were made, or when.

During that time, the 99 proved itself to be strong, accurate, durable, and dependable. Out of the hundreds of models and variations, however, very few are what I would call great hunting rifles. They were all reasonably good, some were better than others, but only a few were "great." Why? Savage always seemed to fit the wrong barrel for a particular cartridge, or misshape the stock. In only one instance, to the best of my knowledge, did the planets align and everything come together in a package that was a little gem. That occurred in the 1920s, and did not last long. The Model E from that era, in .250-3000, capitalized

on the virtues of both rifle and cartridge, minimized their respective drawbacks, and resulted in a stalking rifle that is frankly extraordinary. We look at this rifle in detail in chapter VIII.

An almost endless list of factors can sink the best-laid plans. These include barrel length, rifling twist, stock shape, stock material, safety position and operation, overall weight, action length, the relationship of action length to chamber and maximum overall cartridge length, and a host of ever-more-arcane features. To create a hunting rifle with no flaws—nothing at all we would like to change—requires not only mechanical and technical knowledge, and great attention to detail, but an understanding of ballistics, ergonomics, and shooting itself. Changing any single thing can result in a domino effect that renders an otherwise good rifle practically unusable.

Also, nothing can be done in isolation; we must look at every other feature. For example, when Winchester introduced the .264 Winchester Magnum in 1958, it was originally chambered in the standard Model 70. When that didn't sell well, it was offered in the light, short-barreled Featherweight. It was a disaster. Recoil was very unpleasant, and with the short barrel, the claimed velocity was unattainable while the muzzle blast was a beast.

Making changes to a rifle to accommodate the marketing department, or the company sales force, or the corporate lawyers, is rarely a good idea, because they never take these interrelationships into account. The Savage .250-3000 cartridge is an excellent example. When Charles Newton designed it in 1914, he intended it to shoot a 100-grain bullet at 2,800 feet per second (fps.) The marketing department, however, wanted to advertise a velocity of 3,000 fps which, ever since Sir Charles Ross and his sensational .280 Ross, had been the Golden Fleece of ballistics. To accomplish this, bullet weight was reduced to 87 grains and barrels were given a twist rate of one turn in fourteen inches (1:14). This twist rate limited accuracy in any bullet weight heavier than 87 grains, and also had an impact on effective barrel lengths. Only the intrinsic excellence of the .250-3000 allowed it to overcome these obstacles and become one of the great hunting cartridges of the twentieth century. Without these hurdles, it could well have become as much a standard chambering as the .270 Winchester.

BARRELS, BORES, AND TWIST RATES

In the simplest terms, accuracy depends on the rate of twist of the rifling. The effective twist rate depends on velocity, and velocity depends on barrel length. As I write that, I can hear the chorus of "Well, yes, but . . ." from every rifleman across the land. Of course, the barrel must be straight, the bore good, and the bullet accurate to begin with. My point is that the best bullet, in the finest bore, can be rendered unusable by the wrong combination of barrel length, twist, and velocity.

The purpose of rifling is to impart spin to the projectile and stabilize it in flight. This is the basis of accuracy. It used to be believed that bullets could be over-stabilized, so great attention was paid to having a Goldilocks twist—not too fast, not too slow. In the days of black-powder fouling and cast bullets, twists were generally much slower because a lead bullet could strip in the rifling (not "take" the rifling and spin, but simply plow on through leaving a trail of lead fouling). Such fouling is no longer an issue, and it is now generally believed that over-stabilization is a myth, or at least its effects vastly over-estimated.

Here are some general rules:

Graph that allows calculation of appropriate twist rate for a particular bullet at a given velocity. This graph was printed in the 1962 Gun Digest, *in an article on twist by John Maynard. Today, computer programs for calculating twist are freely available on the internet.*

- The *longer* the bullet, the *faster* the twist required.
- The *slower* the bullet for its length, the *faster* the twist required.
- The *shorter* the barrel, the *lower* the velocity, and hence the *faster* the twist required.

By the same token, a slow twist can be overcome by increasing velocity.

The effects and ramifications of these laws of ballistics spread out like ripples in a pool to affect many other aspects of the rifle. If the magazine is too short (in the case of a box magazine) to allow sufficient cartridge length, either the use of a long, heavy bullet becomes impossible, or it must be seated so deeply that it takes up usable powder space, and velocity is reduced below the minimum required for the given rifling. As a result, you are forced either to use a bullet that is too light, or accept mediocre accuracy.

Comparing two modern 6.5mm's with the old originals, from left: 6.5 Grendel, 6.5 Arisaka, 6.5 Carcano, 6.5x54 Mannlicher-Schönauer, 6.5 Dutch Mannlicher, 6.5x55 Swedish, 6.5x58 Mauser, 6.5 Creedmoor. Long, heavy bullets required very fast rifling twists. The modern trend is to lighter bullets at higher velocities.

In the early bolt-action military rifles in Europe, the 6.5 mm (.264) diameter was popular, using heavy bullets—typically 160 grains. These were often referred to as "pencil-like" because the bullets protruded so far out of the case. Rifles like the Swedish Mauser, chambered for the 6.5x55 Swedish, had a rifling twist of around one turn in eight inches (1:8). This was extremely fast for the time, but necessary to stabilize the long, heavy bullet at relatively low velocities. When these cartridges were chambered in carbines, either military or sporting, velocities were reduced even further, but the fast twist still stabilized the bullet out to reasonable distances.

This lesson was either lost on the engineers at Savage, or simply ignored, when they introduced the .250-3000 in 1915. Twist was 1:14, which would stabilize the standard 87-grain bullet at the advertised velocity of 3,000 fps, but would not if the hunter wanted to use the more effective 100-grain bullet instead. Savage compounded this problem when they brought out the .250-3000 in various carbines, with barrels as short as 20 inches or even, on special order, 18 inches. With a twist of 1:14, and velocity drastically reduced because of the shorter barrel, accuracy suffered. Many of these short-barreled rifles were takedowns, popular in the early part of the twentieth century. They acquired a reputation for inaccuracy, blamed on allegedly "coming loose," when the real culprit was the velocity-twist equation combined with their stubby barrels.

One point should be added. The early 6.5s acquired a reputation for excellent killing power, mostly due to the sectional density of their long bullets, and dependable penetration even on elephant skulls. When later 6.5 mm magnum cartridges tried to increase velocity, it was necessary to use slower-burning powders. The slower the powder, the longer the barrel required to utilize its force. Therefore, combining a bigger case with more powder and a heavier bullet all came to naught if the barrel was too short.

In the days before chronographs, hawkers of wildcat cartridges, and even many factory ones, could claim velocities that simply did not exist. The .264 Winchester Magnum, and its use in the short-barreled Featherweight model in the early 1960s, is a notorious example of all these factors coming together and sinking what is otherwise an excellent cartridge.

SHAPE AND FORM

The shape of a hunting rifle is important, and not just to please the eye of its owner or promote sales. The concept of graceful design is integral to tools of all kinds, and has been throughout history. Great original inventions are refined, usually in two ways: they are made simpler and more reliable, and they are made more graceful and ergonomic.

Ergonomics is a word that was coined in 1857 by a Polish scientist. It's derived from the Greek words for "work" and "natural law," and was introduced to English in 1949, during a meeting at the British Admiralty, which led to the formation of The Ergonomics Society. In North America, it's generally taken to mean "human factors" and how those affect, positively or negatively, the use of any utensil, from cars to coffee pots. Another term would be ease of use, which has roughly the same meaning.

Imagine, if you will, a boat propelled by humans, all lining the rail and wielding paddles. The designers make the gunwales high, to prevent waves washing over. They make the paddles short, because that gives the paddlers the most leverage. In theory, wonderful. In practice, disastrous. The paddlers are positioned too high, their arms are too short, the paddles don't reach the water, and the boat goes nowhere. The designers might argue that the fault lies with the paddlers, whose arms are too short. Had the designers tried using the boat themselves, they would have seen this problem and corrected it.

To continue with this analogy, the canoe is an ancient form of transportation, and over many centuries has been refined into a masterpiece of simplicity. A canoe can be propelled by almost anything—even by the canoeist's bare hands, if need be. Generally, however, some sort of paddle is used. This paddle could be a length of two-by-four, a flagpole, a walking stick; in theory, one could even use a railroad tie. Obviously, all of these present some difficulty either in manipulating them to good effect, or in the minimal efficacy they would have. And so, over many centuries, the canoe paddle has also been refined, and paddles can be found in any sporting-goods catalog.

Just as there are serious shooters, there are serious canoeists, and I've known a few. Their attitude toward store-bought, generic paddles is about the same as mine toward rifles—which is to say, highly critical of the most arcane points. Almost all of them have custom paddles made by paddle-carving *artistes*. They want the right length, a grip on the end that fits their hand, at just the right angle; it must be the correct weight, and the circumference of the shaft must be correct for their hands. It must be made of a wood that affords strength without excessive weight. The shape of the blade must be just right. Some want square corners on the blade, others want it rounded—and in fact, I am given to understand, those features are determined by use: Will the paddle be used by the canoeist in the bow, or the one at the stern who steers the craft? Or, by a *lone* canoeist in the stern, without a front paddler? Will the canoe be heavy-laden, or a light, bobbing craft for competition? I thought I knew a little about canoe paddles. As it turns out, I really knew nothing.

Some of the serious canoeists I've met, given the right paddle, could make a canoe dance like a ballerina, cross a calm lake like a racehorse, or negotiate the most treacherous rapids at warp speed. These same standards of application, usability, and ergonomics apply equally to hunting rifles.

* * *

Sometimes usability is dictated by the technology itself, and the current state of a technology might limit any advance in ease of use. The ancient matchlock firearms are good examples, and from the introduction of gunpowder in the 1200s until around 1790, guns remained clumsy, awkward, heavy, and difficult to use. Little attention was given to form, shape, weight, or fine detail until

A Joseph Manton fowling piece. The Mantons turned flintlock guns into graceful and ergonomic masterpieces, preparing the way for two centuries of superb craftsmanship in rifles and shotguns.

So finely were Manton guns made, inside and out, that locks like these found their way into museums of applied arts. Beau Brummell ranked his Manton fowling pieces on a level with his collection of Sèvres porcelain.

the advent of the Mantons in London. John and Joseph Manton are credited with being the first to treat a firearm not just as a tool, but as a work of art, with the art being in the function of the gun itself. It was this transition that made guns more usable. The immediate result was the rise of wingshooting, beginning with the early box-bird matches. Without guns that handled smoothly and well, shooters were limited to sitting targets. With the Mantons' masterpieces, operation became smooth and reliable, handling was a dream, and the whole concept of shooting at moving targets became realistic.

The entire London gun trade followed in the wake of John and Joseph Manton, and this resulted in several generations of guns that are unquestionably the most graceful—and ergonomic—ever made.

Researching further, we find that while the Mantons introduced the ergonomic concept to fowling pieces, it had already been applied to duelling pistols by makers such as Samuel Nock and John Rigby. Given the stakes, nothing was added to a duelling pistol that would not increase its efficiency and deadliness, but nor was anything omitted. The ability to shoot a duelling pistol accurately and instinctively (to say nothing of reliably) was highly prized. Duelling pistols from the 1780s and '90s are masterpieces of form, function, and grace.

An interesting sidelight on the work of the Manton brothers comes from George "Beau" Brummell, the Englishman who became the arbiter of good taste in everything from men's fashion to public deportment during the Napoleonic Era. The Beau had infallible taste, and his influence lives on in what is, today, proper evening dress for men. We attend black-tie dinners wearing almost the exact outfit decreed by Brummell two hundred years ago. He was most assuredly *not* a "dandy," as he is often characterized, but was in fact the polar opposite. "The surest way to be out of fashion tomorrow," he wrote, "is to be at the height of fashion today." Brummell's formula for proper attire was sober colors, the finest materials, and perfect tailoring. In men's evening dress, he dictated fashion and good taste for the centuries, not just for the next gala. When he died, and his estate was listed for auction, it included, along with his collection of Sèvres porcelain, three Manton fowling pieces. They were, to Brummell's discerning eye, the epitome of perfect form and function.

Just as Brummell's evening dress lives on, so do many of the Mantons' innovations in gun style and design, reflected to this day in Holland & Hollands and Purdeys.

A Safari-grade custom .270 Weatherby—a harmonious marriage of stock, action, barrel, riflescope, and scope mounts. It is beautiful as well as graceful.

As flintlocks gave way to percussion, and percussion to central-fire cartridges, the evolving technology put a strain on gunmakers to maintain, or regain, the level of ergonomics they had previously achieved. The question was how to marry new technology to proven form. Somehow they managed it, although often there was a lag, resulting in guns that were technologically superior but ergonomically inferior. This explains the fairly frequent instances of prominent shooters clinging to older guns with demonstrably inferior firing qualities, because these shortcomings were more than compensated for by their superior weight and handling. Sir Frederick Milbank, one of the greatest of English wingshooters, clung to his Westley Richards pinfires for years after they had been superseded by central-fire, and both Lord Ripon and King George V remained devotees of hammer guns long after hammers had been almost completely replaced by hammerless.

English firms like Holland & Holland had an advantage in designing their rifles, both doubles and single-shots to begin with, and later bolt-action magazine rifles. Their clients would visit the shop and speak personally with the proprietor, as well as with the stockers, barrelmakers, actioners, and others who were actually building the rifle. It allowed them to tailor it precisely in terms of weight, balance, and ease of use and handling. These luxuries—for luxuries they are, in an age of factories and mass production—are not available to the workmen in a big factory, turning out dozens or hundreds of rifles a day. In such cases, fine ergonomic design was sometimes good luck; other times, it resulted from the fact that the workmen were shooters themselves and knew what a good rifle should feel like. As well, early factories employed skilled men to do the final fitting and adjustment of such things

as trigger pull, and if they saw a problem of any kind, they could remedy it before the rifle left the shop.

The problem of ideal form is not one of the stock alone, nor of the barrel and action alone. It requires a harmonious marriage of stock, action, and barrel, and even accoutrements like sights, riflescopes, and slings. A poor rifle can be improved by restocking, but a new stock rarely makes it perfect. The same is true of rebarreling. Assembling all of these disparate parts into mechanical perfection requires either a team of craftsmen who know exactly what is needed and how to do it, working together, or the efforts of one all-around gunmaker who is not only skilled with metal and wood, but knows how to combine them.

You would think, then, that the simple answer is the custom rifle: Have it made exactly the way you want it, and it will be perfect. Alas, no. It is sometimes the answer, when you get a riflemaker who knows what he's doing, and understands what you want. Unfortunately, too often we go to so-called riflemakers who consider themselves *artistes*, who believe they are creating works of art, and have no idea what a good hunting rifle should feel like. Instead, they want the public to admire their exquisite checkering, the fine inletting of the stock, or the gadgets they contrive. The latter may be ingenious, but just as often are completely useless.

If, for example, you pick up a custom rifle by Al Biesen, Jack O'Connor's "genius of Spokane," you know immediately that you have in your hands a rifle made for big-game hunting. Conversely, pick up one by any number of other custom riflemakers, and it feels like just another rifle. It's undoubtedly finely crafted, but not crafted for hunting. Some of these men not only don't hunt, they never shoot a rifle themselves

This custom hunting rifle, built by Al Biesen, is a perfect balance of cartridge and action—a .270 Winchester combined with an FN Deluxe. Completed in the mid-1980s, it includes several custom touches, including a Model 70-style wing safety crafted by Biesen himself, and fitted with a Canjar trigger.

great wine. Until you've experienced it, you can't describe it, but you will remember that feel forevermore, and measure every rifle against it.

It has been known for centuries that gracefulness and ease of use go hand in hand, and this principle has been applied to swords, teapots, buggy whips, ships' wheels, walking sticks, and duelling pistols. Its value and importance should never be underestimated. It is integral to, and inseparable from, the creation of a great big-game rifle.

THE RIFLE ACTION

The action is the heart of any rifle, and most custom projects begin with the selection of an action and proceed from there. Over the past two centuries, any number of action types have been used to build exceedingly fine rifles. In this book, you will find double rifles, lever actions, and bolt actions. There are no single-shots, not because I dislike single-shots, but because I have never owned one that measured up. There is no denying, however, that some exquisite hunting rifles have been built on single-shot actions, to the very highest levels of quality. In fact, I tried to have one built on a Dakota Model 10 action. It was a .250-3000, stocked with a piece of extraordinary walnut. I no longer have it, for the simple reason that when I received the finished rifle, it was not the magic wand I expected. It was simply lifeless—as alluring as a mannequin of a beautiful woman. In fairness, the same thing has happened to me with several custom bolt actions.

It is possible to go wrong with an action, and doom the rifle from the start. For example, if you were to obtain an Oberndorf Magnum Mauser action and then chamber it for the .243 Winchester, you would have an unnecessarily heavy rifle, probably with lamentable balance. Conversely, you could get a Mauser *Kurz* (short)

if they can avoid it. How could they possibly be expected to know what a rifle should feel like?

For that matter, how can a hunter be expected to know this, if he has never had the opportunity to handle a really fine rifle? The human body is very adaptable, as witness how well some shooters have done with rifles and shotguns with lousy balance, reluctant opening and closing, bad trigger pulls, and stocks that are too short. Hefting a fine rifle is like the first time you taste a really action, chamber it for the .284 Winchester, and find yourself doomed to substandard performance because the magazine would not accept a cartridge long enough to allow the use of heavy bullets with appropriate powder charges. This latter has happened many times in the history of factory rifles, generally as a result of trying to offer as many options (calibers) as possible, while at the same time keeping costs down by trying to make one action size do everything.

This is exactly what happened when Savage introduced the .300 Savage in 1920, and tried to duplicate .30-06 performance in a short cartridge and short action. It was, and is, a fine cartridge, but fell short of its potential. It was hamstrung from the beginning by the Savage designers, not unlike the .250-3000 with its slow twist rate, five years earlier.

For these reasons, a great hunting rifle begins with the action, and the choice of a cartridge, and progresses from there.

WEIGHT AND BALANCE

Just as a rifle can be too heavy, it can also be too light. Generally speaking, an ideal big-game rifle weighs between seven pounds, complete, on the light side, and up to maybe ten pounds in heavier calibers, with twelve to fourteen pounds in a double rifle for big elephant cartridges like the .577 Nitro Express. A rifle's *avoirdupois* plays two important roles: It dictates how steady the rifle can be held to make a shot, and it dampens recoil. Also, in bigger calibers, the rifle must have strength (and hence weight) to withstand the repeated destructive force of firing.

After weight, the most important consideration is its distribution. How the poundage is distributed either contributes to or detracts from the positive qualities mentioned above. There is no absolute weight that is ideal for every rifle, in every caliber. And, of course, personal preference and physical ability come into it. A man who backpacks up and down mountains will want a rifle that is relatively light, but if, after all that, he has to take a shot when he is out of breath, and misses because the rifle lacks the heft to hold steady, then he hasn't gained much.

Generally speaking, the more weight there is in the barrel, the steadier the hold. The more weight in the buttstock, however, the shakier the hold, and also the greater the muzzle jump. Weight should be distributed so the rifle has good balance and a lively feel. This will promote better instinctive shooting, such as when you jump a whitetail at close range and have to make a shot without thinking, the way you would shoot at a flushing grouse. You want a rifle that will come up smartly, point naturally, and swing almost on its own.

Since the adoption of the bolt-action rifle as the standard sporter, roughly a century ago, tastes and preferences in weight have come down steadily. In the 1920s, a Springfield sporter with iron sights, weighing nine pounds, was not unusual. Today, such a rifle would be completely unacceptable to the majority of hunters, who think in terms of seven to eight pounds, including scope, sling, and full magazine. Once you dip below six pounds in a big-game rifle, however, you are asking for trouble. It will flutter around like a wand and kick too much, and you may have sacrificed either strength or accuracy to shed the pounds. If shortening the barrel has been part of the weight-reduction plan, you will also be sacrificing velocity.

SIGHTS AND STOCKS

The sights and the stock must be considered together, because the shape of the stock will be largely dictated by the primary sighting equipment. When brought to the shoulder and snuggled down into a secure shooting position, the stock should align the eye exactly with the sights. A perfectly fitted stock should come to the shoulder with your eyes closed and, when you open them, they should be in position to shoot with a minimum of adjustment.

The enduring problem since the 1920s, when riflescopes began to come into common use, has been creating a stock that puts the eye high enough for a scope, yet low enough to use the iron sights. This is a problem that has not been absolutely solved to this day, although Steyr-Mannlicher came the closest to doing so in the 1950s. In a way, however, it is being solved by default, as the use of iron sights becomes more and more rare.

Some ingenious German and Austrian gunmakers, who fitted detachable scopes to their rifles, would sometimes make a movable comb for their stocks. This popped up automatically when the scope was attached, and dropped back down when it was removed. Aside from the expense and sheer finickiness of such an arrangement, it did not lend itself to mass production.

This, of course, is not the only requirement of the stock, but it is a major one. The stock also plays an important part in managing recoil.

Generally, a stock whose length of pull (distance from the trigger to the center of the buttplate) is too short, or has excessive drop, will magnify recoil. Lengthening and straightening the buttstock reduces it.

The pistol grip, if there is one, can be either too steep or too gradual; if too steep, it makes it slow to get into shooting position; if too gradual, it's quick to mount but makes trigger control difficult. Similarly, if the circumference of the grip is too great, it is hard to reach the trigger, and makes the whole rifle seem cumbersome.

Unfortunately, the wrist of the stock is considered to be its weakest point, and because of that, most modern gunmakers make it thicker than really necessary. This is a mistaken belief—or at least exaggerated. Consider how slender the handle of a baseball bat is—much slimmer than a rifle's wrist—and then how much punishment a bat takes before breaking. It's far more than is ever applied to a rifle grip, unless your horse rolls on it or you run over it with your pickup truck. Provided the grain of the walnut is correct through the wrist, it's extremely strong for its size, and with materials like wood laminates or composites, there is no excuse whatever for suffering with a bulky pistol grip.

The forend, which is where the forward hand holds the rifle, has similar requirements. It can

This early Mannlicher-Schönauer exhibits many features of an excellent hunting rifle stock, with a slim forend, a trim, moderate pistol grip, and just the right drop to accommodate its iron sights. Chambered for the 8x57 JS, the drop at heel and comb would not accentuate its recoil unduly.

A .300 Weatherby, one of the last made in Germany by J. P. Sauer, with an Alaskan brown bear taken on Montague Island in 1988. Many dislike the Weatherby's California styling, but ergonomically it works extremely well.

be, in cross-section, like a huge flattened French loaf (a typical target stock,) a triangular slab unfit for human hands (benchrest stock,) an ungainly and awkward "dual purpose" stock, usually called a beavertail, or one that is far too small, usually referred to by anti-slim-stock writers as a toothpick. Early European stocks were very slim, modern American ones are generally too thick and bulky. Given a choice, I'll take the slim one.

Looking at the forend in cross-section, the ideal is either a modest pear shape or a horizontal oval. A beavertail is an oversized horizontal oval, of course, but reduced to a reasonable size it makes a very ergonomic stock. A perfectly round forend is also good, provided it is not too thick. Many modern custom gunstocks have a forend shaped in a vertical oval. This gives large, flat side surfaces, on which it is easy for a checkering *artiste* to apply an elaborate pattern. Alas, it means the only way of holding the forend firmly to help arrest muzzle jump is by pressing the fingertips into the checkering. The

pear-shaped, round, triangular, or horizontal oval allows the fingertips to wrap comfortably around the forend and hold it firmly without having to white-knuckle it.

As a general rule, the less drop at both heel and comb the better for holding a rifle firmly and reducing felt recoil. The American style of stock design flowed originally from the Kentucky long rifle, which was shot exclusively from an upright position. It had so much drop it was impossible to shoot any other way. This style was transferred to plains rifles like the Hawken, then to early lever actions like the Winchester '73. *Schützen* rifles, so popular for off-hand matches in the late 1800s and early 1900s, had similar stock configurations. It was not until the 1920s, as stockmakers began extensive remodelling of Springfield bolt actions, and the bolt rifle began its inexorable ascent, that what we now know as the "American classic" style emerged. It was developed by stockmaking immortals like Alvin Linden and Bob Owen, and today is *de rigueur* for any high-dollar custom rifle. As with any other style, however, the individual features of American classic can be overdone, to the detriment of overall ergonomics.

Jack O'Connor often quoted a rule that originated with Morgan Holmes, a New Jersey stockmaker. It stated that the lines on a fine rifle stock should be either straight or segments of a circle. Also, those lines should blend together into an overall design that is graceful to the eye.

In the 1950s, Roy Weatherby burst on the scene in a big way with what came to be known as the "California look." This was, in many ways, the antithesis of American classic, and when anyone mentions it today, it's usually to deride such aesthetic atrocities as white-line spacers, skip-line checkering, ivory inlays, and varnished wood as flashy as a cheap blonde. Generally, they also mention such exaggerated features as high Monte Carlo combs, with a forward slant to the cheekpiece.

I acquired my first Weatherby rifle in 1975, one of the last made in Germany by J. P. Sauer, and its stock was one of the most comfortable and ergonomic I have ever found—far more so, in fact, than many fully custom, so-called American classics. The forend, flat on the underside and triangular in cross section, was very slim and could be held firmly but effortlessly—essential with a cartridge like the .300 Weatherby. Similarly, while the pistol grip was steep, it was very slim. Overall, the rifle was very handy and not at all cumbersome. Weatherby insists that their stocks today are identical, and that the dimensions have not changed in forty years. Without calling anyone a liar, I beg to differ. New Weatherby stocks have the same general configuration, it's true, but they are toned down, with corners rounded and angles modified. More important, however, they are thicker and beefier overall. So, while the original California look was gaudy and untraditional, it was also very usable. It was no accident, I believe, that Roy Weatherby himself was a serious rifleman who knew his stuff, and the man who designed that stock, Leonard Mews, was an extremely fine stockmaker, albeit one with rather far-out tastes.

If you look at the traditional Weatherby stock, you will find that Mews applied Morgan Holmes's rule. He used more straight lines than most, and fewer radii, but the overall effect is very graceful and appealing. And, very ergonomic.

Weatherby rifles, except for the .460, are absolutely not intended for use with any sights except a scope, which allowed them to use that exaggerated Monte Carlo comb and make no allowance for iron sights. This was not an option for any mass-production riflemaker, like Winchester or Remington, that sold rifles with iron sights already in place. One partial solution is to make the stock with as slight a drop as the iron sights will allow, and then mount the scope as low as possible. This pays dividends in other ways, promoting a very firm, steady hold, and bringing the line of sight down as close as possible to the position of the forward hand. As any shotgunner knows, that makes for the best possible instinctive shooting. Another approach—ingenious in its simplicity—is to make the iron sights higher. By putting the front sight on a ramp and the rear on an island or quarter-rib, you solve the problem, and they do not in any way interfere with the scope.

Some other stock features, such as a forend tip, are purely a matter of taste and not performance. The same is more or less true of grip caps, but the buttplate is another question entirely. Modern custom gunmakers often insist on a steel buttplate, sometimes with engraving to match that on the action. Custom gunmaker Lenard Brownell is quoted as saying that a fine custom rifle with a recoil pad is like a man in evening dress wearing rubber boots. Well, if it's pouring rain, that's actually very practical.

Aside from the real benefits of a good recoil pad on a hard-kicking rifle, there are other good reasons to have a recoil pad (or a hard rubber one) on a big-game rifle. One is standing it up against a tree. Most of us are reluctant to do that if the rifle is wearing a finely engraved custom buttplate. Even the old utilitarian steel buttplates are not very good for that, because they slip. Also, in a pinch, where you find yourself having to use your rifle as an alpenstock, a rubber pad will grip the ground better. If the pad gets battered and tattered, it's an easy matter to have it replaced. This is not the case with either an engraved steel one or the steel skeleton buttplates so beloved of stockmaking *artistes*. Aesthetically, we have mostly dispensed with the ugly ventilated pads and white spacers of years past, and today's solid black or brown ones look very becoming, as well as being very effective.

TRIGGERS AND TRIGGER PULLS

The single most important factor in shooting a rifle accurately is the quality of the trigger pull. No matter what else you have, if the trigger is heavy, rough, and inconsistent, you can never shoot it well. It's possible to adapt to virtually everything else about a rifle, but not that.

There are many types of triggers, and you will find several different ones on rifles in this book. There are single and double triggers, single-stage and double-stage triggers, and both single and double set triggers. Most target rifles have light, crisp, single-stage triggers. The old double-stage was found mostly on military rifles, like the Mauser 98, and those were retained on some sporterized military rifles. The Mannlicher-Schönauer originally was fitted with a double set

The Dayton-Traister was one of several fine replacement triggers that allowed the wholesale conversion of military Mauser 98s into fine sporting rifles.

trigger, and single triggers only became an option later in its production life.

Double triggers, as found on almost all big double rifles, are one of several features that have been demonized to the point of absurdity by American gun writers over the past fifty years. Others include automatic safeties, as found on most English double shotguns, and Damascus barrels. Double triggers, especially, have been condemned as "agents of the devil," which seems to be going a little far. Others have suggested banning automatic safeties by constitutional amendment.

Some shooters are given to flat statements such as, "I just can't shoot a gun with double triggers." Personally, I find that puzzling. Looking down my gun rack, I see both single and double triggers, set triggers, and two-stage triggers. I switch back and forth with no trouble whatsoever.

For a while, it was all the rage to have any double gun with two triggers converted to a Miller single trigger, which were ugly in the extreme and, according to reports, questionable in operation. This outrage was perpetrated on any number of fine English doubles that emigrated to the New World. This is purely an opinion, but I believe anyone who is a competent shooter can adjust to any type of trigger if he puts his mind to it—provided, of course, that it has a decent trigger pull. Certainly, if you acquire a rifle with a particular type of trigger, I would be careful about rushing to replace it with something you perceive to be preferable. It might not be, and you could find that out too late.

The key question with any trigger, again, is quality of release. This has become a rather thorny legal issue, because the last three generations of corporate lawyers have concluded that the way to avoid litigation is to fit firearms with triggers that are abominably heavy. This is the same line of logic that decrees that a sharp knife is more dangerous than a dull one when, in fact, the opposite is true.

Since at least the 1930s, after-market replacement triggers have been manufactured for military rifles like the Mauser 98, as well as better triggers to replace some poor factory ones. Some famous names include Timney, Canjar, and Dayton-Traister. More recent ones are the Jewell and the Jard. One particularly interesting replacement trigger is made by Paul Dressel—a copy of the old Model 70 trigger, which was highly praised, made to fit the Mauser 98. As with any product, some of these after-market triggers are better than others. It appears to my cynical eye that the dark hand of corporate lawyerhood has, if only indirectly, affected the operation of many of these, as well.

Some older triggers were famous, such as those found on Sako rifles in the mid-'80s. It had a release, it was said, like a "glass rod breaking." That particular analogy dates back a long way, but it's still apt for anyone who has ever actually snapped a glass rod. With the disappearance of glass swizzle sticks, a better one for today might be the snapping of an icicle. Those Sako triggers were, indeed, astonishing—and they came that way straight from the factory.

Another legal bugaboo has been the possibility of adjusting triggers for pull weight, creep, and over-travel. It seems that if you make a trigger adjustable, and someone makes it too light and hurts himself, then the manufacturer is liable. If, on the other hand, you do not provide an adjustable trigger, it either puts off potential buyers or forces them to get a replacement like a Timney.

Sako triggers seem to have slipped, and the new factory-trigger champ is the Blaser family of companies, which also includes J. P. Sauer and Mauser. The new (as of 2017) Mauser 98 has the finest factory trigger pull I have ever experienced—better, even, than the legendary Sako. It releases like snapping a stem of fine crystal, and the first one I tested had a trigger pull of two pounds twelve ounces. From pull to pull, it varied no more than an ounce either way, nine times out of ten.

And the worst? The two worst rifle triggers I have ever had the misfortune to experience were on a Ruger 44 Carbine in the 1980s, and a Steyr AUG in 1990. Both had a pull weight of about fourteen pounds, with four or five inconsistent, gritty stages before the rifle finally fired. The AUG at least had an excuse, since it was a semi-auto adaptation of what was originally a full-auto mechanism. There was no excuse for the Ruger, and no remedy either. It got sold down the river, alas, before the Ruger 44 Carbine became a collector's item.

Most of the rifles in this book are sitting on the rack, wearing the triggers they were born with, but three Mauser 98-based custom rifles have replacement triggers. Two of them are the above-mentioned Dressel, the third a Canjar of hallowed memory.

VELOCITY

When the Sirens of the ancient Mediterranean sang to Odysseus and his men, luring them to their doom, it's entirely possible they were promising an additional hundred feet per second for their arrows. The siren song of velocity is at least that old, or so it seems. Every time you think you have found the very first instance of a rifleman (or musketeer, or *arquebusier*) pursuing higher velocities, you stumble on an even earlier one.

It's generally conceded that the modern era of high velocity in rifles began in London in 1851, with James Purdey the Younger. An experimenter and ballistician as well as a gunmaker, Purdey reduced bullet weight, increased the powder charge, and called his new creation an "Express" rifle. The choice of name was certainly inspired, and is with us to this day. For this reason, many believe Purdey originated the pursuit of high velocity.

In fact, it goes back considerably earlier in England, to the soldier and inventor, Lt. Col. David Davidson. He was a Scot who grew up in the Highlands, joined the Bombay Army, and eventually retired as a major. He later commanded a volunteer regiment, earning the rank of lieutenant colonel. During that time, he experimented with both rifles and riflescopes (he is considered the father of optical sights in England) and, in 1851, had his own exhibit at London's Great Exhibition. Prince Albert, Queen Victoria's consort, who was a devoted hunter as well as instigator of many technological advances, examined Davidson's rifles and riflescopes and praised them highly.

Davidson also interested Sir Joseph Whitworth (of steel-making fame), and Whitworth rifles, fitted with Davidson riflescopes, were used to great effect by Confederate sharpshooters during the American Civil War. Partly for this reason,

Davidson is remembered primarily for his pioneering work in sporting optics rather than his high-velocity rifles. Davidson's rifle used a belted ball, whose belts fitted in two spiralling grooves. This was not a new concept in itself. What was new was his use of smaller bores, lighter projectiles, and more gunpowder.

The Great Exhibition of 1851 is most noted in shooting circles for the exhibit of Casimir Lefaucheux, which introduced (from France) the concept of the break-action breechloader. Joseph Lang took the idea and began making the first such English guns, and this was partially responsible for the frenzy of invention and development in English gunmaking that began in the 1850s and did not end until 1914. This was largely due directly to Prince Albert himself. Being the consort of the Queen, he inspired fashion, and one of those fashions was a passion for shooting, both wingshooting and big game.

More shooters meant more demand for guns, but also for ever-better guns. The competition among London gunmakers was intense, with everyone looking for an edge. Purdey found one with his express rifles, and the concept carried over from percussion into the era of the pinfire, and then the central-fire cartridge. Proponents of higher velocity made many of the same claims in the 1860s that we have since heard from Sir Charles Ross (1908), Charles Newton (1911), various wildcatters in the 1930s, and finally Roy Weatherby in the 1950s.

With the advent of breechloaders, the centuries-old round ball finally gave way completely to bullets. As riflemakers searched for ways to increase velocity, some inspired soul took a lead bullet and hollowed out the nose. This not only reduced weight, thereby increasing velocity, but it made the bullet expand on impact with often astonishingly deadly effect—often, but not always. Rapid expansion works to the detriment of penetration, and sometimes animals escaped with ghastly surface wounds. This was in the 1870s, and the debate has continued with only faint pauses from that day to this.

Prophets of high velocity (and they can only be described in religious terms) have made fantastic claims for its effects over the years. David Davidson, who was a big-game hunter from the time of his youth, saw high velocity and lighter projectiles affording two benefits: greater range and flatter trajectory. When combined with his telescopic sights, this turned a 150-yard rifle into, perhaps, a practical and effective 200- or even 250-yard rifle. It was only some decades later that the fantastic claims began, and the belief that velocity *in and of itself* had some magical devastating effect.

Like every other aspect of hunting rifles, velocity cannot be considered in isolation. It is not an absolute, but the result of a combination of factors. In the days of black powder, things were relatively simple. You could only pack so much in, it detonated rather than burned, and you needed a long barrel to capture the full effects of the detonation and get the desired velocity. When black powder was replaced by smokeless, the whole equation changed—on paper, at least. Smokeless powder burned progressively, and it was either "fast" burning or "slow." Early smokeless powders were very fast by today's standards, and the powder story of the twentieth century was a steady progression to slower and slower powders, which allowed the use of larger cartridge cases and heavier bullets. The net result, supposedly, is higher velocities, although that is not always true.

While barrels could certainly be shorter with smokeless powders than with black powder, barrel length was (and is) still a critical factor in achieving the desired velocity. The velocity figures you read in a company catalog may or may not be true, even in their own rifles. Take the .300 Weatherby I mentioned above. You will not find it in this book because it had a critical failing: Its 24-inch barrel could not deliver published .300 Weatherby velocities. It was not until I acquired my first chronograph, in 1990, that I began measuring its loads and realized that, while it kicked like a mule and bellowed like a wounded grizzly, factory ammunition fell far short of delivering "Weatherby" velocities. As personal chronographs became as common as spotting scopes, Weatherby stopped offering the shorter barrel, and the Weatherby magnums became strictly 26-inch-barrel propositions in factory rifles.

Personally, I am neither pro-velocity nor pro-heavy-bullet (the two common divisions). Obviously, you must have some velocity, and equally you must have some bullet weight. Some of my rifles work best with higher velocities, while others prefer heavier bullets, and I make those decisions based on what I want the rifle to do. I have always found the continuing heated debate over velocity versus bullet weight to be pretty artificial anyway, with an awful lot of people who have little real knowledge of ballistics or bullet performance shouting at each other.

In 1988, with my .300 Weatherby, I killed an incoming Alaska brown bear at 17 yards. The next year, I made the shot of a lifetime on a running moose at somewhere around 300 yards. A couple of years earlier, I had made the best instinctive shot of my life on a fleeing caribou, dropping it with a bullet through the neck, and later that week killed another one, standing still, at about 100 yards. When I analyze those four shots, I find myself in a strange situation: If I had known in advance that I would need to make any one of

The .300 Savage cartridge fits exactly into the short Savage 99 action when loaded with a 150-grain roundnose bullet. It functions superbly, but is severely limited, ballistically, by the action length.

those, would I have chosen that particular rifle? The answer is no, and yet it performed perfectly well in each instance. Certainly there was nothing to complain about, although I would cheerfully agree there was a generous proportion of luck involved in the brown bear, the moose, and the first caribou. Velocity (or the lack thereof) played no part in those kills, although I believe the second caribou pretty much disproved the theory that the "shock power" of high velocity would drop an animal in its tracks no matter where you hit it. The animal took a 150-grain bullet at whatever the velocity was—advertised at 3,550 fps at the muzzle, but in that rifle at 100 yards probably no better than 3,100 fps. It hit right behind the shoulder and he stood there looking at me, then walked in a tight circle. A second bullet in almost the same place finally dropped him.

The reason that rifle and I parted company was that it offended my sense of efficiency. What's the point of a rifle chambered for the .300 Weatherby, with all that entails (big, heavy action, stiff recoil, deafening muzzle blast, and expensive ammunition) if you are going to get .30-06 performance?

The one enduring lesson was that velocity should be considered merely one of many different factors in what makes a great rifle.

CARTRIDGES

Traditionally, books on hunting rifles have dwelt at length on cartridges, looking at what each is suitable for, its long-range capability, stopping power, and so on. Not here. There are too many variables to make a blanket statement such as, "The .30-06 is a great deer rifle." Is it? Sometimes yes, sometimes no. A Winchester Model 70 bull gun from the 1930s, in .30-06, would make a very poor deer rifle. The .30-06 is only as good as the individual rifle it's chambered in, and the same is true of every other cartridge.

Several factors come into play, including weight, action length, and barrel length. Take the .300 Savage. In the Savage 99, with its short action, the cartridge's overall length is severely restricted. With anything heavier than a 150-grain roundnose, the bullet is seated so deeply to function through the action that you can't pack in enough powder for adequate velocity. Sweeping statements like "The .300 Savage can take anything in North America, given the right bullet," might be true in a Winchester Model 70, whose long action gave the .300 Savage plenty of breathing room, but it sure isn't in the Savage 99.

Many otherwise fine cartridges have been hamstrung by action length. The .257 Roberts, a real aficionado's cartridge if ever there was one, was bound and gagged early in life by action length. In the case of the Winchester Model 70, the magazine was blocked to fit the Roberts's maximum overall length, which was based on a roundnose bullet. The magazine block could be replaced with one in .30-06 length and, along with a few other modifications, the rifle became much more versatile. Remington, on the other hand, chambered the Roberts in their short-actioned Model 722, condemning an otherwise fine cartridge to a life of mediocrity.

Later in this book you will read about the .250-3000 (.250 Savage). It had problems related to both rifling twist and action length in the original Savage 99, and was also chambered by the Mauser-Werke in their "K" (*kurz*, or short) action. I have never had the good fortune to shoot one of those, but I do have a .250-3000 in an intermediate Mauser action. Its extra length gives the .250-3000 all the space it needs, no matter how heavy a bullet I choose to use.

The Remington Model 600, which came out in the mid-'60s chambered for two "short magnum" belted cartridges, limited both of those by its action length. The 6.5 Remington Magnum should have been a fantastic little cartridge, foreshadowing today's infatuation with 6.5mm cartridges generally, but again it was a matter of the action limiting maximum length, which in turn restricted bullet weight and powder capacity. The same is true, to a lesser extent, of its big brother, the .350 Remington Magnum.

Many short-actioned rifles are rationalized by the questionable tenet that shooters are uncomfortable with longer bolt throws, and will "short stroke" the action in a tight situation. My experience has been the exact opposite. In a tight situation, the bolt gets slammed back so hard it would keep on going were it not for the bolt stop. Sure, you save a few ounces with a shorter action, and there is no doubt the "K" Mauser makes up into a sweet little rifle. If, however, trimming the action by half an inch restricts the capabilities of the cartridge, it's a serious net loss. Most rifle companies seem to give this little thought, however, being caught up in the marketing possibilities of a lighter, handier rifle.

RECOIL AND RECOIL REDUCTION

In one of his books, Sir Samuel Baker tells the story of shooting an elephant with a gigantic muzzleloader. At the shot, the gun spun him around three times, knocked him back several feet, and he fell to the ground with a nose bleed. The question was whether he would get up first and grab another gun to finish off the beast, or the elephant would struggle to his feet and stomp Sir Samuel into marmalade.

Frederick Courteney Selous, a later contemporary of Baker, tells of using an ill-fitting gun for his early African hunting. It had such vile recoil that he was left with a bad flinch for the rest of his life. Ernest Hemingway, ever the merry prankster, wrote about an acquaintance he persuaded to shoot a .505 Gibbs in the basement shooting range of Abercrombie & Fitch, on Madison Avenue in New York. The man suffered a fractured collar bone. Hemingway thought this was hilarious.

With any gun firing a heavy projectile at hunting velocities, the equal and opposite reaction demanded by Newton's third law of physics is going to be noteworthy, no matter how heavy the weapon to dampen the blow. And, another law of physics kicks in, which is that energy can neither be created nor destroyed. Any attempt to divert the kinetic energy of recoil will result in an increase in some other form of energy somewhere else, either creating a whole new problem or aggravating an existing one.

Every rifle has some recoil, although in a heavy target .22 it may be indiscernible to the average person. Like velocity, felt recoil is the result of many different factors, and it can be made tolerable by varying those same factors. Recoil is measured in foot-pounds. There's a formula for calculating this, but in practical terms it's of little value. If you are bothered by the recoil of a light 28-gauge shotgun with one-ounce loads, it does not help in the least for me to point out that the recoil is "only" so many foot-pounds. If it bothers you, it bothers you.

There is also the question of velocity. Over the past thirty years, I have shot, among other things, a .700 H&H, a 4-bore double rifle, various elephant guns from the .465 H&H to the .505 Gibbs, A-Square's late, unlamented .577 Tyrannosaur, and the comparable .585 GMA. I have also fired, a few times, a .378 Weatherby. Of them all, the one I will never voluntarily shoot again is the .378 Weatherby. Experienced shooters of my acquaintance feel the same way. The recoil of the others can be big and bad, but the Weatherby is simply vicious. The reason is the velocity at which the rifle comes back at you. Heavy recoil spread out over a few micro-seconds is one thing, but it's something else when packed

into one micro-second. In one instance you get a big, loud, hard push, while in the other you sustain a blow like a left hook from Joe Frazier.

None of the rifles in this book has what I consider to be even unpleasant recoil, much less unmanageable. Some of them are quite powerful, including a .500 Express 3¼", a .450 Ackley, and a .505 Gibbs. The .358 Norma is no pussycat, either. Only one has any semblance of a muzzle brake—the .450 Ackley—and that's a moderate Mag-Na-Port treatment intended only to dampen muzzle jump, not rein in straight-back recoil. That was done in 1991, and if I could do it over, I wouldn't.

This business of muzzle brakes and other recoil reducers is about equal parts wishful thinking and deliberate fraud. Any muzzle-brake manufacturer who claims there is no increase in muzzle blast is lying through his teeth. There is *always* increased blast. Removable muzzle brakes, intended to be taken off when hunting, can cause all sorts of problems, most obvious of which is a potential change in point of impact. Recoil absorbers, inertia-type gadgets filled with mercury and such that are inserted into the stock, can also change point of impact dramatically, and affect shooting in other ways.

At one time, I had a .500 Nitro Express double, newly manufactured. Unbeknownst to me, the maker (now out of business, thank God) put a pair of mercury recoil reducers in the buttstock, which gurgled like a hip flask. It weighed 12.5 pounds when the proper weight for a .500 is more like 10.5. The extra two pounds in the butt drastically affected its shooting qualities, causing the butt to plunge earthward every time I pulled the trigger, with a corresponding exaggerated muzzle jump. The balance was atrocious. I had the mercury gadgets removed, which moved the point of balance forward into the barrels. That ended the muzzle jump problem. It also carried easier. Alas, the point of impact changed by close to twelve inches at fifty yards, which then had to be dealt with. Even so, it shot vastly better after than before, and I took it to Tanzania and killed a Cape buffalo. Climbing down a cliff in pouring rain, with the rifle in one hand and anything I could grab in the other, I was very happy the extra two pounds were gone.

At various times, manufacturers have tried elaborate collapsing recoil pads, or even entire collapsing buttstocks. Personally, I would rather approach the problem from a different direction.

In 1993, at the Holland & Holland shooting ground outside London, I shot a number of rifles that were under construction, including a .500/.465 H&H double, and a .500 Nitro Express double. In theory, the greater power of the .500 should have translated into greater recoil. Instead, I found the .500 comfortable to shoot (eight or ten rounds worth, as a matter of fact) while the .465 was distinctly unpleasant. They weighed about the same, but the difference was in the dimensions. The .500 was being built for a man with dimensions about the same as mine, while the .465 was quite different. It shows that stock shape and dimensions can go a long way to taming recoil. The .500 NE mentioned a few paragraphs back had been built to my dimensions, too, and with the recoil reducers gone it was very comfortable to shoot.

In the matter of velocity, I have found that a rifle like the .450 Ackley has a magic threshold, above which recoil becomes very unpleasant. Stay below that threshold, and recoil is relatively mild. Practical killing power is not really affected (unless you think 2,250 fps with a 500-grain bullet is a huge difference from 2,400 fps). There are other good reasons for keeping big-rifle loads on the mild side, such as avoiding compressed powder charges and the potential problems those

entail, or high pressures and stuck bolts under the blazing African sun. Recovery time for a second shot is also something to be considered.

A third factor is barrel length. Recoil has three distinct elements: straight-back push, muzzle jump that slams the rifle comb into the cheek, and muzzle blast. The shorter the barrel, the more you magnify the second and third. Keep your barrel to a reasonable length and it helps reduce both muzzle jump and blast.

Of the three, I believe muzzle blast is the worst for causing a chronic and sometimes debilitating flinch. The idea that you can put a muzzle brake on a .460 Weatherby, for example, and then wear ear protection while hunting is, to me, unacceptable. I would no more go into the bush in Tanzania wearing ear muffs than I would a suit of chain mail.

Sir Samuel Baker reserved his big guns for the worst situations. Selous got rid of the villainous weapon as soon as possible, and acquired something more civilized. Hemingway never hunted with a .505 Gibbs, but such was his respect for it that, in *The Short Happy Life of Francis Macomber,* he armed the professional hunter, Robert Wilson, with a .505—"this damned cannon," as Wilson describes it.

Although it's rarely thought of this way, recoil is really one more facet of ergonomics in a rifle. And, it's a very important one. You will never think of a rifle with affection, as an extension of yourself, if you are constantly afraid it's going to bark and savage you. And unless you think of a rifle that way, you will never be able to do your best work with it.

* * *

We began with the analogy of the canoe paddle. We will end with an analogy of the automobile. A car can offer top speed, horsepower, gas mileage, acceleration off a stop light (a nod to my younger days, there), turning radius, road-hugging ability, comfort, and safety, or any combination thereof. Emphasizing any of those to the detriment of the others will turn the car into a specialty vehicle. Top speed is valuable in Formula One, not so much in alpine rallies. A 500-hp V8 does nothing for gas mileage. Building a car out of balsa wood might give light weight and fantastic gas mileage, but the handling would be dreadful and it would give no protection in an accident.

Similarly, a rifle has velocity, accuracy, weight, and power. At various times, manufacturers have keyed on one of these features to the exclusion of all else, and then tried to sell rifles on that basis. This rifle is so accurate, they say, you'll never have to worry about a second shot. Or, it has such high velocity, it doesn't matter where the bullet hits. Power? This cannon will crumple a pachyderm. Climbing mountains? Light as a feather—you'll never know it's there.

In a rifle, tack-driving accuracy is not a benefit if it comes at the expense of weight, stock design, or portability. You can kill a deer with a benchrest rifle under the right conditions, but that does not make it a good all-around deer rifle. High velocity is of little use if the noise is so deafening you live in terror of pulling the trigger and flinch badly when you do. Short barrels may reduce weight, but they also reduce velocity. A rifle may be light enough for you to bound up a mountainside like a chamois, but will you be able to get a steady shot when the oxygen is thin and you're panting for dear life?

The finest hunting rifles of the last 150 years balance all those qualities, emphasizing those that are needed for a rifle's particular purpose, but never to the extent that they compromise other qualities, and turn the rifle into such a specialized tool that it's practically worthless for anything else.

James Woodward & Sons double rifle, in .450 Express 3¼".

CHAPTER I

STALKING-RIFLE PERFECTION, BY JAMES WOODWARD

HEBRIDEAN OVERTURE

In 1810, an obscure Edinburgh lawyer named Walter Scott published a long narrative poem called *The Lady of the Lake*. It took place in the Scottish Highlands, and was a tale of romance and feudal rivalries. The poem sold twenty-five thousand copies in eight months, breaking all sales records for poetry, and set in motion a train of events that rolls on to this day.

Scott's poem inspired an opera by Gioachino Rossini, and major compositions by Felix Mendelssohn and Hector Berlioz; it turned Loch Katrine into a famous tourist attraction (which it still is) and ignited a passion in English breasts for the romantic Highlands which had been largely dormant since the suppression of the Jacobite Rebellion of 1745. Walter (later Sir Walter) Scott followed up *The Lady of the Lake* with the first British historical novel (*Waverley)*, which kept the Highland flame burning brightly. This was in spite of the fact that, at the time, the Highland Clearances were underway, with landlords evicting the clansmen from their ancient homes even as they were being placed on a romantic pedestal by their English neighbors.

Scott's novels, along with the musical paeans to the glories of the Highlands, were largely responsible for a widespread fascination with the clans, the tartans, the glens, and the lochs that pervaded English life through the first part of the nineteenth century. The realities of the Clearances, and the hardships of Scottish forced emigration to the four corners of the world, did not intrude on this fantasy. By coincidence, just as Scott's *Lady* appeared, the future Duke of Wellington was fighting the French in the Peninsular War, and Highland regiments played a major role in his victories. Five years after the Battle of Trafalgar, in the midst of the Napoleonic Wars, the English public yearned for some diversion. Romantic fantasies of misty glens, majestic peaks, and captivating lassies did just that.

The Highlands were home to red grouse and red stag, the two future pillars of British shooting life, but until the 1820s they were rarely hunted with firearms. Such sport hunting as did exist was as Walter Scott described at the beginning of *The Lady of the Lake*. James Fitz-James, one of the main characters, is coursing a stag on horseback. He becomes separated from his companions, his horse dies of exhaustion, he meets the lovely Ellen by Loch Katrine, and the story unfolds. The climate of the Highlands, with its storms and rain, made it almost impossible to hunt deer with flintlocks. Once the Scottish Rev. Alexander Forsyth discovered the explosive qualities of fulminates and ushered in the percussion era, however, the sport of going to "the hill" to stalk red deer became a reality.

In 1995, I traveled to Scotland to hunt for the first time. I rode the overnight train from London to Inverness, sipping tea in my compartment in the grey, rainy dawn as we crossed the Firth of Forth, and then, in a downpour, made my way from the railroad station to a tavern. We stayed in an ancient hunting lodge, and set out each day in that incessant rain, with the burns racing and splashing over their banks. We stood in six inches of water, in the heather, eating our midday "piece," and traversing the hills on foot, hour after hour. Finally, I lay in soaking wet heather for almost two hours, waiting for a stag to rise to his feet. Shooting at a resting stag was simply not done, as my stalker, Davey, sternly advised. Davey wore tweeds and a tie, and a deerstalker cap, and carried our rifle over his shoulder in a leather case. As I lay in the heather, slowly succumbing to a bout of shivering that absolutely precluded any chance of accurate shooting, I reflected that the rules we were following, the customs we were obeying, had been set in place 150 years before, and had been followed to this day by everyone from Harry Flashman to the Prince of Wales.

What I was doing was an almost direct result of events set in motion by *The Lady of the Lake* 185 years earlier. *Oh well*, thought I: *If I die of pneumonia here in the heather, I will be part of that great and grand picture of deer stalking in the Highlands.* It was a comforting thought.

THE ROAD TO THE HIGHLANDS

In the midst of English Highland mania, in 1837, Victoria ascended the British throne and began her long reign. Three years later, she married her cousin, Prince Albert of Saxe-Coburg and Gotha. Prince Albert was to have an enormous influence on English life, and not least in the British passion for deer stalking and shooting. Albert was German, with the traditional German love of firearms, target shooting, and hunting big game. However, he also had a serious interest in science and technology.

As Queen Victoria's consort, Prince Albert had few formal duties of his own to perform, and this left time to pursue such personal interests as promoting the abolition of slavery and improving British educational standards. Queen Victoria adored her husband, and was happy to participate in many of his interests. Since he loved to go to Scotland to shoot grouse and stalk red stag, this led to the acquisition of the estate at Balmoral and the frequent migrations of the royal court to the Highlands. Because the royal family loved stalking and shooting, it became widely popular among all classes, with poorer folk making do with lesser guns and lesser game, while the wealthy and the aristocracy patronized James Purdey and Charles Lancaster, and shot on Scottish estates.

Prince Albert was instrumental in organizing and promoting the Great Exhibition in London in 1851. This turned out to be a technological watershed for English gunmakers. The French gunmaker, Casimir Lefaucheux, exhibited his early break-action pinfire breechloader, and within a few years Joseph Lang had marketed the first such gun in London.

It is now generally believed that this first gun was actually made by an out-worker to the trade, Edwin Charles Hodges. Having seen the Lefaucheux gun at the exhibition, and an article about it in the *Illustrated London News*, Hodges built the gun and sold it to Lang, who took the design from there. This was established practice in the English gun trade and remained so for a century. Edwin Hodges himself was an extremely skilled gunmaker. He died in 1925, at the age of ninety-three, having seen the complete revolution in firearms from the fashioning of this first English pinfire with his own hands, to the use of machine guns mounted on aircraft. Truly an extraordinary life.

In the quarter century between 1850 and 1875, the world of guns and rifles changed dramatically and completely. During this time, so many developments occurred that it's difficult to summarize them. However, guns progressed from muzzleloaders to breechloaders; from pinfire cartridges to central-fire; from paper cases to brass. The primer was invented, as were different forms of rifling to suit the new elongated bullets that replaced round lead balls. Most of all, from the point of view of passionate deer stalkers who made annual pilgrimages to the Highlands to pursue their favorite game, rifles were developed that were vastly more weather-proof, durable, and simple to operate. They were deadly at longer ranges, and eminently reliable.

Looking back at the form we now see of double-barreled rifles, both with and without hammers, it would seem that all of this perfection of mechanism—there is no other term for it—is eminently logical. Like looking at the wheel and wondering why it was not invented earlier, the modern (that is, within 150 years) double gun is a masterpiece of logic and simplicity. The hammers, the top lever, the sliding bolt, the hinge pin, the ejectors—all of these fit so beautifully together, they just seem obvious. They were anything but. Progress from the beginning in 1851, to the level they'd achieved in 1875, was a labyrinth of different approaches, false starts, dead ends, promising but disappointing ideas, and hundreds and hundreds of patents—the vast majority of which came to nothing at all.

Donald Dallas, today's foremost historian of the British gun trade, and a social historian by profession, notes two watershed events that profoundly affected the development of guns. One was the Great Exhibition of 1851. The other was the overhaul of the patent act in 1852, which made it both easier and cheaper to patent new designs. A third element—an absolute essential for any industry to thrive—was demand. Demand for guns from all classes of people and levels of income also blossomed after 1850, largely due to Prince Albert, the activities of his family, and the astonishing impact of royal tastes on public fashion.

By 1860, breechloaders had surpassed muzzleloaders in sales, and the early '60s became the years of the pinfire. As the popularity of shooting grew, so did the number of gunshops and gunmakers, and the most talented group of craftsmen in the history of gunmaking embarked upon a fifty-year stretch of intense (and sometimes bitter) competition to improve guns, rifles, and ammunition.

In 1851, James Purdey coined the term "Express" to describe his high-velocity muzzle-loading rifles, and higher velocities became a goal for riflemakers as breechloading progressed through the pinfire era to the development of

The .577 Snider, in its early paper-cased design (left) and later drawn-brass cartridge, was the critical pioneering development in the evolution to central-fire cartridges in England.

central-fire cartridges. Again, a Frenchman was involved (Eugene Schneider), and again an Englishman saw the potential and carried the development further. This was George Daw of London, often called the "father of centerfire," who filed the initial patents in 1862. As central-fire ammunition evolved, guns were adapted to use it. In the case of rifles, the .577 Snider, for the converted Enfield musket, was the critical pioneering development. Proceeding from Daw's innovations, it was adopted by the War Office in 1866; by 1870, the English were well into the wholesale development of drawn-brass cartridge cases, loaded with black powder, ignited by Boxer primers (invented by Col. Edward Mounier Boxer of the Royal Arsenal at Woolwich), and rifles to shoot them.

So many developments were proceeding simultaneously, with one invention feeding off another, and making possible yet a third, and then a fourth, it is impossible to tell the story from just one aspect. It was like a game of high-speed technological leap-frog, with barely a year—or even a month—going by without *The Field* (the bible of shooting and outdoor recreation, founded in 1853) reporting yet another revolutionary development.

* * *

James Woodward was a London gunmaker who apprenticed to Charles Moore in 1827 and became a partner in the firm (Moore & Woodward) in 1844. Eventually he took over the business, brought his two sons into it, and in 1872 it became James Woodward & Sons. The company was to last as an independent gunmaker until 1948, when the last of the Woodward family sold the firm and its patents to James Purdey & Sons.

During that century, Woodward gained a reputation as a "gunmaker's gunmaker," producing rifles and shotguns of a quality second to none.

If James Purdey was at the "top of the tree," some smaller firms such as Boss & Co. ("Builders of Best Guns Only") and James Woodward & Sons were perched on the top branch beside them and, sometimes, surpassing them. In fact, throughout its existence, Woodward considered Boss & Co. its real competition. Much later, when the attention of the London trade turned to developing an "under-and-over" gun, it was Boss and Woodward that produced the two successful, iconic (and now revered) designs.

The advent of the drop-barrel breechloader in 1851 was a watershed, but it was only the start. As ammunition and actions evolved, it became necessary to solve several nagging problems, such as developing a dependable gas seal and finding a strong and reliable method of bolting the barrels in place. With central-fire cartridges, it was also necessary to have a means of extracting the spent cases and, later, ejecting them automatically. A third requirement was a method of conveniently locking and unlocking the bolting system. Many approaches were tried, separate from the bolts themselves. Hundreds of patents were filed. Most fell by the wayside, but a surprising number were adopted and manufactured, if only by their gunmaker-inventors. A few designs were so good that they were generally recognized as a genuine step forward, became standard features, and were widely adopted throughout the trade.

A major advance was made in 1859 when Birmingham gunmaker Henry Jones patented the Jones underlever. With this mechanism, the barrel flats were locked to the action by means of two opposing lugs, operated by a lever under the trigger guard that swung out to the side. Because the lugs were mated to slanting surfaces, like a very coarse screw thread, the barrels were cammed down into place, giving an extremely strong and solid lock-up. It was what was called

The Jones underlever was widely used on double rifles because of its strength, simplicity, and reliability. This is a Holland & Holland, built around 1895.

Underlugs for the Jones underlever (top) compared to the Purdey double underlugs. Note the tiny pivoting cam in front of the hook that eases movement of the extractors. This was a Woodward refinement.

an "inert" system—that is, the lever had to be moved by hand back into its locked position after the barrels were closed. It was simple, strong, and reliable, but slow.

This was the beginning of the great age of driven shooting of birds, with ever-increasing emphasis on large bags. Shooters commonly used pairs of guns, or trios (garnitures), with one or two loaders, and gunmakers were constantly searching for ways to make loading faster and easier.

In 1863, James Purdey introduced his double underlugs, which were initially operated by a "thumb-hole" lever in front of the trigger guard. Two years later, in 1865, William Middleditch Scott, the "son" of W&C Scott & Son of Birmingham, improved the system greatly by locking and unlocking them with the Scott spindle and top lever. Purdey recognized the advantages and the two companies came to an arrangement, with Purdey holding the rights to the combination for London and W&C Scott for Birmingham and the regions. Over the next fourteen years, until the patent expired, each

collected a royalty of two pounds Sterling per gun manufactured employing the system—a substantial amount. Purdey underlugs combined with the Scott spindle are the double-gun standard to this day.

With their higher pressures, rifles required a different treatment than shotguns. As the inventions came thick and fast, tumbling over one another, rifles generally lagged behind shotguns in adopting the newest and latest. Riflemakers wanted features well proven in actual use before adopting them. For these reasons, the Jones underlever not only became a mainstay of double-rifle production, it remained in common use until well into the twentieth century.

The only real drawback to the Jones was that it was slower to operate than the Purdey-lug, Scott-spindle combination. The latter was also a "snap" action—the lugs and top lever moved back into position automatically as the gun was closed, powered by springs. All the shooter (or loader) needed to do was snap the barrels closed and it was ready to shoot, whereas the Jones underlever required a separate movement on the part of the shooter to lock the barrels down again. Eventually, a full-snap version of the Jones was introduced, as well as a partial-snap, but it was too late to overtake Purdey—which in any event was a more compact, elegant, and intuitive system that eventually became the standard even for double rifles. However, the Jones underlever remained in use for decades, preferred by many, especially for large-bore, powerful rifles. Since it did not depend on springs that might break in the middle of nowhere, it was absolutely dependable, practically foolproof, and much less complex. As well, it required fewer machine cuts; less steel was removed from the frame, leaving it stronger overall.

Still, the snap action had great appeal. George Daw, in his initial patents for the central-fire cartridge, included a break-action design with a "push forward" lever under the trigger guard, and this approach lent itself to a snap action. This became known henceforth as the "Daw lever," and variations were used by many different gunmakers. Purdey's thumb-hole patent was one of them.

James Woodward went a slightly different direction. They liked the underlever concept, and wanted a lever that pushed down and forward, like the Daw, rather than swinging out to the side. However, they also wanted a means of cocking the hammers automatically as the gun was opened, saving the shooter a few more steps. The push-forward lever lent itself admirably to this and, in 1876, Woodward patented their "Automatic" or "Automaton" action. This mechanism was very adaptable, and was used for both hammer- and hammerless guns. James Woodward became known for its underlever guns, and continued to make them for many years.

The name "Woodward," incidentally, is not uncommon in the British gun trade. There were more than a dozen different Woodwards (individuals or firms) registered in Birmingham alone between 1838 and 1910. Thomas Woodward, the son of one of these, became Holland & Holland's long-time factory manager, and prominent in the London trade in his own right. Many were inventors and patentees as well, so anyone encountering a Woodward rifle or shotgun should pay close attention to the address on the rib, as well as to the proof and maker's marks, to determine exactly who made it and when. Only James Woodward & Sons of London were makers of the very finest in guns and rifles.

Because the snap underlever was a popular method of bolting and unbolting a gun, there were many variations. Some gunmakers simply did not want to pay royalties to Purdey, but others (James Woodward and John Rigby & Co., to name two) believed they were superior for some applications. Aside from its "Automatic" action, Woodward used the simpler (non-cocking) snap underlever on some of its later hammer guns.

The hammer mechanism, by this time, had been around for centuries in one form or another, all the way down through flintlocks, percussion, pinfire, and now central-fire. It was proven and dependable. This did not mean it could not be improved, however, and it was. The manufacturing of lock mechanisms was a specialist trade,

James Woodward & Sons double rifle, with bar-action locks and a snap underlever.

and all the great gunmakers bought their basic lock blanks from outside suppliers. Sometimes these were made to their own patent, sometimes they were generic. The most prominent lockmaker during the hammer era was John Stanton of Wolverhampton.

With the advent of central-fire, and strikers that were struck by the hammer and which, in turn, struck the primer, a problem arose that had not existed before. With the hammer pressing against the striker and the striker tip lodged firmly in the primer, it could become difficult, if not impossible, to open the gun. It was necessary to pull the hammers back to their half-cock position to release the strikers. It was not long until strikers were fitted with coil springs to withdraw them into the frame, but the hammers still needed to be lifted off them manually.

Half-cock was a useful position for carrying a loaded gun as well. When firing one barrel, the second hammer could be left at half-cock, neither ready to fire nor resting against the striker and the live primer of the second barrel. Either of those positions risked firing the second barrel inadvertently. As an additional precaution, some rifles were fitted with sliding safety bolts on the lockplates that allowed the shooter to lock the hammers in half-cock. These were known as "stalking safeties," and had to be pulled to the "off" position before the hammer could be drawn back.

John Stanton devised a method of not only returning the hammer to half-cock, but of eliminating the need for stalking safeties. This was his "rebounding" hammer, patented in 1867. A V-spring in the lock would automatically lift the hammer back to half-cock after the gun was fired and position it firmly, held in a stout notch. In this position, it could not be pressed down upon the striker without pulling the trigger. Stanton's rebounding hammer was one of the major advances of the hammer era.

According to Crudgington & Baker (*The British Shotgun, Vol. One, 1850-1870*), James Woodward was the first London gunmaker to recognize the value of the new lock. As early as November, 1867, a letter appeared in *The Field* extolling the advantages of a Woodward gun fitted with "rebound" locks.

It's worth noting, however, that not every advance instantly swept the land, rendering all other designs obsolete and changing the landscape forever. As with the Jones underlever, some mechanisms and features had sufficient virtues that they remained in use for years. The hammer era overlaps hammerless for decades, while the Jones, Woodward, and Rigby underlevers remained long in use, as did stalking safeties on rifles. This was at least partly because older shooters were used to them, or distrusted the new designs, or simply liked them better. When a man ordered a new gun in 1890, for example, he could have it made like his old one from 1875. Checking patent dates is useful in dating a gun, but generally only in reverse. You can usually—but not always—determine that a gun might have been made *after* a certain date, but you can never say for certain that it *could not* have been made after. In the case of rebounding hammers, Stanton's innovation was so simple and elegant that earlier hammer guns could be retrofitted with the system. Therefore, you cannot look at a gun with rebounding hammers and say for certain that it was made after 1867.

Riflemakers, inherently more conservative than shotgun makers, did not rush to embrace innovations in bolting systems, nor did they immediately adopt the rebounding hammer. Climbing mountains and crawling around in the heather raised more potential problems for a shooter than did standing in a butt as birds were driven toward you. In such circumstances, the idea of a firmly locked safety was very attractive.

Generally speaking, there were two types of lock mechanisms in the hammer era: bar action and back action. In the case of the bar action,

the spring that powered the hammer was forward (located in the bar of the frame, which was recessed to accommodate it) while in the back action it was located behind. Both worked very well, but it became general practice to use back-action locks for rifles because they required milling less steel from the frame, leaving it stronger. Both bar- and back-action locks carried over into the hammerless era, as was this custom of usage in rifles. Back-action locks did have an old-fashioned look, to which some objected, so in some hammerless designs ingenious gunmakers devised a way of putting the spring behind the tumbler while giving the lockplate the trim, modern appearance of a bar action.

Between gunmakers' preferences and clients' tastes and prejudices, one could find an almost infinite variety of designs and features in guns and rifles made between 1865 and 1900.

The practice of deer stalking in Scotland was popular before Prince Albert, but he was instrumental in making it highly fashionable. The Scottish Highlands are the natural home of the red stag, and going to "the hill" to stalk them had been a custom for centuries, involving everyone

Although made well after the advent of rebounding hammers, this Woodward double rifle was fitted with non-rebounding locks and stalking safeties.

The back-action lock is seen on the H&H (top) while the Woodward has a bar action. The H&H uses a Jones underlever. The Woodward has a snap underlever that pushes forward rather than swinging out to the side.

from Scottish kings to clan chieftains to common poachers. The Scottish red stag is the same animal found on continental Europe, but longer winters and harsher conditions have made the Scottish deer both tougher and smaller bodied.

Through the late 1800s, train travel made it possible to visit the Highlands relatively easily, and many Highland estates became the stag and grouse moors of wealthy Englishmen. This was the stag that inspired Sir Edwin Landseer's *Monarch of the Glen*, painted in 1851 for the House of Lords, and which has become world famous through its depiction on labels of both Dewar's and Glenfiddich whisky.

It is the sacrosanct Scottish tradition of "deer stalking" that the practice is exactly that: *stalking*. Even a landowner is normally accompanied by a stalker, or gamekeeper, and his word is law both as to what you shoot and when you can shoot it. Rarely does a stalker allow a shot beyond two hundred yards, and one hundred is preferable. The thrill of the chase lies in stalking as close as possible, then making a clean kill with one shot, not blazing away at an animal at long range.

The usual deer-stalking rifle was a single-shot or double, and this carried on into the central-fire cartridge era. It's no accident that many great British single-shot designs originated in Scotland (Alexander Henry, Daniel Fraser, Farquharson), but London gunmakers produced stalking rifles for their monied clients, too. Such companies as Charles Lancaster and John Rigby became especially noted for rifles, but Purdey, Boss, and Woodward also billed themselves as "gun and rifle makers" and produced rifles of the highest quality.

During this period, these gunmakers also produced rifles for use in British colonies all over the world, including Africa and India. They were used by army officers, civil servants, and sportsmen who traveled far to hunt big game such as elephant, rhino, Cape buffalo, lions, tigers, and everything on down. While these rifles developed in one direction, the dedicated deer-stalking rifle for Scotland developed in another, and became a particular type on its own. There was no difference in quality or durability, but the Scottish stalking rifle could be just a little bit more specialized.

While James Purdey (probably the Younger) coined the term "Express" for his high-velocity rifles, he was not the first to use the concept. Lt. Col. David Davidson, while an officer of the Bombay Army in India in the 1830s, experimented with both rifles and optical (telescopic) sights. His rifles employed deep two-groove rifling, and specially cast balls with a belt to fit into the grooves. The projectiles were lighter, the powder charge heavier, velocity higher, and trajectory flatter. Combined with his telescopic

Alexander Henry's legendary hammerless single-shot, chambered for the .450 Express 3¼". A classic stalking rifle in every way.

sights, Davidson developed an early, accurate, long-range stalking rifle. At the Great Exhibition of 1851, he displayed his rifles and optical sights, and Prince Albert himself handled and admired them. According to Donald Dallas, author of *Purdey, The Definitive History* (Quiller, 2001), the first "Express" rifle listed in the Purdey numbers book was built in 1851, and followed Davidson's principles: Purdey reduced the bore size, increased the powder charge, gave it slower rifling twist to allow higher velocity without fouling, and created a conical bullet with two wings that fit the rifling grooves.

This was right at the end of the percussion era, but with the coming of breechloading, the same principles could be applied once a method was found of giving the breech a secure gas seal. Drawn-brass cartridges and central ignition solved that problem, and once that was accomplished, the dam burst. Eley Brothers, and later Kynoch, designed cartridges which they released to the trade, and then provided ammunition. Popular early black-powder "express" cartridges included the .577 and .500, but the one that became the best all-around cartridge, and perfectly suited to traditional deer stalking, was the .450.

Ever since the Whitworth rifles of the 1850s, .450 had been recognized as the best all-around bore diameter for a military rifle. The .577 Snider was merely a stop-gap, to allow conversion of existing Enfields while the military searched for a permanent replacement. Alexander Henry of Edinburgh was one of the foremost riflemakers in the United Kingdom, and in 1860 introduced his famous Henry rifling. He wanted to enter a falling-block single-shot of his own design, using his proven rifling pattern, in the competition to choose a new military rifle.

Working with Col. Boxer from the Royal Arsenal, Henry developed a new cartridge for

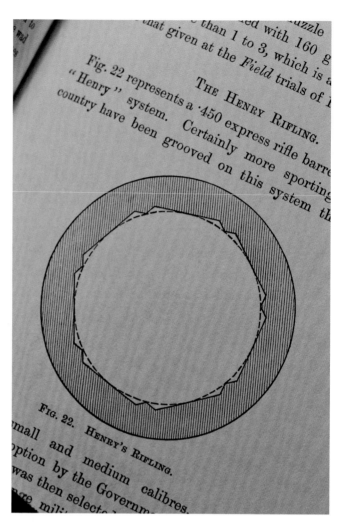

Alexander Henry's famous rifling pattern, patented in 1860 and used in the Martini-Henry rifle. It was one of the most accurate rifling patterns of the black-powder era. This is an illustration from **The Modern Sportsman's Gun and Rifle, Vol. II, by J. H. Walsh ("Stonehenge"), published in 1884.**

the trials, the .450 Express 3¼". It had a straight, tapered case, loaded with 120 grains of black powder behind a 270-grain lead bullet. This achieved a velocity of 1,975 feet per second at the muzzle. At 150 yards, the mid-range trajectory of the .450 Express was just under five inches, and it had a maximum effective range of about 300 yards.

In 1871, the War Office adopted the Martini rifle to replace the Snider-Enfield conversion.

Henry himself later wrote that it was a technically sound decision because his rifle was cocked manually, while the Martini was automatic. Recognizing the value of Henry rifling, however, the War Office chose that for the bore, and the new rifle became the Martini-Henry. Alexander Henry's .450 cartridge also found favor, but it was too long for the Martini action, so the army lengthened the existing .577 case, necked it down to .450, and created the .577/.450 Martini-Henry. Obviously, what was good for the military was also good for hunting, and civilian .450 cartridges followed, both straight and bottleneck, long and short. In fact, .450-diameter cartridges proliferated as gunmakers began designing and marketing their own, and by the 1880s, there were at least a dozen in existence.

Early .450s, from left: .577/.450 Martini-Henry, .450 Express #1, and .450 Express 3¼".

The one that became best-known, however, and which is one of the great cartridges of all time, was Alexander Henry's .450 Express 3¼". While the Martini was noted for having particularly unpleasant recoil, the .450 Express 3¼" could be chambered in a nine-pound rifle and still shoot very comfortably. It was also perfectly suited to double rifles.

By 1875, the London gun trade was in its glory. The greatest names were all in place: Woodward, Boss, Purdey, Lancaster, Grant, Holland & Holland, Rigby. In fact, James Woodward, Stephen Grant, Thomas Boss, and John Rigby were all in a cluster on St. James's Street in their own little "Who's Who in Gunmaking." It was the great age of the hammer gun. Central-fire was firmly established, rebounding hammers were the state of the art; Purdey underlugs, combined with the Scott lever and spindle, gave them a sleek elegance like never before. At 64 St. James's Street, home to James Woodward since 1843, the company had now become James Woodward & Sons (1872) and James the Younger was hard at work on the advanced design that was to become the "Automatic."

By this time, Prince Albert had been dead for fourteen years, but his influence lived on. Particularly, his eldest son, the Prince of Wales, had inherited his love of shooting and, having little else to do, devoted himself to society life, shooting, and beautiful women. Several generations of aristocrats emulated him in every way they could afford—and some they could not. Driven shooting, for red grouse, partridge, and pheasants, was almost a national mania. Travel to and from Scotland to shoot was nearing its peak.

Sometime around 1878, a client approached Woodward and ordered a rifle for deer stalking in Scotland. It was to be a .450 Express 3¼" double with non-rebounding hammers and stalking safeties. The barrels were twenty-six-inch "best" Damascus. Within a year, and probably much less, he took delivery of Woodward rifle number 3610. Who the client was, where the rifle went, and what it did during its long career, are all mysteries. While the Woodward records for those years are intact, there is no mention of this particular rifle, for reasons to be explained. However, I surmise it was a rifle intended for deer stalking. By its condition, it has the look of a rifle that did not brave Africa or India, but was kept close to home and was well looked after—a thoroughbred that never saw a plough.

Having handled many rifles from that era, British, American, and European, one comes to expect shortcomings of various descriptions. Sometimes, a rifle is a victim of simple poor design, but more often its faults result from the limitations of the technology of the time. London gunmakers enjoyed one great advantage, and that was that they spent time, face to face, with their clients. Clients were measured for their guns, to ensure the wrist was neither too thick nor too thin, that it was not too heavy, the length of pull too long, or the triggers out of reach. Because happy clients typically returned to the same gunmaker over and over, any complaints or suggestions they might have were listened to, and acted upon.

Knowing nothing about the Woodward's original owner, it's impossible to say if he was a regular client, or whether this was his first rifle or his fifth. However, just by its feel and elegant appearance, one can draw some conclusions. First, the Woodward comes to hand with the feel of an aristocrat. At almost exactly eight and a half pounds (8 lbs., 7.6 oz.), it is slightly on the light side for a .450, but it's comfortable both to carry and shoot. It comes to the shoulder (mine, at least) with the sights perfectly aligned, without requiring even the slightest adjustment. There are two sling eyes, one out on the barrel, the other just forward of the escutcheon in the stock, so it is fitted out to be carried to "the hill" either in a case or with a sling.

The barrels are of best Damascus steel, and have Henry-style rifling, suggesting that the basic rifle was probably made by Alexander Henry for James Woodward. Henry rifling was, at the time, considered to be the best. It was common practice in London for gunmakers to do out-work for other gunmakers of comparable quality. I have, for example, seen a John Dickson shotgun built on a Woodward "Automatic" action, with the basic work by Woodward and finishing by Dickson. My rifle would be the reverse, with the rifle made by Henry but finished by Woodward. Both barrels are stamped "JW&S," because

James Woodward & Sons, rifle number 3610 in .450 Express 3¼". It is a thoroughbred that never saw a plough.

Woodward wanted no name or initials anywhere on their guns except their own. The barrels do, however, each have "Henry's Patent" stamped on them, along with the numbers 237 and 238. This is in line with standard Scottish practice of "patent usage" numbers assigned to each individual barrel or mechanism. Donald Dallas lists a .450 Express 3¼" rifle made in 1873 by Alexander Henry, whose barrels are stamped "2223." This is a much higher patent usage number, on a rifle made five years earlier than the Woodward, but there are several possible explanations. Probably, the barrels on the Woodward were made and numbered earlier, but actually used on a rifle much later. It was standard practice to produce barrels and frames in lots, assign them individual numbers for record-keeping purposes, and then keep them in stock, sometimes for years, to be used later when an order came in. Anyone exploring the numbers books of British gunmakers must be prepared for such anomalies, or go mad.

If the basic rifle was made by Alex. Henry for James Woodward, it would explain the lack of an entry in the Woodward numbers book, since the action and barrel numbers would never have been entered when production began, and this was also normal practice. Other records from early in the Woodward years have either been lost or are incomplete.

The rifle is a bar-action hammer gun with half-cock positions and stalking safeties, rather than rebounding hammers. It is bolted with Purdey underlugs, with the bolt operated by a snap push-forward lever. There is one standing sight (150 yards) and one folding (250 yards). The buttstock has a distinctively "Scottish" curve to the pistol grip, with two triggers in easy reach. There is a cheekpiece with a shadow line, and the grip cap and buttplate are of horn. The forend is

held in place with the Harvey lever, rather than either the Anson plunger or Deeley latch, the two most common types of snap forend fastener. The Harvey was patented by Charles Harvey in 1866. While not as convenient as either the Anson or Deeley system, the Harvey lever (like the Jones underlever) was very solid and secure, and became popular for use on double rifles. In fact, John Rigby & Co. used it so often that it is often mistakenly referred to as a "Rigby lever."

Having used both rifles and shotguns with push-forward underlevers, I have discovered that it is every bit as natural to use as the Scott

The Woodward is a bar-action hammer rifle with non-rebounding hammers, stalking safeties for the half-cock positions, and a snap underlever.

top lever, if not more so. If, after shooting a few rounds with the push lever, I then go back to a top-lever gun, I find myself reaching for the push lever for a long time afterwards. The reverse, however, is never the case. Switching to the push lever is easy; switching back is not. The intuitive and ergonomic qualities of the underlever principle also explain the enduring popularity of American lever-action rifles. Much the same is true with hammers, and after shooting hammer guns of various types, I began to understand the reluctance of men like King George V and Lord Ripon in refusing to give up their hammer guns even long after hammerless actions had taken over.

THE WOODWARD AS HUNTING RIFLE

James Woodward & Sons was known more for its shotguns than its rifles, but those it did make were exquisite. Alex. Henry, on the other hand, is one of the most famous names in British rifle-making. The firm was established in Edinburgh in 1853, and eighteen years later, in 1871, its patent rifling (#2802, 1861) was adopted for use in the Martini-Henry military rifle. Henry filed more than a dozen patents between 1860 and 1882, most related to rifle actions. In 1872, Alex. Henry received a royal warrant as riflemaker to "His Royal Highness the Prince of Wales," and the following year was commissioned to build a rifle for Queen Victoria, which was given as a Christmas present that year to her long-time friend and retainer, John Brown.

Henry rifling has seven grooves, and in the Martini-Henry, a twist rate of one turn in twenty-two inches (1:22). In the Woodward rifle, the rate of twist is 1:28, or about three-quarters of a revolution in the length of the barrels. Henry rifling is instantly recognizable by a pointed ridge lying between each of the lands, which are flat. A perfect circle drawn around the bore would touch each land in the center, as well as the peak of each ridge. This stabilized the bullet, while reducing powder fouling and cleaning problems.

It has been said that if the action of a rifle is its heart, then the barrels are its soul. In the later 1800s, as cartridge development progressed, as bores became smaller and velocities greater, such legendary riflemakers as Alexander Henry, George Gibbs, and William Metford all strove to find a rifling pattern that provided the greatest accuracy while, at the same time, minimizing

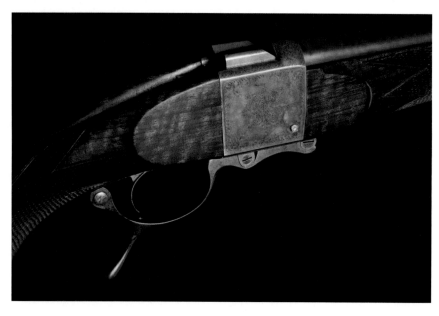

A later Alexander Henry hammerless single-shot rifle, in .450 Express 3¼". Henry was deservedly recognized as one of the foremost riflemakers in Britain.

both powder fouling and difficulty in cleaning. Shallow rifling was generally acknowledged to be a key element in achieving this. Later, when cast bullets were superseded by jacketed, such shallow rifling was found to be too delicate and prone to wear. Metford rifling, for example, was used in the earliest Lee bolt-action military rifles (Lee-Metford) but was later replaced by a deeper pattern designed at the royal arsenal at Enfield Lock (Lee-Enfield). Through the heyday of black powder and lead bullets, however, Henry rifling enjoyed a stellar reputation for both target shooting and stalking.

James Woodward No. 3610 has a doll's-head third bite, which was probably unnecessary but which was deemed essential for secure lock-up by such authorities as Dr. J. H. Walsh, editor of *The Field*. During the early years, there was some doubt—long-since dispelled—about the strength of Purdey sliding underlugs, especially when used on a rifle. Some sort of third bite was common, even used by Purdey themselves.

The Woodward has another intriguing feature which I have seen only on Woodwards, and is also found on my Woodward hammer shotgun. Both are fitted with extractors, not ejectors. Normally, the extractors are pushed up by a solid arm that projects from the knuckle of the action at about a 45-degree angle. As the gun is opened, the end of this arm comes in contact with the end of the extractor and pushes it up as the barrels drop. On the Woodward, however, this arm does not contact the extractor itself but rather a comma-shaped bearing that pivots on a pin in the forward end of the front lump. Functioning much like a roller bearing, it transfers pressure effortlessly from the end of the arm to the end of the extractor, eliminating any friction that might make opening the gun more difficult. Such a feature was typical of Woodward's, who had a

The Woodward has every little nuance of fine gunmaking, including perfectly timed pins inside and out.

reputation for flawless finishing. Any alteration that would improve functioning, no matter how tiny, was worth doing to make a Woodward the absolute best.

Needless, perhaps, to say, all the screws (pins) are timed—that is, the slots align fore and aft—and there is a very good reason for this beyond elegant appearance. With the screw slots timed, one can tell at a glance if a screw is backing out and needs to be tightened. If a screw that attaches metal to wood can be tightened beyond the correct alignment, it shows the wood has shrunk slightly or, conversely, expanded. This was no small concern in the rains of the Scottish hills and the dry plains of Africa and India, and it was common practice with all British gunmakers. Today's machine screws, with Allen heads and the like, do not alert the owner to such nuances.

The Woodward has a flat, file-cut rib of Damascus steel that dips ever so slightly forward of the rear sight, then rises to provide a ramp for the front sight. The sight itself is a prominent platinum bead or "moon" sight intended for low light and close range, but it also has a second blade, very thin, for finer work at longer ranges. The blade is locked in place by a tiny set screw, which makes it easy to switch the sights if necessary (and provided you have a suitable tiny screwdriver).

The rear sight has one fixed and one folding blade on a base dovetailed into the rib. A set screw holds it tightly, and it can be adjusted for windage by loosening this screw. Adjustments to elevation could be made by installing a higher or lower front sight.

By English express-rifle standards, these sights are remarkably simple, but then it was early in the game, and ammunition was standard at one bullet weight and velocity. Later, as more manufacturers produced ammunition, it became customary to stamp on the rifle exactly what bullet weight and powder charge the rifle was regulated for. Front sights were developed with folding moon sights, so either was instantly available. Rear sights became increasingly elaborate, with as many as four or five folding leaves, regulated for ranges from fifty to five hundred yards. Unless they are properly made by expert craftsmen, however, such sights can be more trouble than they're worth. They need to be held in place by springs or detents to ensure they do not move, either up or down, under recoil, or when snagged by a piece of heather. Having to

constantly check sights to make sure you have the right one up is a distraction no one needs, especially when trying for a quick second shot on a moving animal.

In this sense, this Woodward is extremely simple, and therefore extremely desirable. In the field, there is no need to decide which front sight to use, while there is only one folding sight in the rear and you can tell instantly if it is up or down even while peering through the sights.

The Woodward's 26-inch barrels are somewhat unusual, since 28 inches was more common at the time and, with black powder, greater length delivered greater velocity. Obviously, the deer stalker who ordered the rifle felt that the increased agility of the rifle was worth any loss in velocity. One may also deduce that he was very disciplined and knew the limits within which he would shoot, with two hundred fifty yards being the longest range. In theory, the .450 Express 3¼" was capable of killing cleanly at three hundred yards, but in practice such extreme-range shooting was dubious because of the coarseness of the sights, and the difficulty in range estimation combined with the arc of the trajectory.

Here we have a perfect example of the basic difference in their approach to hunting compared with today. Modern riflemakers try to build in as many adjustments and variations as possible, to both rifle and sights, so that the rifle can be adjusted to fit any situation. In 1878, the ideal was to make the situation fit the rifle, and this was done by combining stalking skill with knowledge of the terrain and habits of the animal.

Even for 1878, the James Woodward is conservative to the point of being old-fashioned. It has hammers, when hammerless designs were already available, including Woodward's own "Automatic." The hammers have half-cock positions and stalking safeties, when rebounding hammers had become standard. It employs an underlever, when Purdey lugs and the Scott spindle and top lever had been available for fifteen years, and were well on their way to becoming standard. The rifle has extractors only, and the forend is firmly held in place with the Harvey lever.

Every one of these features was almost sure to have been at the client's request. While Woodward was a maker of the very finest quality,

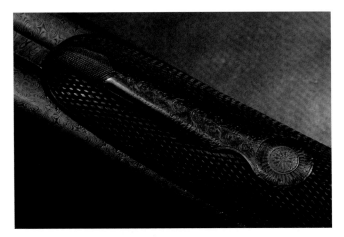

The Harvey lever that holds the forend was also widely used by John Rigby—so much so that many call it a Rigby lever, and believe it was a Rigby invention.

it also had a reputation for being at the technological forefront: It was the first London maker to embrace rebounding hammers, and one of the first to develop self-cocking and hammerless actions. Obviously, the Woodwards were not a family inclined to persuade clients to go with older designs when newer (and possibly better) ones were available. All of this leads me to believe that the original purchaser of Woodward rifle No. 3610 was a deer stalker of considerable experience who knew what worked, and what he wanted.

For the traditional deer stalking of the Scottish Highlands, creeping in close, braving snow and rain and high winds, lying for hours in soaking heather and making shots under the poorest of conditions, this rifle is almost perfect: It is light to carry, balances beautifully, and comes to shoulder and eye like a fine bird gun. It is uncomplicated and completely reliable. It may not be the perfect stalking rifle, but it is very difficult to see what improvement could be made.

* * *

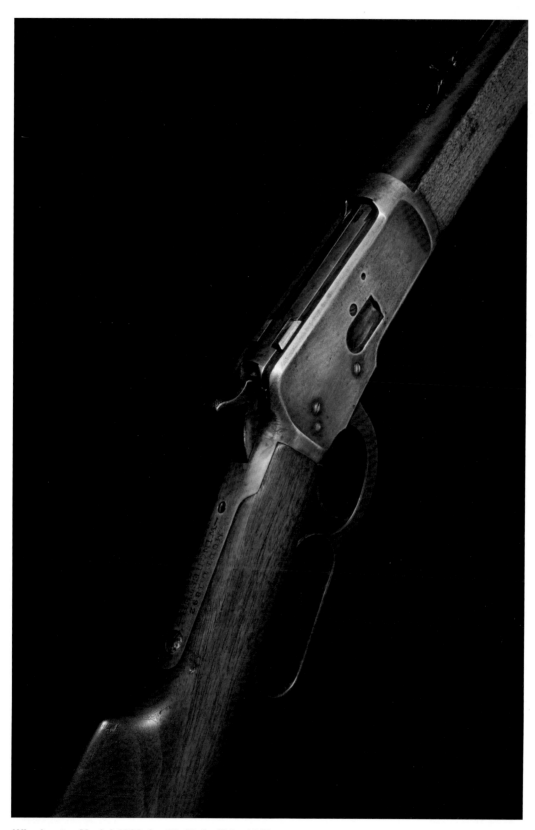

Winchester Model 1892, in .38-40, built in 1912.

CHAPTER II

WINCHESTER'S MODEL 1892—ERGONOMICS, AHEAD OF ITS TIME

STILL-HUNTING—A PRELUDE

In 1882, a previously unknown writer by the name of Theodore S. Van Dyke published a book on hunting that was destined to become a classic and have a profound effect not only on the way men hunted but, by extension, on the rifles they used.

The book was called *The Still Hunter*. The origin of the term "still hunting" is not absolutely certain, but it's generally believed to be derived from "stealth" hunting, which is exactly what it says, and is remarkably close to the British practice of deer stalking. In fact, in an early chapter of his book, Van Dyke says that still-hunting and deer stalking are one and the same. Although we might assume that hunters in the 1880s were hardy outdoorsmen, moving through the woods like Indians, and deadly shots with whatever weapon came to hand—the prevailing myth of the American frontiersman and his trusty Kentucky rifle, or the mountain man with his Hawken—such was not the case, and not by a long, long way. In fact, so unlike this vision was big-game hunting in the late 1800s that Van Dyke felt the need to write his book in an attempt to persuade hunters to at least try his methods.

We should remember that *The Still Hunter* appeared shortly after the final demise of the great bison herds of the West, and at a time when big-game populations were either in peril or terminal decline due to expanding settlements and the prevalence of market hunting. While Van Dyke's book is aimed primarily at whitetail deer hunters of the East, his theories and methods can be applied to any big-game animal. Particularly, he mentions how they could be readily applied to pronghorn antelope.

In the East, the preferred method of hunting was to drive deer, with lines of guns spread out while the animals were stirred up and moved either by hounds or human beaters. By contrast, Van Dyke advocated hunting on your own, on foot, in wilderness areas. Van Dyke's still-hunter moved silently and slowly through the bush, always watchful, reading sign, gauging the wind, hoping to catch sight of an animal before it saw him, or flushing it from its hiding place and getting a snap shot as it disappeared.

In 1882, American hunters had two basic types of rifle available. One was the big single-shot like the Sharps, which had been used to wipe out the buffalo, and was preferred by most big-game hunters. The other, in its infancy at the time, was the lever-action repeater such as the Winchester Model 1873. The lever actions of that time were chambered for relatively light, short-range cartridges like the .44-40, but had the great advantage that their tubular magazines held a dozen or more rounds. While not ideal as hunting rifles, especially for really large game like elk, bison, and grizzly bears, they were very good multi-purpose guns for the man who might encounter hostile Indians or bandits during his travels through the West.

Van Dyke devotes relatively little space in his book to discussing rifles, except in general, and none at all to specific types, styles, or calibers. He does, however, examine some individual aspects of them, such as the concept of express rifles, with their light, high-velocity projectiles, and the practice of exaggerated long-range shooting. On subjects like the above, he could just as well have been writing in the 1980s as in the 1880s—or, for that matter, today.

WINCHESTER'S TRIUMPH

The era of the breechloading center-fire rifle began, in the US, with Smith & Wesson's .22 Short in 1857, and progressed, more or less in parallel, with development of central-fire breechloaders in England and Scotland. Like Col. Boxer's primer in England, Col. Hiram Berdan's self-contained primer, patented in 1866, spurred similar development in the US. The Sharps falling-block rifle was the earliest big-game cartridge rifle, and the Henry the first widely successful repeating rifle.

The series of Winchester lever actions, which began with the Model 1866 and progressed through the '73 and the '76, became gradually

The Sharps falling-block rifle, the earliest big-game cartridge rifle, dominated hunting on the Great Plains during the era of the great bison herds.

more powerful, more accurate, and more usable for big-game hunting. Generally, however, they were too heavy and awkward for the minimal power they delivered. Cartridges like the .44 Henry Rimfire were, to put it mildly, anæmic, while the rifles themselves had stocks with far too much drop at heel, resembling the early Pennsylvania and Kentucky long rifles. These were suitable for offhand shooting but little else. They were usually fitted with a deeply curved steel buttplate which needed to be carefully positioned in the shoulder, precluding much in the way of accurate instinctive shooting. At the same time, the barrels were unnecessarily long, adding considerable weight in themselves, and when the full-length tubular magazine was filled with up to fifteen cartridges, they were very barrel-heavy as well. This overall configuration might have worked for offhand target shooting, except that the rifles and cartridges were not accurate enough to make this worth the effort.

The turning point came in 1879, when a previously unknown Utah gunmaker and inventor named John Moses Browning sold Winchester a design for a falling-block single-shot rifle. He also assigned them first rights to any subsequent gun design. What Browning had in mind was a lever action unlike anything that had been made up to that date. This became the Winchester Model 1886, an action that was strong enough to handle the most powerful cartridges made, was long enough to accommodate even big buffalo rounds like the .45-90, and was both sturdy and dependable. In his book *Winchester—An American Legend,* historian R. L. Wilson calls Browning's designs masterpieces of "unadulterated functionalism," and quotes him as saying "Anything that can happen with a gun probably *will* happen, sooner or later." Browning was obviously a man of extensive practical experience.

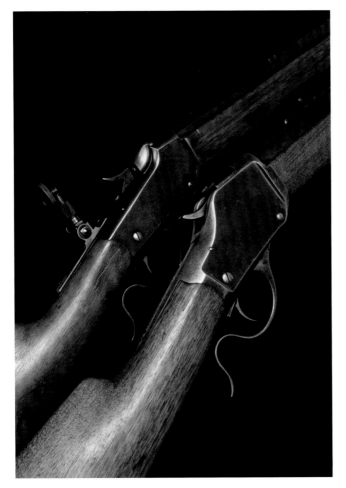

John M. Browning's famous single-shot rifles, the Winchester Low Wall (top) and High Wall, were the first in his long collaboration with Winchester Repeating Arms.

The Winchester Model 1886, considered by many to be the greatest lever-action rifle ever made. This is an original '86, chambered for the .40-65, restored by Doug Turnbull.

"His (Browning's) guns were sturdy, supremely practical, and functional," Wilson writes. "And, in accordance with the adage of form following function, they were generally supremely handsome, even graceful."

Wilson also notes that John Browning and his brothers were serious hunters in the wilds of Utah, and tested his finished models in the countryside around their home in Ogden.

"John was an excellent shot," Wilson noted, "And he and his brother Matt . . . were (on) the leading trap and live-bird shooting team of Utah in the 1890s."

Obviously, John M. Browning could bring to his design work a practical experience and understanding of what made a great hunting rifle, and what did not. The Winchester Model 1886 has a claim to being the greatest lever-action ever made, and very few would dispute that. It was unquestionably powerful, accurate enough, and reliable. It was also, however, heavy and relatively awkward in handling. Although it was several cuts above the Winchesters that had gone before, there was still considerable room for improvement.

Jumping ahead, the most famous lever action of all time was also a John Browning invention:

the Winchester Model 1894. It came out in that year, chambered for the first small-caliber, smokeless-powder big-game cartridge, the .30 Winchester Center Fire (WCF), later known as the .30-30. With more than eight million rifles and carbines produced over the course of 120 years and counting, there can be no dispute as to the '94's qualities as a hunting rifle. Almost certainly, more whitetail deer have been killed by still-hunters using '94s in .30-30 than with any other rifle and cartridge combination. In its later carbine form, with a 20-inch barrel (rather than 26 inches), it was light, fast-handling, and quick to load and reload. However, the rifle that is in this book representing the John Browning genius is not the Winchester '94 but its slightly older, slightly smaller brother, the Winchester Model 1892.

The '92 is a scaled-down version of the 1886 action. It was introduced in 1892, chambered for four cartridges: the old .44-40 and .38-40 (which originated with the Winchester '73), as well as the diminutive .25-20 and .32-20. Appearances to the contrary, in terms of power there is very little to choose between the .44-40 and the .38-40. The .44 is actually a .42, while the .38 is .40-caliber, and while the .44-40 shoots a 200-grain bullet, the .38-40 uses a 180-grain. Neither one is much good for deer beyond 125 yards, but within that

range any practical difference in power lies largely in the imagination.

For the seething Model 94 devotees who might be reading this, a further explanation of its exclusion is necessary. No one disputes its history or its reputation, but it does have practical limitations. If its .30-30 cartridge has more power than the .38-40, it only really matters beyond 150 yards, and to make use of that power, you need better sights than the open leaf on the barrel with which the rifle was equipped. A scope is a problem because of the rifle's top ejection, which makes a receiver or tang aperture sight the only practical alternative. Also, with its 20-inch barrel, the rifle is barrel-light, which makes accurate shooting difficult without a rest.

On all of the above counts, Browning's Model 1892 outshines the '94. My particular rifle is a .38-40. With its 24-inch barrel, the full-length tubular magazine holds fifteen rounds—enough that one could fill the magazine and go out for a day's hunting, and not have to carry any extra ammunition. For the dedicated still-hunter, divesting one more thing to carry is a blessing. The Winchester '86 is rightly noted for having the smoothest lever action ever invented, and I will cheerfully accept that. This smoothness was carried over into the scaled-down '92 which, because of its size and weight, seems even easier.

The Winchester 94, this one in rifle configuration with a 26-inch barrel, is both ergonomic and comfortable to shoot.

With my usual tendency to try to perfect any rifle that comes into my possession, I scoured the gun auctions looking for a Lyman tang sight for the '92. When I found one, I removed the rear sight and replaced it with a dovetail blank. I used the rifle like this for about half a season, when it dawned on me that I was really gilding the lily since all my practice shooting was being done at 125 yards or less. I removed the tang sight, reinstalled the open rear leaf, and found that I could shoot the rifle every bit as accurately, and with more ease. In fact, I began shooting it almost like a shotgun, instinctively, with both eyes open.

Ever since I began reading gun magazines and books in my impressionable teens, writers have been condemning the open sights with which all rifles come equipped from the factory. And, I learned, they had been doing it for fifty years before that. In almost all cases, I agree with them, but one exception is the Winchester Model '92. In either .44-40 or .38-40, the '92's open sights are perfect for the rifle's purpose.

With its 24-inch barrel, the '92 is longer than the '94 carbine, and weighs a few ounces more (6 lbs. 13 oz. versus 6 lbs. 8 oz.). Those few ounces are all out front, which makes the rifle remarkably steady for offhand shooting, but also very smooth and stable on moving targets. As Larry Wilson pointed out, Browning's designs are usually graceful, and this translates into ergonomic operation. The '92 has a straight stock (no pistol grip) and a slim forend. As with a good English game gun, I find that a straight stock and slim forend (splinter, as opposed to beavertail) contributes mightily to fast, positive handling. After 1918, as lever actions lost ground to bolt-action sporting rifles in the United States, Winchester and other lever-rifle manufacturers tried to "modernize" them with pistol grips, bulky forends, and even Monte Carlo stocks and

cheekpieces. All this did was negate the lever gun's natural handling advantages, without in any way allowing it to compete with bolt actions on their home ground, which was high-velocity cartridges, longer range, and more precise accuracy using riflescopes.

For still-hunting, few bolt actions can even begin to compare with a fine, traditional lever rifle. As they came from the factory, the '92 (and also the '94 and various Marlins) had no sling swivels, and while this might have seemed like a drawback, it was actually an advantage in still-hunting. Prowling through the woods, prepared for a quick shot across a clearing, or a buck bursting out from behind a log, a rifle on your shoulder is no use whatever. It should be in your hand (or hands) 100 percent of the time. Carried at the trail (the military term for balanced in one hand, down at your side), the rifle can be brought up to the shoulder and grasped with the other hand in fractions of a second. When it is carried across the chest, it's as quick into action as a game gun on a grouse.

The Winchester '94 is without question the most famous deer rifle in history, and has probably taken more whitetails than any other. This one is a .32 Winchester Special, and yes, it took that very whitetail.

No less an authority than Jack O'Connor stated in various places that he would no more go hunting with a rifle without a sling than he would go without his pants. I am a strong sling admirer myself, but looking back I can recall several occasions when I would have had a fighting chance at a deer had my rifle not been slung on my shoulder. Particularly as the day wears on and the weary miles pile up, the temptation to sling your rifle becomes almost irresistible. There is also the argument that, if you do get a deer, it is much easier to drag it out with your rifle slung on your shoulder. Or, should you have to climb a bluff and need both hands to do so, your rifle can be on your back. All of this is true, but those situations can be accommodated by something as simple as carrying a length of twine in your pocket and looping it over barrel and buttstock in a makeshift arrangement. Every still-hunter should carry some twine or cord anyway, so it's no additional burden.

If there is one tiny quibble with the '92, it's the deeply curved rifle-style buttplate, which has a sharp steel toe that could be used to split kindling. If the cartridge were any more powerful, or the rifle any lighter, recoil might make this a problem. As it is, with any of its factory cartridges, the '92 is very comfortable to shoot and, if you bring the rifle quickly to your shoulder and don't manage to seat the buttstock properly, there is no harm done.

Overall, the Model 1892 rifle, as John Browning designed it and the Winchester factory delivered it, was well-nigh perfect for the traditional still-hunter of whitetail deer. No, I would not recommend it for elk on a mountainside, moose in the muskeg, or grizzly bears anywhere, but for whitetails in thick timber? Absolutely.

* * *

The Model '92 stayed in the Winchester line until 1937, during which time about one million rifles were made. Several variations also came and went. The Model 53, introduced in 1924, was essentially a '92 with a nickel-steel barrel, half-magazine, and "modernized" buttstock and forearm. It was offered in the same calibers as the '92, minus the .38-40. About 25,000 were manufactured before it was replaced, in 1933, with the Model 65. The 65 was originally offered only in .25-20 and .32-20, but later the .218 Bee was added. The Bee was a .224-caliber varmint cartridge made by necking down the .32-20. It used the 40-grain Hornet bullet, but at considerably higher velocity (approximately 2,800 fps.) Only about 7,000 Model 65s were manufactured, and it is, today, a prized collector's item.

In both the 53 and the 65, the Model '92 action was modernized and updated, including some internal changes. Philip B. Sharpe compared the 65's action to the Model 71, which

The Winchester Model 1892.

was an improved version of the original 1886, and short of tearing all these actions apart and comparing the bits and pieces, it's difficult to be exact about what was changed, and how it was an improvement.

Most authorities praise the '92's smoothness of action, although Sharpe himself says he did not find it as smooth as the '86, and in the case of the Model 65, it was not as smooth as the Model 71. With a lever action, smoothness counts for a great deal. It allows the shooter to keep the rifle at his shoulder, with the sights aligned while loading and shooting, loading and shooting. Personally, I have no complaints about the '92 in that regard, even with the limiting effects of a shoulder injury sustained while elk hunting in the Idaho mountains twenty years ago.

In 1979, Browning Arms Co. came out with a thoroughly modernized version of the '92 called the B-92. It was very similar to the original, except it had a 20-inch barrel, and was chambered for the .357 Magnum and .44 Magnum. Rechambering or rebarreling '92s to .44 Magnum had a brief flurry of popularity during the 1960s, and this undoubtedly influenced Browning in offering the B-92. Removing four inches of barrel, along with four inches of magazine and the three extra rounds it would accommodate, was questionable in terms of handling. The '92's desirable, slightly barrel-heavy quality in the rifle version was eliminated, muzzle blast increased, and the extra power of the .44 Magnum gave it a very unpleasant recoil.

Rechambering original '92s to .44 Magnum, aside from enraging Winchester collectors, was pretty questionable given the softer steel from which both the barrels and frames were made, but of course this did not apply to the B-92.

The Model 65 in .218 Bee provides an interesting example of how ideas that seem good in

marketing meetings can fall flat when offered to a public that is considerably more knowledgeable and discerning than the marketing committee itself. In the 1930s, there was wholesale pursuit of high-velocity .22 varmint cartridges. The king of these was the necked down .250-3000 (Savage), which came to be known as the .22-250, or Varminter. But there were many others, too. The goal was a high-velocity, light bullet accurate out to 250 or 300 yards, mainly for shooting crows and woodchucks.

Such performance was only possible with a spitzer bullet, and utilizing pin-point accuracy was only possible with a riflescope. In the case of the .218 Bee, neither was an option. With its tubular magazine, loading spitzer bullets was perilous because it placed the sharp point of one bullet up against the primer of the cartridge in front, so the Bee was offered only with flat- or round-nosed bullets. And, with the 65's

Three original chamberings of the Model '92, from left: .32-20, .38-40, and .44-40, also known as the .32 WCF, .38 WCF, and .44 WCF. All have been used to take deer, and all are capable of doing it—in the right hands, and under the right circumstances.

top ejection, a scope was tricky to impossible. Finally, when serious varmint hunters were experimenting with such solid lock-up actions as the Mauser 98 for maximum accuracy, the perceived sponginess of the lever action was a drawback. Add them all together, and you have a rifle which can best be described as a white elephant.

The one possible advantage of the 65 in .218 Bee was that it was a factory rifle and readily available, but in the cash-strapped 1930s, anyone serious enough about varmint hunting to lay out any substantial amount of money could do far better than the Bee—and obviously, most did. It was gone from the Winchester line when war came, and never reappeared.

About the best any authority could say about the Model 65, .218 Bee combination was that accuracy was "surprisingly good, considering . . ." One would think that marketing executives would learn from such examples but, alas, it appears not. At least, not considering all the remarkably similar mistakes that were made with other rifles and other cartridges throughout the 1950s and '60s, and right up until today.

During its forty-five-year lifetime, the Winchester Model 1892 was offered in the usual bewildering array of configurations. There were both round- and octagonal-barreled rifles; barrel lengths ranged from 30 inches in a "military"

model to 14 inches in the "Trapper." Some were made with outsized lever loops, made famous in various movies and in the 1950s TV series, *The Rifleman.* Spinning the rifle around to work the action became a highly questionable stunt, comparable to fanning a Colt .45. It is also more difficult than it looks, especially with longer barrels, and gives shooting instructors apoplexy because of the safety aspects. However, it sealed the '92's reputation as a smooth action.

Magazines were offered in both full- and half-lengths. Buttstocks were made with both "rifle" and "carbine" buttplates.

In the end, however, the prize for being the most ergonomic and perfect for its purpose is the original, 24-inch barreled rifle, in .38-40 or .44-40, with the original lightning-quick open sights (or the ability, at really short ranges, to do without the sights altogether.) Some years ago, I took one of the carbine-shooting courses at Gunsite, in Arizona. I took both my '92 and a Ruger Mini-14. The '92 was a bit tongue-in-cheek. The instructors at Gunsite take it all very seriously, and most of them, replete with rigs and harnesses that would do credit to a paratrooper, festooned with handguns, back-up guns, and deep-secret back-ups to the back-ups, regarded my '92 with something approaching contempt.

Amid the plethora of ARs, AKs, and various hideously unergonomic modern rifles, the

The Model 1892 in rifle form, with a 24-inch barrel. Even with its curved rifle-style buttplate, it is highly ergonomic and handles like a charm.

'92 stood out in that it was both fun and comfortable to shoot, *and* it was highly effective at knocking over steel plate after steel plate with rhythmic regularity. It shoots readily from the shoulder, from the hip, and anywhere in between. Instinctive shooting comes naturally to the '92, and this is often valuable in hunting situations. The obvious one is a charging animal, which one would hope would not occur with something as diminutive as a '92, but a buck that bursts out from behind a log right in front of you, and offers a split-second chance at a shot, certainly requires instinctive shooting. A hunter who's good with a '92, using relatively amiable cartridges like the .38-40 and .44-40, can get off three very accurate shots in a remarkably short period of time.

At Gunsite, these qualities quickly evinced themselves. It's an interesting exercise to take several guns to a range, with several shooters of varying degrees of experience, and see which ones they gravitate to. Which do people line up to shoot, simply because they are either fun to shoot or because they shoot well with them? These two qualities, I have found, are closely related—and also connected to the question of gracefulness in a rifle that we looked at earlier. A rifle that is fun to shoot will be shot a lot. A hunter who shoots a particular rifle a lot will become better with it, more comfortable with it, and more confident in his ability. This, in turn, contributes to calm and accurate shooting, and fends off attacks of buck fever, which are largely due to lack of confidence and fear of failure.

In the early years of computers, Apple aired a series of television commercials in which a couple of senior executives of a company watched employees at work on different computers. It was common for a company to own one or two Macs, for special purposes, but outfit everyone else with cheaper IBM PCs. The two executives noticed that the employees would line up to use the Mac, because it was ergonomic and intuitive, and simply fun to use. As a result, they became comfortable with it and very good at using it, whereas they continually struggled with the PCs. Exactly the same principle applies to big-game rifles, and it doesn't matter if it's a .250-3000 for deer or a .505 Gibbs for pachyderms.

John M. Browning was a hunter and a shooter, and I do not think it's any accident that the original Model 1892 was such a near-perfect combination of barrel, cartridge, sights, weight, and balance, for a big-game hunter in the thick woods. All the later modernizations and variations only took away from Browning's practical, ergonomic design, rather than adding to it.

* * *

Holland & Holland .500 Express (3¼").

CHAPTER III

HOLLAND'S .500

THE 1883 "FIELD" RIFLE TRIALS

A. J. Liebling, the great boxing writer for the *New Yorker* through the 1940s and '50s, noted that one could trace a continuum through boxing history based on who had punched whom, with one man punching another, who in turn hit another, all the way from Rocky Marciano back to Tom Cribb. Boxing is as inseparable from its history, he wrote, "as a man's arm from his shoulder."

The same is true of gunmaking, with Charles Lancaster learning from Joseph Manton, and passing it on to his sons, who taught this barrel-maker or that one, right up to the modern day. Another example would be hunting writers.

Captain William Cornwallis Harris was an English army officer. In the 1830s, on medical leave from his posting in India, he traveled through the *terra incognita* of southern Africa, and returned to write a book called *The Wild Sports of Southern Africa*. The English of the Victorian era were great readers, great seekers after knowledge, and insatiable when it came to books about far-off lands. Captain Harris's work was a great success, and is today regarded as the first real "hunting" book as we now know them. Beyond enriching the lives of Englishmen, huddled by a coal fire on a rainy winter's night, *Wild Sports* inspired others to emulate Capt. Harris, to travel thousands of miles and embark on major expeditions in search of elephants, rhinoceros, lions, and all the other great game animals of Darkest Africa.

From the great Victorian era of hunting, exploration, writing, and, not least, rifle development.

At that time, for an Englishman, big-game hunting consisted of deer stalking in Scotland and little else. Images of elephants and tigers, rhinoceros and lions, were magical. Among those inspired were such great men as Sir Samuel Baker and Frederick Courteney Selous. Both were not only hunters but writers. Baker inspired Selous, who inspired Roosevelt, who inspired Ernest Hemingway, who inspired Robert Ruark, who inspired (among others) me. Were it not for Robert Ruark (and, by extension, Harris, Baker, and Selous), I might never have taken an intense interest in rifles and hunting, and I would not be writing this book.

Of course, things are never that directly linear, and simple cause-and-effect is rarely simple. Other names are equally important. One whose contribution should never be overlooked or underestimated is Dr. J. H. (John Henry) Walsh, a.k.a. "Stonehenge," long-time editor of *The Field,* author of *The Modern Sportsman's Gun & Rifle* (1882 & 1884), and originator of the long series of *Field* trials that began in 1858 and ended in 1883. J. H. Walsh was instrumental in turning Holland & Holland from just another London gunmaker into one of the most famous and respected names in riflemaking—a reputation that endures to this day.

* * *

When J. H. Walsh took over the fledgling magazine, *The Field,* in 1857, the London firm of H. Holland had been in business only twenty years. Founded by Harris John Holland, a tobacconist, in 1837, Holland's began around the time that Joseph Manton died, and is one of the few top-tier London gunmakers that cannot trace some sort of direct connection back to the Manton brothers. Holland began by buying and selling guns and rifles to his tobacco customers, and slowly moved into making and selling new guns. These early guns were brought in from Birmingham, a common practice; later, Holland's forged a relationship with W&C Scott, one of the

finest Birmingham gunmakers, and together they built a reputation for excellent quality.

In 1860, Holland's fourteen-year-old nephew, Henry, joined the firm as an apprentice, and eventually became the driving force that transformed Holland & Holland (as it became in 1876) into a riflemaking powerhouse. It was Henry Holland's close friendship with Sir Samuel Baker that gave H&H its connection to the real world of hunting large and dangerous game in far-off countries, and Baker had a great influence on Holland's rifles and cartridges right up until his death in 1893.

Meanwhile, over at *The Field,* J. H. Walsh was making his presence felt in such a wide range of outdoor activities that it's hard to know where to begin. *The Field* was founded in 1853, the brain-child of Robert Smith Surtees, creator of the famous fictional character Jorrocks, and was intended as a weekly devoted to country life and outdoor sports. Its mainstays were fox hunting and farming, but subject matter ranged as far afield as angling, greyhound racing, croquet, and, of course, shooting. Walsh, born in 1810, trained as a medical doctor, but an early mishap with a muzzleloader cost him the thumb and one

Holland & Holland was founded by Harris Holland in 1835. It is now located on Bruton Street in London, just off Berkeley Square.

finger of his left hand, and he eventually gave up medicine to become a full-time writer.

J. H. Walsh was a true "all-rounder," to use the English term. He rode to hounds, kept and raced greyhounds which he trained himself, trained hawks, trained his own pointers and setters, and coached rowing crews. He put his medical knowledge to use in developing physical fitness programs for his rowers, and the latter resulted in a book, *Athletic and Manly Exercises*. Another book was his *Manual of Domestic Economy*, dealing with making ends meet for families of all incomes; he wrote authoritative tomes on dogs and horses, and a complete compendium called *British Rural Sports*, which endured through many editions. Somehow, Walsh found time to design "The Gun of the Future," (Patent #5106, 1878), a hammerless design of almost astonishing ugliness that went nowhere, and did so purely on merit. Although Thomas Bland manufactured a few of them (and we may speculate on his motives for doing so), it was one of Walsh's few failures in life.

Dr. Walsh was a great one for full and comprehensive testing of *everything*. His own experience with that faulty muzzleloader made him almost obsessive about safety. Perhaps, given the contribution he later made to guns and shooting as a result, we should feel grateful to the unknown gunmaker who cobbled the treacherous gun together.

Dr. Walsh seemed to be fascinated by everything, and went to great pains to educate himself on anything in which he became interested. He was forty-seven years old when he took over editorship of *The Field*, and occupied that position until his death in 1888—still at his desk until the day he died. As we have seen, the modern era of gunmaking in England was in its infancy in the 1850s, and Walsh became involved almost immediately. As a scientist, he was a great believer in organized testing and evaluation. In an age when the most outlandish claims could be made for any new invention or discovery—and usually were—he became devoted to the principle of proving (or disproving) claims in full public view, and publicizing the results in the pages of *The Field*.

Dr. Walsh had been in the editor's chair barely a year when he set up the first *Field* test, in 1858, pitting muzzleloaders against the early pinfire breechloaders. The muzzleloaders won, but it was such a close contest that it was plain the writing was on the wall. This was followed, in 1866, by trials for pattern and penetration of shotguns; in 1875, trials of choke bores versus cylinder tubes; the 1878 trials of explosives, involving black powder and the earliest smokeless powders; and, in 1879, trials that pitted large bores against small. *The Field* thrived on controversy, and many debates over such arcane subjects as choke boring and single triggers were fought to the bitter finish in its pages, not least in the letters to the editor. As Donald Dallas points out in *The British Sporting Gun and Rifle*, Dr. Walsh would allow controversial subjects to heat up to breaking point, then step in, organize an actual test, and publish the results.

In 1883, he staged what became the most famous *Field* test of all: the rifle trials. By this time, gunmakers were becoming known according to specialty. Some companies were noted for their shotguns (Purdey, Boss, Woodward) and others for rifles (Charles Lancaster, Alexander Henry, John Rigby). There were many areas of dispute in riflemaking, from rifling patterns (Lancaster, Henry) to bolting systems, sights, and barrel lengths. Many were the claims of riflemakers, and Walsh decided to put them to the test. On July 14, 1883, he announced a trial that would take place in just two months. Although later criticized for giving such short notice, it was intentional and served a purpose: Walsh wanted to ensure that makers could not build special rifles just for the trials, but would have to use their standard products.

According to the magazine's official history, *The Field 1853-1953,* the "chief object of the trials was to determine and ascertain accuracy and trajectory of express rifles" out to 150 yards. An express rifle was any bore size from .400 to .577.

After twenty-five years of conducting such tests, the staff at *The Field* had amassed considerable expertise. They knew what needed to be done, but also what needed to be *seen* to be done in order to head off criticism from either the losing participants or members of the public. Further, Dr. Walsh was quick to see ancillary benefits that could be gained by expanding the trials in one way or the other, not just to test rifles themselves, but to compare methods of testing.

In his two-volume work, *The Modern Sportsman's Gun and Rifle,* Dr. Walsh describes the rifle trials in complete detail. Volume one (shotguns) was published in 1882, and volume two (rifles) followed in 1884, the year after the trials. In retrospect, new drugs have come to market with less testing than J. H. Walsh put into the 1883 *Field* trial. He explains all that he hoped to accomplish with them, including comparing the accuracy of calculated trajectories based on chronograph readings and ballistic coefficients, against the actual measured trajectories using bullet holes in screens. Velocities were measured on a Boulengé chronograph, and Dr. Walsh enlisted the assistance of Major W. McClintock of the Royal Artillery, assistant superintendent of the Royal Small Arms Factory at Enfield Lock, to calculate the trajectories. Major McClintock's calculations proved remarkably accurate, and this ability to calculate trajectory was very useful to riflemakers in the future. Another contributor to the findings was J. H. Steward, described as "official optician to the National Rifle Association," who took meteorological readings every day at precisely 11:30 a.m., Greenwich Mean Time (GMT). These readings were published with the test results, and included barometric pressure, wind direction, wind strength in relation to the north-south alignment of targets, and temperature readings from both "dry and wet bulb" thermometers.

Dr. Walsh's most important collaborator in the tests was Frederick Toms, a gentleman seldom mentioned but whose contributions were substantial. This is not due either to neglect or a desire to give Dr. Walsh all the credit. Frederick Toms seems to have been a retiring and self-effacing individual. He is identified in Dr. Walsh's book only as "T," which was a common Victorian practice. He was Dr. Walsh's assistant at *The Field,* and succeeded him as editor after his death. Toms then held the editor's chair himself for ten years. The Victorians worshipped erudition and learning the way modern America worships ignorance, and Toms was a living example of this. He was born in Hertford in 1829, the son of a "malthouse clerk," apprenticed to a printer at the age of fifteen, and when his father died three years later, found himself supporting his mother and a younger sister and brother. To educate himself, he attended night classes and joined *The Field* as a printer shortly after its founding. Toms became Managing Printer in 1855, then transferred from the composing room to the editorial office (highly unusual!) and assisted with the first gun trials in 1858.

Frederick Toms was what the Victorians would have described as a "philomath"—one who is a "lover of learning, particularly of mathematics and natural philosophy." In *Who's Who*, published at the turn of the century, his recreations were listed as "rural sports, mathematics, and philology." The latter is the study of "the structure and development of language." In 1896, he wrote a paper that was delivered before the economics section of the British Association for the Advancement of Science—quite an accomplishment for a largely self-taught man who began as a printer's apprentice.

J. H. Walsh had, by his own admission, "little personal liking for arithmetical calculations," and attended to the mechanical and inventive side of the trials while leaving the higher mathematics to Frederick Toms. In Dr. Walsh's book, Toms, identified as "T," wrote the chapter devoted to the calculations and methods used to determine trajectory. The results he arrived at were considered "authoritative" by officials at the Royal Arsenal at Woolwich, and on his death, one official stated that the world had "lost a gunnery expert whose place it would be difficult to fill."

These, then, were the men Dr. Walsh gathered around him to conduct the 1883 *Field* trials of express rifles.

The trials also gave Dr. Walsh an opportunity to test the usefulness of machine rests, and he employed one made by William Jones of Birmingham (inventor of the try-gun). Another benefit, dear to the exact mind of such a one as Dr. Walsh, was that the trials defined, for the first time, the term "express rifle." Henceforth, to qualify, a rifle would be required to have a muzzle velocity of at least 1,600 fps, and a mid-range trajectory, out to 150 yards, no greater than four and one-half inches.

By this definition, rifle sights could be regulated in such a way that the shooter could allow for differences in range, not by aiming higher, but simply by adjusting his sight picture. In books from that time, we read of hunters taking a "fine" bead, or a "full" sight. With a maximum midrange trajectory of four and a half inches, the difference could be allowed for all the way out to two hundred yards simply by taking a bead that was full, fine, or somewhere in between. Since hunters depended only on their own judgment and experience in determining range, and most were very good at it, practice with their rifles allowed them, simply by using this method, to put their bullets exactly where they wanted them within ethical shooting distances. Hence, the importance of Dr. Walsh's definition of exactly what constituted an express rifle.

William Jones's machine rest was not used for any of the accuracy tests. These were carried out by individuals—either the riflemaker or a designated shooter—firing the rifles from a standing rest.

Although the original test was for express rifles only, this was expanded to include rook rifles, on the small side, as well as large bores at shorter ranges. There were ten classes altogether. Participants were allowed to enter two rifles per class, up to a maximum of fifteen in total. The entry fee was £2 per rifle. In an age when a skilled craftsman lived well on a weekly wage of £3, this substantial fee ensured only serious entrants.

The classes were:

1. Single-barrel rook rifles, at ranges of 50 and 75 yards.
2. .400-bore double rifles, at 50, 100, and 150 yards.
3. .450-bore double rifles, at 50, 100, and 150 yards.
4. .500-bore double rifles, at 50, 100, and 150 yards.
5. .577-bore double rifles, at 50, 100, and 150 yards.
6. 12-bore double rifles, at 50 yards.

7. 10-bore double rifles, at 50 yards.
8. 8-bore double rifles, at 50 yards.
9. 4-bore double rifles, at 50 yards.
10. 12-bore double smooth-bore, at 50 yards.

The rules were extensive, detailed, and stringent. Each entrant was to specify the amount and type of gunpowder used, but bullets could be of any metal. Cartridge-case shape and size was specified for rook rifles, but open for all others. A rook rifle (or, more properly, Rook & Rabbit) is what we would now call a small-game rifle, roughly akin to the American .25-20 or .32-20. Trigger pulls could not be less than three pounds, and ordinary (open) sights were required except for rook rifles, where aperture sights were allowed. Cartridges would be inspected before each round, targets were specified, and order of shooting was determined by a draw, carried out at the *Field* office several days in advance.

The shooting contest followed the practice of the day, and was similar to modern benchrest matches. In those days, there were two ways of measuring results. One was the "diagram." This was what we would call a group, but it was measured differently. It was customarily ten shots, and a rectangle would be drawn through the centers of the outermost holes. All the bullet holes were then inside the rectangle, and the dimensions of the rectangle constituted the size of the diagram. An alternative method, and the one employed at the trials, was "string measure." Five shots were fired from each barrel. The gunmaker then chose the centre-point of his group and measured the total distance to each of the ten holes from that point. The total of the ten measurements constituted "string measure." The *Field* varied this slightly; instead of using the total, it used the average length of measurement.

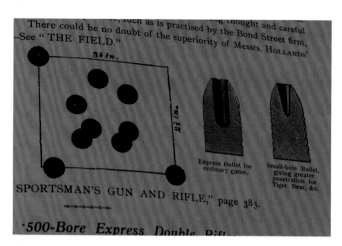

A ten-shot "diagram," taken from the Holland & Holland catalogue of 1900, and reprinted from **The Modern Sportsman's Gun and Rifle**, *by Dr. J. H. Walsh.*

Diagrams were shot at all three ranges, and the three string-measure averages were then averaged for a final "figure of merit." If a gunmaker had two rifles entered, his score would be the average of the two.

Never one to miss an opportunity, Dr. Walsh also prepared diagrams for each rifle in each round, which he could then compare with string measure to see if there was any discrepancy in ranking performance. The only difference he found was that, using a diagram rather than string measure, two Thomas Bland rifles that finished fourth and fifth in the .500 class would have switched places. Dr. Walsh had thus demonstrated that the two methods were equally sound.

A criticism, leveled later, was that the overall results were not valid because many noted riflemakers did not participate. This list included George Gibbs, Alexander Henry, Charles Lancaster, and John Rigby & Co.—all big names, then and now. Although they gave various reasons, such as being too busy preparing for exhibitions in foreign countries, the real reason seems to be that Holland & Holland had already gained such a reputation in rifle circles that other makers stood to gain little from competing with them. The best they could hope for was to maintain the reputation they already had whereas, if they lost, it would be damaging.

The other participants in the rifle trials were Thomas Bland & Son, Watson Bros., and Adams & Co., all of London, and Lincoln Jeffries of Birmingham. William Tranter, the Birmingham revolver maker, was a late entrant in the rook-rifle class.

For its part, Holland & Holland embraced the challenge. It was the only company to enter all ten classes, and when the smoke had cleared, Holland's emerged as the winner in every class. In only one category were they threatened: In the .500 double express rifle class, Lincoln Jeffries won at 50 and 100 yards, but finished third at 150, while Adams won at 150 yards. H&H finished second at all three distances. When the averages were taken, however, H&H was first, Jeffries second, and Adams third.

Holland & Holland's string-measure average for their .500 Express—thirty shots in total at 50, 100, and 150 yards—was 1.719 inches. That is truly spectacular, but Lincoln Jeffries's score was almost as good, at 2.060 inches. There are few hunting rifles today, with modern powder and bullets, that could do as well. While Holland & Holland, as a company, received the accolades for the victory, much of the credit for this extraordinary performance must go to William Froome. If, as stated, Henry Holland designed all the rifles that were entered in the competition, and oversaw their regulation, it is also true that the actual regulating was done by William Froome, who also shot every H&H rifle in the competition. Given the power and recoil of some of these rifles, that alone is testimony to his skill and endurance. Froome fired 190 shots in total, with the reputation of his company riding on each one.

William Gilbert Froome played a critical role in the development of Holland & Holland as a riflemaking company, every bit as important as Henry Holland himself, or Sir Samuel Baker. He eventually became a partner and director of the firm, after the death of Harris Holland in 1896. Donald Dallas states that Froome was responsible for "creating the reputation of Holland & Holland rifles," a reputation that has lasted more than a century and is untarnished to this day. It's difficult to argue with that assessment. If Henry Holland was a man of ideas, William Froome was a man of practical application and great skill. It would be a mistake, however, to think of Henry Holland as merely a manager. He was certainly that—and a brilliant one—but he was also an ingenious and inventive gunmaker.

Donald Dallas: "Henry Holland had incredible talents combining business acumen with inventive genius. He expanded Holland & Holland in the late nineteenth century to probably the biggest gun business in London; he set up the first large, modern gun factory, specifically designed for gun manufacture; he ensured Holland guns and rifles were an essential throughout the British

After winning the 1883 Field trials, and right up to the 1930s, every Holland & Holland rifle and trade label bore this inscription.

Empire and, by the time of his death in 1930, had amassed considerable wealth.

"As an inventor, he must rank as one of the most prolific gun inventors of all time. He took out his first patent in 1879 and by the time of his last patent in 1927, a total of forty-seven patents were in Henry Holland's name."

It was, as Dallas notes, an "incredible tally and achievement." These inventions included the Holland "Royal" action, and the Holland ejector, single trigger, self-opening mechanism, and many innovations related to cartridges.

Holland's triumph at the 1883 *Field* rifle trials was the beginning of the firm's golden age. Solidly established as London's preeminent riflemaker, Holland & Holland embarked on a series of improvements and innovations in both rifles and cartridges. A year earlier, Holland's had introduced a rifling pattern in their rook rifles they called "semi-smooth bore." Such small-game rifles had been a Holland specialty since the 1860s. The new rifling was reduced to the barest minimum required to grip the bullet, and consisted of narrow, shallow ridges and wide, smooth lands. This technique reduced fouling to a minimum, and since fouling was a major cause of deteriorating accuracy, it was a break-through. In the *Field* trials, the H&H rifles were fired thirty times each without cleaning, while their competitors cleaned their bores after every ten shots (as allowed by the rules.) After the rifle trials, Holland's use of semi-smooth bore rifling was expanded to larger bores. In some rifles, at least, the bore tapered near the muzzle by five thousandths of an inch, a feature that was found to improve accuracy.

The 1880s were a time of great change: Smokeless powder was just coming into use, hammerless actions were well on their way to displacing hammers, and the shotgun world had

Holland & Holland capitalized greatly on its success in the 1883 rifle trials.

largely settled on Purdey underlugs combined with the Scott spindle and top lever. However, the 1880s were still the heyday of double rifles chambered for black-powder express cartridges, with external hammers and Jones underlevers. This was a proven design, extremely durable, dependable, and simple.

After 1883, Holland & Holland settled on a couple of cartridges that became a specialty. One was the .500 Express, the rifle that snatched victory from the grasping clutches of Lincoln Jeffries at the trials. That rifle was probably chambered for the cartridge we now know as the .500 Express 3¼", but it's not certain. There are elements of mystery attached, and Holland & Holland itself does not have records of which cartridge it was.

By the rules of the contest, a .500 had to employ a charge of five drams (approximately 135 grains) of gunpowder, and a bullet not more than 3.5 times the weight of the powder. Therefore, the maximum bullet weight was 472 grains. This, however, does not tell us much. That was the *minimum* powder charge, and the *maximum* bullet weight. Using those parameters, the case length had to be 3¼" simply to accommodate the powder.

Although it became customary to specify, on the rifle, not only the caliber, but also the exact cartridge, powder charge, and even bullet weight for which it was regulated, the information on this H&H .500 Express double does not tell us much.

Exactly which cartridge the H&H .500 rifle was chambered for, we don't know. Information published later stated it was loaded with 138 grains of powder, while the stated bullet weights were either 414 or 435 grain—both odd weights for that caliber. Later, H&H made published reference to their "special bullet," but exactly what that was remains a mystery. The recorded velocity of Froome's ammunition was 1,784 fps at the muzzle, loaded with 138 grains of powder and using either a 414- or 435-grain bullet (reports do not agree).

In the years that followed the trials, Holland & Holland developed its own .500 Express (3¼") and maintained a proprietary hold on its exact configuration, including bullet weight, powder charge, type of powder, use of wads, and so on. As a result, when we read glowing accounts of the performance of a "Holland's .500 Express" from the 1880s, there is some question as to exactly what it consisted of.

Regardless of that, H&H settled in to make large numbers of hammer rifles in .500 Express,

with back-action locks, Jones underlevers, and rebounding hammers. Until Henry Holland built his first dedicated factory at 507 Harrow Road in 1893, these rifles were almost certainly produced in their basic form by W&C Scott, and then regulated and finished by Holland's in London. These rifles remained extremely popular in India and Africa, among army officers and colonial administrators, well into the twentieth century. Ammunition was plentiful and it was a proven quantity. Although, in black-powder form, the .500 with its 340- or 380-grain bullet was no elephant gun, it was perfect for both lions and tigers—and tigers were the primary target of most hunters in India. Jim Corbett, who began hunting tigers around the turn of the century, started his career using a .500 express rifle. For a young Englishman heading out to the colonies in the 1890s, intending to hunt big game, a .500 hammer double was almost standard equipment.

* * *

The rifle you see pictured here is a Holland & Holland from that era. According to its serial number, it was probably made in 1892, which means it likely originated with W&C Scott. Russell Wilkin, now retired as technical director of Holland & Holland, told me they had no specific record of the rifle; it was produced "for stock" and sold retail to its first owner. According to the gold stock escutcheon, this was Captain F. W. Heath, an officer in the Royal Artillery, but of course the escutcheon could have been installed by a later owner.

After 1883, and right up until the 1930s, Holland & Holland incorporated the line *WINNERS OF ALL THE "FIELD" RIFLE TRIALS. LONDON* not only on their trade labels, but on the barrels of rifles themselves. Because of the wide range of ammunition available from Eley

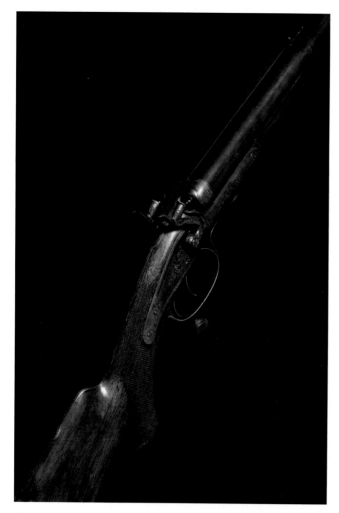

Fitted with rebounding locks and Jones underlever, chambered for the .500 Express (3¼") this rifle, probably made in 1892, was produced "for stock," not in response to a bespoke order. Note the over-the-comb tang, fitted to strengthen the wrist against the formidable recoil.

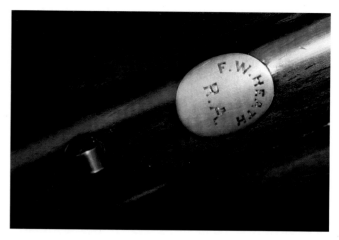

The rifle was probably sold to Captain Heath as a retail item from the Holland & Holland shop, having been made "for stock." Because there is no record of the rifle in the H&H numbers book, we can only speculate on where it went with Captain Heath in his career with the Royal Artillery, or what he might have hunted with it.

Brothers, Kynoch, and other makers, it also became the custom to show the exact cartridge and powder charge for which the rifle was regulated. This was true of most British riflemakers. On my rifle, this information is engraved on the left side of the frame, and reads *CHARGE 5 DRAMS. CASE 3¼ INCHES.*

The rifle's barrels are 26 inches long, with the usual wide flat rib, cross-filed behind the rear sight to eliminate glare. There is an express rear sight with one standing and two folding leaves. The folding leaves are marked "200" and "250," while the standing leaf (with a wide, shallow "V" and vertical line,) is marked "50" on the left and "150" on the right, denoting the respective ranges for a "fine or full" bead. The rib is polished immediately ahead of the rear sight, but rises to a front ramp, where once again the surface is cross-filed. The front sight is a blade fixed in its slot with a pin, and has both a fine bead and a folding ivory "moon" bead.

The rifle weighs 9 lbs. 12 oz., with a sling, and ten pounds on the nose with a cartridge in each chamber. The stock is fitted with a leather-covered recoil pad, installed many years ago, and has an elegant cheekpiece with a shadow line. There is an over-the-comb tang, and the lower tang extends the full length of the pistol grip to the grip cap. Both features strengthen the stock through the wrist. The forend is fastened with a Harvey lever. The front trigger is cross-hatched,

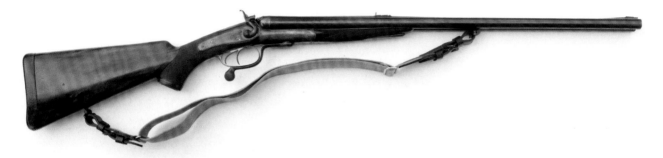

This is a typical example of the superb H&H big-game rifles, made for use on lions and tigers in India and the Colonies, produced in the 1880s and '90s. Built before Holland's opened their factory on Harrow Road, it was produced in basic form by W&C Scott and finished at the H&H shop in London.

while the rear one is smooth, and the front is articulated to protect the finger from bruising.

The Jones underlever is a "partial snap" mechanism. When the action is closed, the lever comes back about two-thirds of the way, and is locked in place with the fingertips. To prevent doubling, the rebounding hammers are held at half-cock in a notch or "bent," not merely by spring pressure.

If one set out to define the ideal lion and tiger rifle, as envisioned in the 1890s, this would be it. It is lacking none of the finer details, but nor is it burdened with any extra non-essential features. As a company that began as a retailer of rifles and shotguns, and only moved into full production for themselves in 1893, Holland's was always conscious of keeping guns in stock for men who wanted to buy off the rack, walk out with a rifle,

and catch the boat for India. As such, they had standard shotguns and rifles made up to fit their own ideas of what was suitable and what was not. In this, Henry Holland received invaluable advice from his good friend and client, Sir Samuel Baker, one of the foremost big-game hunters and rifle experts of all time.

THE .500—A SPECIALTY

The cartridge for which this rifle is chambered deserves some attention. It was not merely a generic .500 Express. Anything but! In the fifteen years between the London rifle trials and the dawn of the nitro-express (smokeless) era in 1898, Holland & Holland made a specialty of the .500 Express (3¼"), carefully tailoring ammunition to their rifles. The .500 Express (3¼") was

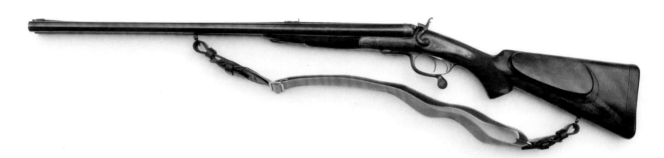

The sling is a recent addition, and the leather-covered recoil pad was probably added after the rifle was made. Note the shadow-line cheekpiece.

98, New Bond Street, LONDON, W. 19

·500 BORE DOUBLE BARRELLED EXPRESS RIFLES.

WINNERS OF ALL THE "FIELD" RIFLE TRIALS.

GOLD MEDAL INVENTIONS EXHIBITION, LONDON, 1885.

Holland & Holland have paid special attention to these rifles, and their great experience as rifle makers, combined with the large amount of information obtained from their customers from all parts of the world, enables them to supply sportsmen with an express which is unrivalled for accuracy, power, and handiness.

One of the first desiderata in a ·500 express is that the crushing power may be relied upon when shooting dangerous game.

It will be found that our ·500 bores shooting 140 grs. (5 drs.) of powder and special bullets, is, in this, and other respects, the most reliable weapon of its size made.

In the *Field* Rifle Trials our ·500 bore beat all other competitors, chiefly through the great accuracy of both barrels, viz., shooting together. This, of course, was not so marked at the short ranges, but at the longer distances our rifle ran away from all others.

In the *Field* report on these trials the Editor says: "Mr. Holland had, however, so fixed his weight as to serve him well all through, and this was one great source of his success. The fact is, that the construction of double rifles and the proper adjustment of their charges require long thought and careful trials, and it is only by the combination of theory and practice, such as is practised by the Bond Street firm, that success can be achieved. . . . There could be no doubt of the superiority of Messrs. Holland's rifles, and they have swept the board."

See *Field, October*, 1883.

Winning Diagram. "Field" Trial, 10 yards, 100 shots.

Mean deviation 3 ranges (50, 100, and 180 yds.) 1·719, area of diagram 3 ranges.

16·47 other competitors from 31·85 to 91·83.

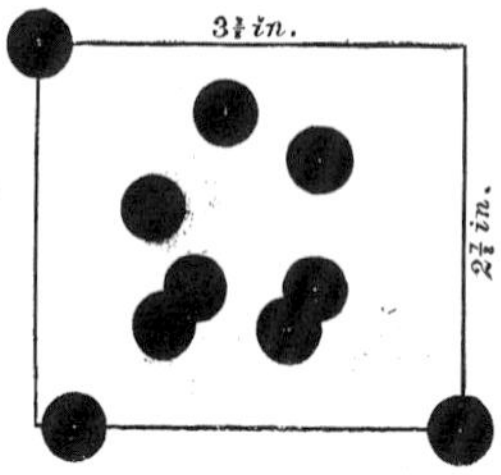

Muzzle Velocity 1784 ft. per second, striking energy, 3134 ft. lb., trajectory at 100 yards 1·52"

Also see "Modern Sportsman's Gun and Rifle," page 383.

Our ·500 bores are constructed with our special non-fouling rifling, which gives the greatest accuracy with the least amount of friction. In the *Field* Trials we fired over thirty shots without cleaning out; the other competitors wiped out at each range.

In 1900, although the first nitro-express (smokeless) cartridges had already appeared, traditional black-powder express loads and rifles were still the order of the day, and still a mainstay of Holland & Holland's business.

a cartridge that had a short life span, but was considered in its day to be the best lion-and-tiger round the world had ever seen.

Look up the .500 Express (3¼") in almost any cartridge book and the information will be sparse. The very first edition of *Cartridges of the World* (COTW) gave it barely a mention, lumping it in with the 3" version as just a variation on the theme—black-powder ancestors of the great .500 Nitro Express.

If you include both available case lengths, and then multiply by the original black powder, the later Cordite, and the in-between nitro-for-black loads, there are six variations, and they do tend to look alike from a distance of more than a century. But delve into a little history—history that is spread in bits and pieces through different books, catalogs, old magazine advertisements, and even the loading information engraved on the frame of an H&H hammer double—and the differences start to come into focus.

Although later editions of COTW expanded on the British .500s, they never did go into the particular history of the .500 Express (3¼"). As it turns out, however, that cartridge was more than just some gunmaker's attempt to be a little different.

The 3" version was introduced sometime in the 1860s, which makes it one of the very first central-fire rifle cartridges. The round numbers are logical: A half-inch bullet in a three-inch case just makes sense. Initially, these "express" cartridges followed the pattern of the original express muzzleloaders as initiated by James Purdey, and fired a relatively light cast bullet in front of a maximum charge of black powder. In the case of the .500, standard bullet weights came to be a 340-grain hollow point and a 380-grain solid.

There were certainly other bullet weights loaded in the .500 (3"), but for stag stalking and general plains-game hunting in India, those two were the accepted standards. The cartridge belonged to no gunmaker in particular. This was before the later practice of proprietary cartridges really became established; there were several metallic-cartridge makers in Britain, and all of them loaded variations on the .500.

During this period, guns for really big game continued to be the proven 8-bores and 4-bores, with wide use of 10- and 12-bore rifles as well.

The three main variations of the .500 Express, from left: .500 Express, by Kynoch; .500 Express (3¼"), and the .500 Nitro Express, which was a descendant of the shorter black-powder round.

By comparison, the .500 was a "medium" at best. But by the 1870s, hunters and gunmakers alike were starting to see the possibilities of smaller rifles on the larger game. Sir Samuel Baker was an unquestioned admirer of the ultra-large guns, but he championed the development of a .577 rifle even for elephants.

The .500 Express (3") as it existed had potential, but it also had limitations. The standard bullet was paper patched. You could increase the weight to make it more effective on bigger game, but that would reduce powder capacity; if you packed in more powder, it meant you had to reduce bullet weight. Someone hit on the idea of extending the case length by a quarter of an inch, which allowed a 100-grain increase in bullet weight while still managing to afford a little more capacity for powder.

By the way, the configuration of the 340- and 380-grain bullets is identical; the weight difference comes from hollowing out the cavity, so seating depth, overall cartridge length, and so on, are the same for both.

The longer .500 Express (3¼") would accept 440- and 480-grain bullets, and even with these, powder capacity increased to 142 grains from 136. The new cartridge was the ideal rifle for lions and tigers.

* * *

Over the years, I have had the privilege of shooting many different double rifles by many different makers, old and new, English and otherwise. Probably two dozen of them were made by Holland & Holland, ranging in size from .375 H&H up to the largest, a 4-bore double that was being built in 2009 for an American client. In between, there were a .700 H&H, a .577 NE, a .500 NE, and a .500/.465. Then, of course, there is my own black-powder .500 Express (3¼"). All of these rifles were of excellent quality and superb workmanship, but like all rifles, each had its own personality. Partly this was dictated by the dimensions, weight, and balance. The 4-bore double weighed in the neighborhood of twenty-four pounds, which is a lot of *avoirdupois* to hoist to one's shoulder, hold there while it steadies, and then take careful aim. The same is true, albeit to a lesser extent, of the .700 H&H, which was a couple of pounds lighter.

Of the nitro-express rifles, my favorite to shoot was the .500 NE. It was under construction in 1993, at the same time as the .500/.465, but the dimensions of the two were quite different. The .500, while more powerful, belted me around considerably less than did the .500/.465. It just felt natural in my hand, and friendly even in its recoil. By some freak of fate, my .500 Express

(3¼") hammer rifle fits me much like the .500 NE did in 1993, and in its handling and balance, it feels lighter than it is. In both rifles and shotguns, that is a key element: When a gun feels lighter than it weighs, then it is well balanced. It mounts like a shotgun, and comes to my shoulder with the sights already aligned with my eye.

On the basis of those experiences, I believe the .500 Express hammer doubles that H&H produced toward the end of the black-powder era were the prototypes for the superb H&H nitro-express doubles to come. Unlike many black-powder rifles, which differ considerably from what followed, it was as if Holland's had perfected their lines and balance, and learned how

The later, great nitro-express cartridges, from left: .450 NE (3¼"), .500 NE (3"), .577 Nitro Express, and .600 Nitro Express. Holland & Holland built double rifles for all of them, and these are highly prized (and expensive) today. Much of Holland's expertise was based in their experience with the .500 Express (3¼") hammer rifles that traveled to every corner of the British Empire.

to weave all the differing factors, and weld all the disparate parts, into a finely tuned mechanism that could perform like a Stradivarius. Having mastered the secrets of weight and balance, when black powder gave way to smokeless and the heavy nitro-express cartridges, it remained only to give those powerful rifles the same eumatic qualities (see chapter XII) as their black-powder predecessors.

Dedicated users of .500 Express doubles, such as Jim Corbett in India, only gave up the big .500s when something lighter yet more powerful came along. In Corbett's case, it was a .450/.400 NE double, augmented by a .275 Rigby, as the rifle that he carried, henceforth, more than any other. The coming of smokeless powder changed everything in the realm of big-game rifles, but it does not in any way diminish the excellence of that which went before. The Holland & Holland .500 Express (3¼") is one of the great hunting rifles of all time.

Such a magnificent rifle!

The Commission '88 bolt-action rifle.

CHAPTER IV

THE MILITARY BOLT ACTIONS

On continental Europe, rifle development through the nineteenth century concentrated more on military than sporting use. The situation there was completely different than in Britain, both culturally and politically, and these differences evinced themselves not only in the way rifles were manufactured, but also the purposes for which they were made.

Britain, with its vast empire, was always on the verge of war somewhere, although these were usually tribal wars or border skirmishes. There was no threat that an enemy might appear with a serious technological advantage in the form of modern weapons. The only real wars Britain fought in the mid-nineteenth century were against Russia in the Crimea (1853–54), and against its own sepoys in the Indian Mutiny in 1857. Russia was not an industrial power, and the Indian Mutiny was fought with the British Army's own weapons. With its army focused largely on imperial policing, the War Office was more concerned with saving money than enhancing firepower. As for the great nations on the continent, there was always the possibility of war with France, but that was more force of habit than actual threat. And if the French did become belligerent, the United Kingdom had its private moat in the English Channel, patrolled by the ships of the Royal Navy.

An entire generation of military historians, after 1918, sought explanations for the great arms races of Europe, from 1850 to 1914, and the origins of the "merchants of death." These latter included familiar names: Mauser, Fabrique Nationale (FN), Mannlicher, Luger, Krupp, Skoda, and Steyr. If one were willing to go that far, one could trace the origins of it all back to Vercingetorix and the Romans. Not venturing quite so far, it's safe to say that age-old enmities between, mainly, France and Germany were at the root of it all. Both France and Germany were essentially land powers, and their strength lay in their armies. France had not been a real naval power for centuries, and any lingering pretensions in that direction ended at Trafalgar in 1805. Germany never had been a naval power, nor really wished to be.

The French Army of King Louis XIV, and later the *Grande Armée* under Napoleon, had dominated Europe, and despite various defeats, the French Army was still reckoned the most powerful on the continent. The Prussians had challenged this, occasionally with some success (such as Blücher's involvement at Waterloo), but were generally left in a position of trying to catch up to the French in order to hold their own. The third great European power was the Austro-Hungarian Empire. While it had a fleet in the Mediterranean, it was also largely a land power, with a substantial army. It had steadily lost ground since the Napoleonic Wars, and was preoccupied, first, with staving off Ottoman advances into Europe, and later the turbulent politics of the Balkan region. These conflicts called for well-trained infantry armed with rifles, not for ships of the line. If the Austro-Hungarians were politically weak, however, they did have significant industrial assets, and a first-rate arms-making industry that went back centuries.

The uniting of the disparate German states really began with King Frederick the Great of Prussia, and the rise of Prussia at the expense of the older states of Poland and Russia was the great catalyst. Once Prussia became the dominant German-speaking state (outside of Austria), it was logical for the many Teutonic kingdoms, principalities, palatinates, duchies, and electorates to eventually combine into one country. The man responsible for this was Prince Otto von Bismarck, a Prussian aristocrat. Until the unification was completed, Prussia acted on her own or with allies drawn from among the German states. The consolidation of Germany, and the establishment of Prussia as a force to be reckoned with in Europe, took place partly through a series of wars. The Prussian Army already had a reputation throughout the world that outstripped its actual size, which was never very large. It was, however, extremely good. *Extremely*. Prussian militarism, which became an object of faith in France and England, had its roots in Prussian culture all the way back to the Teutonic Knights of the twelfth century. An army career was as natural for a Prussian as entering the Royal Navy was for an Englishman. As Voltaire observed, "Where some states have an army, the Prussian Army has a state." This was repeated more and more—usually by Frenchmen—in the years after Waterloo.

As a child learning history, I was taught that the Franco-Prussian War of 1870–71 was won by the Prussians because they possessed the Dreyse needle gun. This glib statement is, at best, only partly true. One might say that, had they not possessed the Dreyse, they might have lost, because the French infantry rifle at the time, the Chassepot, was vastly better. Unfortunately for the French, their generalship was vastly poorer.

Prussia adopted the Dreyse in 1842, and at that time it was state of the art. It was an early bolt-action that employed a paper cartridge containing a bullet, powder, and a primer. The firing pin was a long needle that penetrated the rear of the paper cartridge and passed through the powder charge to strike the primer at the base of the bullet. While the rest of the world was still using muzzleloaders, the Prussians were armed with a breechloader.

Where the Dreyse did have a decisive influence, both in military terms and in the history of rifles generally, was at the Battle of Königgrätz in 1866, during the Austro-Prussian War. This was the second of Bismarck's wars that was instrumental in forging a united Germany. The Prussians, armed with the Dreyse, defeated the Austrians, who were armed with the muzzle-loading Lorenz. The Lorenz was a fine military weapon for its day, but its day had passed with the coming of the Dreyse. The major advantage of the Dreyse is the fact that it can be loaded and fired while the shooter is lying on the ground or kneeling, whereas the Lorenz must be loaded standing up. Against concentrated, accurate Prussian fire, a standing line of infantry was at a huge disadvantage.

By the time of the Franco-Prussian War, four years later, the French were armed with the Chassepot, also a bolt-action breechloader. It was lighter than the Dreyse, more dependable, had greater velocity and range, and was a superior rifle in every way. The Prussians more than compensated for this disadvantage with better artillery, superior tactics, and superb generalship.

The lasting impact of the Battle of Königgrätz on rifle history was that it inspired a young engineer to abandon his career with the Austrian railway and turn his inventive hand to fire-arms. That engineer was Ferdinand Mannlicher (later Ritter von Mannlicher), one of the great geniuses of firearms development. A patriot, he was determined to help arm his native Austria to defend herself against possible attacks from Russia, which was seen as the immediate threat post-Königgrätz. Mannlicher allied himself with Josef Werndl, founder of the Österreichische Waffenfabriks-Gesellschaft at Steyr, and together they not only provided Austria-Hungary with a succession of highly effective rifles over the next fifty years, they turned the Steyr works into one of the world's great rifle manufacturers—a company that is still in business, and still making fine rifles, to this day.

For its part, Prussia defeated the French finally and almost irrevocably at the Battle of Sedan in 1871, but they recognized the superiority of the Chassepot rifle, and set about finding an up-to-date replacement for the Dreyse.

* * *

By 1871, the military world was well into the era of breechloading rifles and self-contained cartridges. Even the British, never exactly trend-setters when it came to arming their infantry, were using the Snider-Enfield with its drawn-brass cartridge case, and looking ahead to a permanent replacement for that stop-gap measure. The replacement they chose was the Martini-Henry.

After Königgrätz, the Austro-Hungarian Empire was restructured to become the "dual monarchy," consisting of the Austrian Empire and the Kingdom of Hungary, with Emperor Franz Joseph as both Emperor of Austria and King of Hungary. It was a very cosmopolitan empire; Franz Joseph was fluent in seven languages, which allowed him to speak in their native tongue to most—but by no means all—of his subjects. The political cracks that appeared after Königgrätz may have been papered over, but they were still there, and getting wider all the time. This resulted in political stagnation on the one hand but had far-reaching effects in other areas. An unintended consequence affected the Österreichische Waffenfabriks-Gesellschaft at Steyr, where Werndl, Mannlicher, et al, were laboring to arm the empire. If the British were frugal in their military spending, the Dual Monarchy was positively miserly. The arms factory at Steyr could not depend on purchases by Vienna and Budapest to keep its machines running, and was forced to look for export markets. Thus did Steyr become one of the foremost "merchants of death," although they certainly did not see it that way.

After 1871, with the development of the self-contained brass cartridge, almost all the European powers adopted single-shot rifles as a stop-gap while they worked on repeating rifles.

In Germany, two brothers, Paul and Wilhelm Mauser, had gone into business as gunmakers in the 1860s. Paul was the talented designer, Wilhelm the manager. The history of Mauser is well known, and has been written many times and from many angles—from that of a mechanical engineer, to a military historian, to a social historian horrified by the Mauser company as a merchant of death. However, because the story of the Mauser brothers and their rifles is integral to our story here, it deserves recounting in some detail.

From the beginning, the Mauser brothers were interested in military rifles and government contracts, not in making rifles for either hunting or target shooting. Their initial customer was the Prussian government which, in 1871, adopted Mauser's Model 71 single-shot rifle to replace the Dreyse. The Model 71 was a turnbolt-type action,

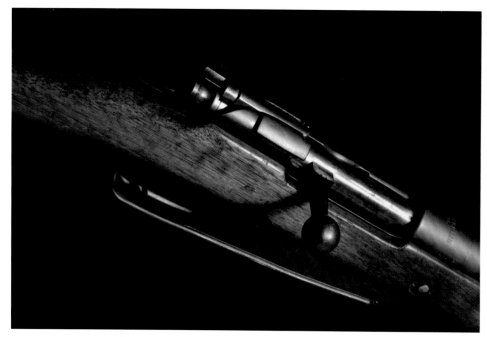

and Mauser seems prescient in having settled on a basic mechanism that is the most versatile rifle action ever made, and which—with many adaptations and improvements—became the dominant military action throughout the world until 1945. Later, a tubular magazine was added to make the Model 71 into a repeating rifle (the Model 71/84). By that time, so many other developments were taking place in cartridges, magazines, and repeating mechanisms, the German government decided it once more needed a completely new rifle that would put it on the cutting edge of military hardware. It appointed a commission of the Prussian government to decide on a design.

Ferdinand Mannlicher was already in full stride at Steyr, in Austria, developing his own turnbolt actions, and concentrating on different methods of storing and feeding cartridges. Today, it's easy to forget that in this era, strides were being made almost daily in every area of rifle design and function. Cartridges were evolving, and calibers becoming steadily smaller; new smokeless powders were beginning to make an appearance, with higher pressures and higher velocities. It was

the chicken-and-egg question multiplied by ten. An improvement in a rifle action led to a new cartridge that could take advantage of it; a new cartridge allowed further improvements in magazines, and this led to more sophisticated actions. Virtually every aspect of rifles and cartridges that we now take for granted (and which look so simple and obvious in retrospect) required long periods of evolution, trial, and error, before they were perfected.

In what may be the only instance of a truly fine rifle being designed by committee, the German 1888 Commission rifle was adopted and began a long and illustrious career. In official German military use, it lasted only until 1898, but it was exported all over the world and saw use by many different armies on many different battlefields. Large stocks were manufactured and kept in storage, and were being issued to reserve units in Europe as late as 1945.

The Commission rifle, as it is generally known, is variously claimed as a Mauser or a Mannlicher, but while it incorporates features that are definitely one or the other, it is neither a Mauser nor

The 8x57 JS (right) beside its equally famous offspring, the 7x57. Although both began life as military cartridgeso, both went on to be great hunting cartridges as well. Many of today's favorite hunting cartridges are descended, directly or indirectly, from the 8x57.

The Mannlicher "packet" system of holding cartridges. The entire clip is inserted in the magazine well. When the last cartridge has been fed into the chamber, the empty clip falls out of the action. This system was used in the Commission '88 rifle as well as in later Mannlicher designs, including the Model 1895 straight-pull military rifle.

a Mannlicher. It's a turnbolt repeating rifle with a magazine forward of the trigger guard that utilizes Mannlicher's "packet" system. This was almost a Mannlicher trademark. Cartridges are held in a steel clip, and the entire packet is pushed into the magazine well. The bolt strips the cartridges out one at a time, with the remaining cartridges pushed up into position by a spring-loaded arm. When the last cartridge is chambered, the empty steel clip falls out the bottom of the action. This was Ferdinand Mannlicher's most obvious contribution to the design. Paul Mauser's was the dual opposing locking lugs near the head of the bolt, but Mannlicher is credited with its removable bolt head. The Commission made a contribution of its

own, with the introduction of the 8x57 J (or "I," for *Infanterie*) rimless cartridge. Whichever anonymous member or members of the Commission came up with the 8x57, he or they missed a golden chance at immortality. It was, and is, one of the great cartridges of all time.

In the mountainous, forested regions of central Europe, including the German states, Austria-Hungary, and Switzerland, there was a

The Commission '88 (top) not only provided inspiration for sporting rifles, such as this Haenel-Mannlicher New Model, but many '88 military rifles and carbines were converted to sporters and used all over the world.

strong tradition of both big-game hunting and target shooting with rifles. These traditions went back centuries, and during that time certain styles and patterns had emerged. They were not only accepted, but almost mandatory. The target rifle was a single-shot, intended for either offhand shooting or from a bench, at ranges from 100 to 300 metres. These rifles were as intricate and elaborate as cuckoo clocks. The standard form of hunting rifle was a single-shot or a double, with the trend in double rifles favoring the over-and-under. They also developed and made a specialty of multi-barreled combination guns. The most common is the *drilling*, or three-barreled gun, which combined rifle and shotgun into one. Such weapons were mostly produced one at a time, in small shops, by independent gunmakers. In Austria, the town of Ferlach was the center of this activity, dating back centuries. Ferlach's counterpart in Germany was Suhl. Like any craft, gunmaking was regulated partly by government decree and partly by guilds that set standards of craftsmanship and skill.

The great arms-making factories, like Steyr and Mauser, were generally located in other towns, where water power, rail access, and the varied requirements of modern industry could be met. The mass-production arms industries of Europe grew up apart from the traditional crafts of gunmaking. Partly for this reason, and partly due to conservatism, European hunters look down on rifles with military origins. They don't want their big-game rifles to be, or look, in any way military. There were exceptions, of course, and gradually these prejudices were overcome. There was also a feeling, not entirely dispelled to this day, that repeating rifles (that is, with more than two or three shots) were unsporting. Both the Mauser factory at Oberndorf and the Steyr works in Austria, however, eventually became major manufacturers of hunting and target rifles.

Big-game hunting in Europe resembled stag stalking in Scotland, but only to a degree. In the Alps, hunters either climbed in search of game, or set up stands where they could overlook trails or alpine meadows. The rifles they used reflected

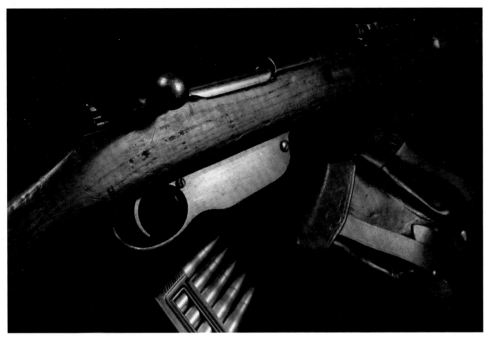

The Mannlicher Model 95 straight-pull rifle, using the packet system of loading, was the main military arm of the Austro-Hungarian Empire from 1895 to 1918.

this. The Alpinist wanted a light, handy, single-shot rifle he could strap on his back; the occupant of a *hochsitz* (high seat) wanted a heavier, accurate rifle; a prowler of woods and meadows might want a drilling with a shotgun barrel for birds, a high-powered rifle for red stag, and a small-caliber barrel for roebuck or capercaillie.

When the self-contained brass cartridge was perfected, German and Austrian gunmakers embarked on a spree of designing cartridges for their own rifles. They then provided loaded ammunition to their clients, and countless numbers of specialty cartridges appeared, for short-range and long-range targets, big game, small game, and anything else that appealed to a gunmaker's fevered imagination in the wee hours. A few of these creations became standard, with ammunition supplied by large companies.

The debut of the German Commission rifle of 1888 was a watershed for riflemakers, although they could not have known it at the time. It was produced under contract at many different factories, including the Austrian rifle works at Steyr, and it was produced in quantity. Its bolt-action

system was the best one to date at that point, but did not remain so for long. The Mauser brothers were designing one turnbolt rifle after another, each one an improvement on what went before: 1891, 1893, 1894, and so on. Similarly, Ferdinand Mannlicher in Steyr was improving with each successive model, although he concentrated on straight-pull bolt rifles, with most using his packet system.

The packet method of loading was excellent for military rifles but poor for a hunting rifle. Paul Mauser had developed a box magazine in which cartridges were staggered, lifted into position by a spring-powered follower, and this was recognized as a good system for a hunting rifle. It was also versatile: It could be adapted to different cartridges much more easily than a pre-formed, sheet-steel, "packet" clip.

The Commission rifle used packets, but independent gunmakers saw how it could easily be reworked to include a box magazine similar to the Mauser. They also recognized that in the ultra-smooth and silent Commission action, they had the basis for a first-rate modern sporting

The Mauser 98 (shown here in K98 form) was not only the dominant military rifle from 1898 to 1945, it was also the basis for outstanding hunting rifles, either purpose-built at Oberndorf, or converted military actions.

rifle. Although its bolt handle jutted out at right angles, topped by a bulbous knob, this could be reshaped into something graceful and unobtrusive as well as ergonomic. With warehouses full of Commission rifles, and many gunmakers experienced in manufacturing them, the stage was set for the first real attempt to make a first-class hunting rifle out of a military bolt action.

* * *

There was one last step in the perfecting of the military bolt action in Europe, and that was Paul Mauser's Model 1898. This was the rifle that replaced the Commission '88 rifle in the German Army, and from the moment of its introduction it became the rifle that every other designer tried to beat for the next hundred years. Some came close in both military and civilian applications. There were bolt actions that were more accurate, there were some that fired more rapidly, and there were others that had greater cartridge capacity. One or two, it could be argued, were stronger.

But none could be unequivocally termed *better* in every way.

Over the next fifty years, the Mauser Gewehr 98 evolved into the K98, and was then manufactured in several different countries, some of which made genuinely valuable improvements. What set the 98 apart from its rivals, such as the American Springfield or the British P-14 (both of which were frankly modeled on, derived from, or copied the Mauser), was its capacity for refinement, and for alteration to suit a specific purpose. The Mauser 98 has no single perceived weak point that cannot be eliminated if desired. When riflescopes became standard, it was possible to replace the Mauser's over-the-top three-position safety with a horizontal safety on the shroud, or a trigger safety as part of a complete new trigger mechanism. For that matter, although its two-stage military trigger was very good, replacement trigger mechanisms became almost a growth industry. So did more elegant bottom metal, and new bolt handles. The standard military action could be cut down and then welded back together to create a shorter (*kurz*) action suitable for smaller cartridges, or the standard could be opened up to accommodate longer or fatter ones. As for cartridges comparable to the military 8x57 JS, the K98 could handle just about any of them, and with a reasonable minimum of alteration.

The roughest military action salvaged from some battlefield on the Russian Front could be cleaned up by a good gunsmith, and with some polishing here, grinding there, a new trigger and bolt handle, and the application of some gun-making skills, become a custom rifle that would command $50,000 at a Safari Club auction.

After the 98's introduction and adoption by the German Army, the Mauser company expanded its operations and, for the first time, seriously entered the sporting-rifle market. From its factories at Oberndorf, it began exporting Model 98 actions, barreled actions, and entire rifles to London where, through its English agent, John Rigby & Co., it supplied such riflemakers as Holland & Holland, W. J. Jeffery, and Westley Richards. Rigby was instrumental in persuading Oberndorf

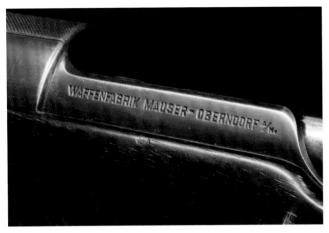

The last Oberndorf sporters were assembled from existing parts in 1946.

to produce the famous magnum action, which made possible cartridges like the .416 Rigby and .505 Gibbs.

Some Oberndorf sporters are excellent rifles, others not so wonderful. The same is true of the London-vintage 98s, bearing names like Rigby, Jeffery, and Holland & Holland. Both German and American gunsmiths have done wonders with Mauser 98 actions, producing some sporting rifles that are nothing short of exquisite, and a

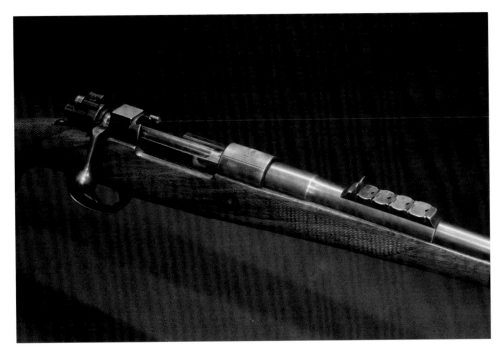

Square-bridge commercial Oberndorf Mauser sporting rifle, complete with express sights and the Mauser banner on the action ring. Such rifles are rising, inexorably, in value.

few chapters hence we will look at some individual rifles that show exactly what can be done with the Mauser 98.

For many years, Oberndorf sporters were common, and relatively inexpensive. Altogether, it is estimated that the factory produced about 125,000 sporting rifles, in three main grades: Types A, B, and C. The Model A copied the style and features of a London-made "magazine rifle" sporter, as produced by John Rigby. The Model B had more European styling of stock, barrel, and features, while the Model C was the plainest and least expensive. How many individual actions and barreled actions were produced for export, or for sale to German gunmakers, is unknown, but they are included in the above estimate of 125,000. Within those model categories there were any number of variations possible, including different calibers, stock styles (such as the three-quarter length "African" style), and different sights.

Oberndorf actions were made in a wonderful array of styles and sizes. Smallest was the "K" or *kurz* action, and rifles were built on it chambered for the .250-3000 and similar deer and small-game cartridges. The standard action was suitable for the 8x57 JS or .30-06, and magnum actions for such as the .416 Rigby. Some were military style with a round bridge, others had square bridges, or even a double-square bridge (both bridge and receiver ring with a flat plateau for scope-mount bases). The early German style for mounting scopes followed that of Austria or Czechoslovakia. A detachable mount was preferred, usually with some variation of a claw mount, and normal practice was to carry the scope in a leather pouch and only attach it to the rifle when needed. Often, these mounts had tunnels through which the iron sights could be seen with the scope in place. For this reason, as

The Mauser banner today.

well as to allow clearance for the safety and the bolt handles, mounts were customarily quite high by American standards—sometimes absurdly so. Curiously, unnecessarily high scope mounts are still the German custom, and you have to fight them tooth and nail to get rings that place the scope as low over the action as the bolt handle will allow.

Today, Oberndorf sporters in fine condition command prices from collectors comparable to the rarer original military rifles. Not extortionate, but not cheap, and no one in his right mind would buy one today, strip it down for the action, and rebuild it into a custom rifle. Nor would a collector have scope mounts installed if they were not there already. As for using one for its original purpose, in its original condition, that is certainly possible. None would be considered suitable for shooting beyond 250 yards or so with open sights, but many of them so equipped would make very good stalking or still-hunting rifles. They carry well, feel good in the hands, and mount quickly, and fulfill in many ways my criteria for a good hunting rifle.

The last Oberndorf sporters were put together from existing parts in 1946, under French authority, and that was the last of the K98

Oberndorf sporters. The Mauser name continued in existence, under different owners, for the next seventy-five years. In 2000, it was acquired by Michael Lüke, owner of Blaser in Germany, where it now resides with its own plant in the Blaser complex at Isny im Allgäu. During those seventy-plus years, the company made several different types of hunting and tactical rifles, but never a 98. Even as the prices of original Oberndorf actions skyrocketed, during the height of the custom-rifle boom from the 1970s to 2010, Mauser stubbornly refused to manufacture 98s, even though a 98 action with the genuine Mauser banner on it would find a ready market, competing with such 98-clone actions as those produced by Granite Mountain and others. There was one abortive attempt to make a "made by Mauser" 98 in 2008, using a magnum action produced by Prechtl, a small company in Germany. But,

priced at $40,000, it was not surprising that few were made.

When Michael Lüke acquired the John Rigby name in 2011, rescuing it from varying degrees of American fast-buck fraud and moving it back to London, there arose a demand for original Mauser actions on which to once again build genuine John Rigby magazine rifles. Apparently, that was enough of a spur to cause the Mauser company to return to building the 98, both for Rigby's use and their own. In 2015, the company began producing magnum actions, and followed this up two years later with the first Mauser-made standard Mauser 98 sporters in seventy years. The first ones arrived in America in 2017, while in London, John Rigby & Co. was busy producing stalking rifles like the ones they had made a century before. These rifles are not inexpensive, by any means, but they are worth many second looks.

* * *

A modern (2017) Mauser sporting rifle, manufactured at Isny im Allgäu. The quality more than matches those produced at Oberndorf. This one is chambered, fittingly, in 8x57 JS.

The Haenel-Mannlicher New Model.

CHAPTER V

STEYR AND THE MANNLICHERS

THE HAENEL-MANNLICHER NEW MODEL

Successful European arms designers were highly regarded in the years before 1914, and grateful countries rewarded them for their efforts. In 1892, Ferdinand Mannlicher was knighted by the government of Austria-Hungary and became Ferdinand, Ritter von Mannlicher, a permanent member of the upper house of the Austrian parliament. For von Mannlicher (as we shall henceforth refer to him) this was but one of the rewards of his genius.

There have been many talented gun designers throughout history, but not many warrant the term "genius." Von Mannlicher was one. During his career, from 1869 to his death in 1904, he patented dozens of different designs for rifles and pistols, bolt actions and semiautos, and even machine guns. W. H. B. Smith, one of the foremost firearms historians of the twentieth century, considered von Mannlicher to be comparable to John M. Browning, and even superior to him in some respects. He was a man gifted with the prescience to anticipate developments in cartridges and their ballistic capabilities, and to design weapons that were far ahead of their time. According to Smith, every significant development in small arms that was made through 1945 had already been anticipated by von Mannlicher and included in one or another of his patents. Not all were manufactured, and of those that were, not all were successful, but they planted the seed for others that followed. For example, the eight-round packet that provided the

firepower for the American Garand rifle in the Second World War was derived from a Mannlicher concept.

The astonishing thing about von Mannlicher's career was that his rifles were made at a time when the self-contained cartridge was evolving almost daily. His career spanned black powder and smokeless. When he began, the rimmed centerfire 11.4mm (.43) black-powder military round firing a lead bullet was state of the art; when he died, his rimless, bottleneck 6.5x54 was starting on its way as one of the great hunting cartridges, using a .264-diameter jacketed bullet powered by smokeless powder.

Because of the workings of the Prussian small-arms commission that developed the Commission rifle, it is not clear exactly who was responsible for which features. It's generally conceded, however, that von Mannlicher had an influential hand in the design of the bolt with its dual opposing locking lugs and detachable bolt head. Undoubtedly, Paul Mauser was involved as well, but von Mannlicher's contribution has led to the action being referred to as a Mannlicher in its subsequent incarnations as a sporting rifle.

Exactly who first came up with the idea of converting Commission rifles into sporters is a question that will never be answered. Possibly, several firms began doing it around the same time. These included some famous names in gunmaking, including V. C. Schilling and C. G. (Carl Gottlieb) Haenel, of Suhl. Both companies were involved in producing the military Commission rifles, and had a variety of tooling in place. The first Haenel-Mannlichers were chambered for the 8x57 J, and had the original Mannlicher packet-type magazine. These dispensed with the Commission rifle barrel shroud, had sporter-style stocks with Prince of Wales grips and Schnäbel forends, and the bolt handle was turned down into a wide, swooping "butterknife."

Two prominent New York firms, Von Lengerke & Detmold, and A. H. Funke, imported Haenel-Mannlichers. Funke also imported a later model, much modified from the original, called the Haenel-Mannlicher New Model. Although this rifle is often listed as appearing in 1909, it was advertised in various shooting journals as early as 1902. Oddly enough, these two rifles are described in *Mauser Bolt Rifles*, by Ludwig Olson, in the chapter titled "Mauser Sporters by Other Makers." They are "Mauser sporters" by only the broadest of definitions, but to the best of my knowledge this is the only book of that era that deals with them at all.

Although the Haenel-Mannlicher New Model was based on the Commission action, it bore about as much resemblance to the original as a later, full-blown, Mauser-actioned custom rifle bears to a battered military K98. The essential elements are there, true enough—honed, bevelled, and polished—but virtually everything else has been either modified or replaced.

The major change in the New Model was the replacement of the packet system and original magazine with a box magazine, flush with the stock, similar to the Mauser 98. Where it differed substantially was in its spring-powered arm that lifts the cartridges into position for feeding. Instead of a simple steel follower with a "W"-shaped spring, it is a precision mechanism that folds back as the floorplate is opened. The

The Haenel-Mannlicher New Model floorplate release is a precision mechanism. Physically, it resembles the later commercial Oberndorf Mauser, but the operation is quite different. The New Model also came with a double-set trigger.

floorplate itself is held in place and released by a knurled button inside the front of the trigger guard. It is similar in appearance (but not operation) to later Oberndorf Mauser sporters. Because it did not depend on packets, the New Model could be offered in different calibers, and 7x57 and 9x57 were added to the standard 8x57 J.

At the time, gunmakers were still learning what was and was not necessary on a sporting bolt-action rifle. The New Model had a stock similar to the original Haenel-Mannlicher, with a Prince of Wales grip and Schnäbel forend. The forend was held to the barrel by a barrel bolt, an ancient method of fastening that can be traced back to flintlocks. As well, to ensure strength in the stock where it had been hollowed out to accommodate the action, there were raised wooden panels on each side. These are sometimes described as merely decorative, but they were originally intended for strength. Later, as bolt-action sporters evolved, both the barrel bolt and side panels were dispensed with as unnecessary.

The Haenel-Mannlicher New Model was fitted with a double-set trigger as standard. The bolt was modified to employ a pivoting ejector,

The Haenel-Mannlicher New Model has a gas shield ahead of the bolt shroud and the bridge is split to allow passage of the bolt handle.

similar to the Mausers, and was fitted with a gas shield in front of the bolt shroud, just behind the bridge. Like the Commission rifle, the bridge was split to allow passage of the bolt handle. Two other differences mentioned by Olson were a separate firing pin tip that could be replaced without requiring an entirely new striker, and a thumb cut on the left receiver rail to facilitate the use of stripper clips. The bridge had a slot to accommodate these.

Exact original technical specifications for the Haenel-Mannlicher New Model do not seem to exist, and no two examples of the rifles are ever quite identical. This may be due to vagaries in production at the C. G. Haenel factory, where an improvement or alteration could be incorporated, seemingly at the whim of the foreman, without bothering to inform the importer. Alternatively, a rifle could be a custom order from the factory. With importer-retailers like Funke, this was not uncommon. Finally, some changes could have been effected by Funke or a gunsmith to accommodate a client. The example shown by Olson has a front base dovetailed into the receiver ring for a claw mount for a riflescope, but this was probably installed much later, along with the mount for the rear base.

In the rifle shown in this book, several alterations have been made. It's chambered for the 9x57, a cartridge comparable to the .358 Winchester in power and recoil. Somewhere along the line, an owner had the original steel buttplate replaced by a ventilated recoil pad with a white-line spacer. The pad was pretty dilapidated when I acquired the rifle, and I subsequently had it replaced with a solid brown pad. This is more effective as well as quite handsome. Had the rifle been in original condition, I could never have brought myself to alter it in this way, but I am grateful to that unknown owner of years past.

This Haenel-Mannlicher New Model has been altered by the addition of the recoil pad, and by the trimming of the Prince of Wales grip to a stylish (for 1910) squared-off pistol grip. Note the side panels and barrel bolt.

The recoil of the little rifle is attention-getting, to say the least, even with the pad.

Another change was the addition of a Lyman Model 36 receiver sight. This sight was created by Lyman in 1907 for the newly introduced Mannlicher-Schönauer Model 1903 and 1905 rifles, which we shall come to shortly. The Lyman 36 would also fit the Haenel-Mannlichers. The entire sighting system on this Haenel deserves a closer look because it's carefully thought out and extremely practical. It includes a front sight, iron sight on the rib, and receiver sight, combined in a system that is adaptable to any target practical with iron sights.

The Haenel-Mannlicher New Model came from the factory with a half-octagon, half-round

This Haenel-Mannlicher is fitted with a half-octagon barrel of Krupp steel.

barrel, wearing a full-length rib beautifully file-cut to eliminate glare. Like the Woodward double rifle described in an earlier chapter, the rib dips ahead of the rear sight, then rises into an integral ramp for the front sight. The front sight has two blades; when one is pushed down, the other pops up through its slot, and vice versa. In operation, it functions exactly like a teeter-totter, held in the center by a tiny transverse pin. One blade has a fine, blued steel bead, and is 20/100ths of an inch lower than the other, which has a larger bronze bead. There is a spring that holds the large bead in place when it's up and prevents any accidental "half-up, half-down" position. Presumably, this is the bead one would use in most circumstances, especially at close range with an animal like a running boar. The entire front-sight mechanism is a dovetailed insert held in place by a set screw, and machined to match the rib surface perfectly. Such inserts may have been a factory option, but it's doubtful.

The rear sight, also dovetailed into the rib, is a Lyman No. 6 with two folding blades. One is a broad, deep "V," the other is a low, straight blade with an engraved triangle to catch the eye. Designed by Lyman as an auxiliary sight for use with either a tang or receiver aperture sight, the blades fold down out of the way so as not to impede use of the aperture. There is a tiny screw

on each side of the pivot point. The one on the right adjusts tension of the folding blades, and can be tightened to compensate for wear.

The Model 36 aperture sight has a spring-loaded arm that oscillates out of the way as the bolt is operated. It's adjustable for elevation by a thumb lever. If the open sights are being used, the arm can be folded back out of the way. The Model 36 does not have interchangeable screw-in apertures, but there is a tiny hinged aperture that allows you either a large view for close, fast action, or a pinhole for more exact work. In any kind of hunting, the pinhole is best left folded back out of the way, but this is one more variable that allows the shooter to tailor the sight to his immediate need.

Taken as a whole, this sighting arrangement appears complicated, but in actual use it is elegantly simple and eminently usable. If any sight is not needed, it can be stored out of the way. Nothing need interfere with anything else. One problem that commonly occurs with all sights that fold down, up, or out, is a tendency to move under recoil. On a dangerous-game rifle, this can be life-threatening, but it's a constant annoyance

Lyman No. 6 folding rear sight with two blades, both of which fold down flat when the receiver sight is used.

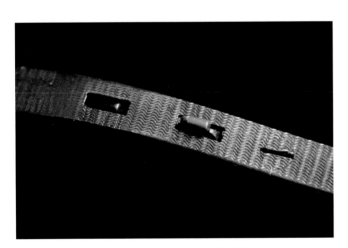

The double front sight has two beads. When one is pushed down, the other pops up.

The Lyman Model 36 receiver sight, created by Lyman in 1907 to fit the new Mannlicher-Schönauer Model 1903 rifle, works perfectly on the Haenel-Mannlicher.

if you take a shot at an animal and need a quick second shot, only to miss and find out later that your long-range blade popped up unannounced and you shot over. Once a hunter realizes that his sights won't stay put, constantly checking them becomes not only a distraction but an annoyance. For this reason, and with most sights, simplicity is a virtue beyond price. The sights on this rifle, I'm happy to say, stay exactly where they are supposed to unless invited, even under the sharp recoil of the 9x57.

The rifle saw one other alteration, incidentally, which I'm at a loss to explain. The Prince of Wales grip is a gradual half-pistol with a rounded tip. My rifle has had this tip cut off, and the end left flat. Possibly there was some damage that could not be repaired any other way. The alteration is only apparent because it lopped off part of the checkering pattern on both sides.

* * *

My Haenel-Mannlicher weighs 6 lbs. 15 oz., unloaded but wearing a sling. The barrel is 22 inches long. Factory ammunition for the 9x57 ranged from a 205-grain bullet at 2,400 fps, to a 281-grain bullet at 1,920 fps (RWS). Either would be more than a handful in such a light rifle, especially without a recoil pad. However, loaded with any of the excellent 225-grain bullets available, such as the Sierra GameKing spitzer or Nosler Partition, at a velocity of 2,290 fps, this rifle is comfortable to shoot and capable of taking on just about anything in North America. In fact, given the range of .358-diameter bullets available, including jacketed hollow-points intended for the .357 Magnum revolver, various cast bullets, and the excellent Speer 180-grain flat-nose, the 9x57 becomes a remarkably versatile cartridge.

It's impossible to say who first took a military bolt-action rifle and modified it into a hunting

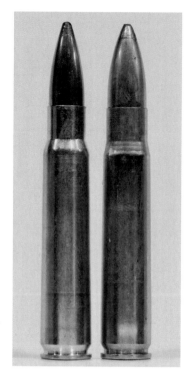

The 9x57 (right) is the original 8x57 JS necked up. In power, it is comparable to the later .358 Winchester.

rifle. The rifle may have been an early Mauser, Mannlicher, or Lee-Metford—all of which were floating around by 1900. The *formal* adaptation of a military design to a civilian one, however, probably lies with Mannlicher, at Steyr, since Lyman was designing receiver sights for Mannlichers with split bridges as early as 1895, and there were already hunting reports about the performance of the 6.5x54 in its rimmed version.

Most of these military conversions that I have handled have seemed heavy, ill-balanced, awkward, or clumsy. In America, when gunsmiths began converting Springfields after 1906, the first ones were nothing to write home about, and in fact sporting Springfields did not really become usable until the 1920s. Even then, it took the efforts of talented metalsmiths like James V. Howe, and stockmakers like Alvin Linden, to map a path for others to follow.

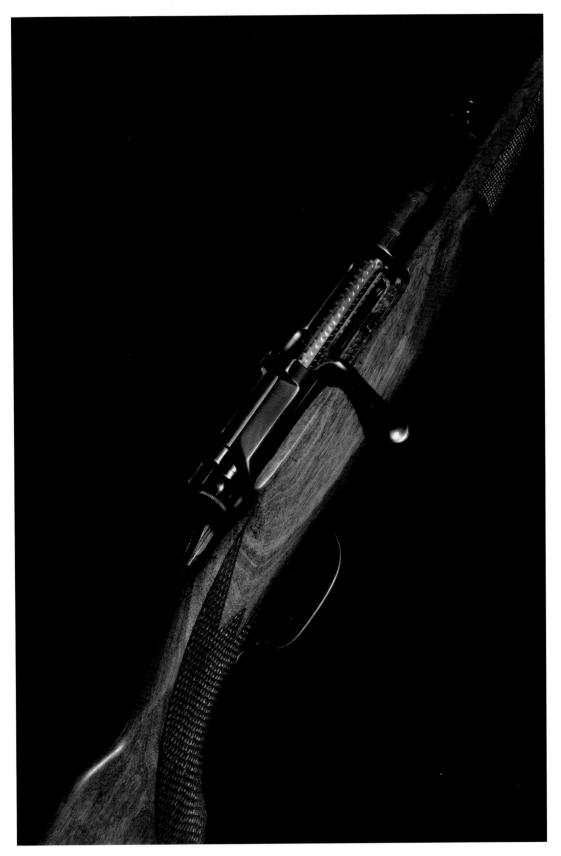

The Mannlicher-Schönauer Model 1903.

What sets the Haenel-Mannlicher New Model apart is how slim, trim, and well balanced it is, with a barrel perfectly suited to its caliber. It need be no longer than 22 inches for the 9x57, but nor would you want it shorter. Carried at the military "trail" position, it balances perfectly in one hand, and when fast action is anticipated, it carries like a quail gun. Except for the cheekpiece, the stock is much like a fine game gun of that era, and the cheekpiece itself is very modern-looking, not the usual pancake style found on English rifles or old Mannlichers. The front edge drifts forward to lose itself in the lines of the grip. This is a style made popular in America much later by Alvin Linden. It was suggested to him by an artist client, so exactly what its origins are is impossible to say. Probably, it simply evolved from some of the *schützen* designs.

The rifle comes up like a bird gun, too, with the eye perfectly aligned with the sights. For fast, instinctive shooting, it would be difficult to find better.

The Haenel-Mannlichers did not stay on the market for long. For one thing, they were expensive. In 1905, they were listed in the Stoeger catalogue for $24.50. In the US, the favorite hunting rifle was the lever action, and bolt rifles were new and awkward. In Europe, Mauser-Werke very quickly got into the sporting-rifle business after the introduction of the Mauser 98, and at Steyr, Mannlicher was making dedicated, from-the-ground-up hunting rifles, in a big way, from 1903 onwards. These shaded the Haenel-Mannlicher in many ways, and the latter disappeared from the market.

Today, anyone seeing a Haenel-Mannlicher is likely to assume it is either an early Mannlicher or, if more familiar with that era, recognize the unique features adopted from the Commission '88. It is undoubtedly a hybrid, and the 9x57 is no match ballistically for today's cartridges. But

for a rifle for still-hunting the forests, or taking on wild boar in thick bush, it would be difficult to find anything made today that is demonstrably better without having sacrificed some of the Haenel's virtues along the way.

MANNLICHER-SCHÖNAUER MODEL 1903

More than any other country in Europe, Austria is a land of mountaineers and big-game hunters. Drive through any village in the Tyrol and you will find inns with antlers over the door—usually red stag—and the walls festooned with roebuck antlers and chamois horns. The mountains, the forests, and the game animals are important even to Austrians who do not hunt, and the annual report of the local gamekeeper on the state of the game is a cherished public ceremony. The small town of Ferlach, in the Alps just north of the Slovenian border, is the traditional home of Austrian gunmaking, where skilled craftsmen produce a wide range of elaborate single-shot and multi-barrel rifles. These are made for both hunting in the mountains and the traditional Teutonic sport of target shooting.

The production of military rifles, and the making of sporting rifles, remained separate industries through the 1880s and into the '90s. Repeating rifles were considered neither appropriate for most hunting, nor accurate enough for target shooting. By 1900, that was about to change.

Through the 1890s, Ferdinand von Mannlicher was designing military rifles at a furious pace, with a new patent and design appearing every year or two. He was perfecting both his turnbolt and straight-pull designs, as well as experimenting with, and refining, different approaches to magazines and the feeding and ejection of cartridges. Every time a major design went into production, Steyr seemed to find a customer for

The Model 1903 action was the basis for sporting rifles in various models over the next seventy years.

it among its main markets, which were the countries of eastern and southern Europe.

In 1900, Mannlicher produced a rifle with a turnbolt action and a spool-type magazine (also called a rotary or spindle) designed by his colleague at Steyr, Otto Schönauer. It was a heavily modified version of the 1893 Rumanian Mannlicher, which had used the packet system of loading. Outwardly, with its split bridge, the Rumanian action bears a physical resemblance to the Commission '88, but arms historian W. H. B. Smith says it is "entirely Mannlicher" in design.

"It employs a form of turning-bolt action developed by Mannlicher which is nearly as simple as the famous Mauser bolt and is cheaper to manufacture," he wrote, in *Mannlicher Rifles and Pistols*. Von Mannlicher disagreed with his German contemporary, Paul Mauser, on a number of basic points of design and manufacturing processes. Most important was Mannlicher's detachable bolt head, which allowed for both simpler machining when producing the bolt, and easier repair if the bolt head became worn or damaged. Its disadvantages were that it made it necessary for the locking lugs to be positioned slightly farther to the rear, which slightly weakened the action for use with high-intensity cartridges.

Arguments can be made in favor of both systems. It is usually suggested that the Mauser eventually won out, but in reality, both survived, did very well, were in production for many years, and were chambered for comparable cartridges.

The 1893 Rumanian rifle became the basis for the 1895 Dutch Mannlicher, and both were chambered for a new rimmed 6.5mm cartridge. When von Mannlicher turned to his 1900 rifle, he drew on the Rumanian/Dutch design in several ways, one of which was to produce the 6.5mm cartridge in rimless form, and call it the 6.5x54.

The rifle and cartridge were adopted by Greece as its official military rifle in 1903.

The Greek Model 1903 was to Steyr what the Gewehr 98 was to Mauser, and thereafter followed Steyr's first attempt at large-scale production of a sporting rifle. It was destined to become one of the world's all-time great hunting rifles and stay in production, with only minor modifications, for the next seventy years.

The Mannlicher-Schönauer Model 1903 is the Greek Mannlicher modified into the perfect rifle for mountaineers hunting chamois in the Alps, or stalking roebuck in the forests on the lower slopes. The bolt handle is turned down and reshaped into the famous butterknife, which was one of the Mannlicher's two trademarks for three-quarters of a century. The other was its full-length stock, with a forend that stretched to the muzzle, capped with a steel forend tip. Such stocks were common on military carbines

for cavalry or artillery use, including the Mauser Model 71 and the Swedish 1894 Mauser, and like the Model 1903 those carbines had very short barrels. The Mannlicher 1903 barrel is 17.7 inches. The 1903 was the first sporting bolt action to employ the full-length stock, and today any carbine with such a stock is routinely referred to as a "Mannlicher." There is only one genuine Mannlicher, however, and it was made in Steyr. The Model 1903 was chambered only in 6.5x54, and in this particular model it gained fame both in hunting and in literature.

The Mannlicher-Schönauer Model 1903 was chambered in 6.5x54 M-S, and had a shorter barrel (17.7 inches) than any subsequent model. It was the ideal mountain rifle for those who scaled cliffs and carried their own rifle.

This is the rifle with which Margot Macomber shot her husband in Ernest Hemingway's *The Short Happy Life of Francis Macomber.* Hemingway

The Mannlicher-Schönauer Model 1903 was chambered in 6.5x54 M-S, and had a shorter barrel (17.7 inches) than any subsequent model. It was the ideal mountain rifle for those who scaled cliffs and carried their own rifle.

The 6.5x54 M-S (left) with the later 8x56 M-S, introduced in 1908.

was a great admirer of the Mannlicher, kept one on his fishing boat, the *Pilar*, and mentioned it by name in his later novel, *Islands in the Stream*. He also makes admiring reference to the Mannlicher in *A Farewell to Arms*. Both W. D. M. (Karamojo) Bell and Charles Sheldon were famous turn-of-the-century hunters—Bell on African elephants, Sheldon on mountain sheep—who were known to use a 6.5mm Mannlicher. Bell used a Model 1903, but Sheldon's rifle is open to debate. In Mozambique, as late as the mid-twentieth century, professional hunter Werner von Alvensleben killed more than a thousand Cape buffalo, shooting on control, with a Model 1903 6.5x54. Finally, Annie Alexander, who led a biological expedition to Alaska in 1908, guided by the famous brown-bear expert Allen Hasselborg, used a Mannlicher 6.5x54 to collect brown-bear specimens along the coast, and on Montague Island in Prince William Sound.

No one today would recommend the 6.5x54 for hunting elephants, brown bears in dense brush, or as a mountain rifle for Dall and Stone's sheep. For that matter, few would consider it as a mountain rifle for chamois, the diminutive mountain goat of the Alps. And yet, the 6.5x54's modest ballistics belie its performance. As originally designed, it used a long, round-nosed 160-grain bullet (approximate weight) at around 2,250 fps. In either soft-nosed or solid, this bullet has very high sectional density. It penetrates and keeps on penetrating. That was the secret of its success when used by Bell, and others, on elephants. It also made it very effective on brown bears and grizzlies.

The 6.5x54 has a rather looping trajectory, but since few hunters would attempt a shot beyond 250 yards even on chamois or Dall sheep, preferring to stalk closer if possible, this was not a huge drawback. Ammunition was light and compact—an added bonus.

On a personal note, in 1995 I hunted in the Austrian Alps for the first time. It was part of a longer European trip with several stops, and I was advised that a rifle would be provided to save me the trouble of traveling with one. I was given a Weatherby Mark V in .257 Weatherby, fitted with a huge scope of extravagant power range—3-12X, or something like that, and with a 26-inch barrel. Our ammunition was factory 117-grain round-nose. The owner of the rifle went hunting the first morning, ambushed some chamois still down in the valley as dawn broke, handed the rifle over to me, and went home for breakfast. It was then left to me to climb that particular Alp in pursuit of the chamois which, following chamois practice after their night in town, had promptly started climbing and were now back home, in some gravelly basin high above the treeline.

With my backpack and that Weatherby cannon, I climbed for the better part of six hours.

At one point, we traversed a narrow ledge with overhanging rock, on which the rifle barrel banged mercilessly as I gripped a cable put there to assist climbers, edging along on my toes. Down the valley, a helicopter hovered. "Recovering the body of a climber who fell," my guide explained. By mid-afternoon, we had reached the peaks and the basins, found some chamois, waited for a clear shot, and decked one at about 100 yards, maybe 150.

More than any other time in my life, at that moment I understood clearly why the Mannlicher Model 1903 had been designed the way it was. As well, I heartily wished that I was carrying one instead of a completely unneeded long-range, high-powered rifle, with an unnecessarily big and heavy scope, firing a load intended for use on elk at long range, not on an animal the size of a golden retriever at one hundred yards.

* * *

The Mannlicher-Schönauer derives the second part of its name from Otto Schönauer, who is credited with designing the superb rotary magazine that remained an essential feature of this rifle throughout its life. Schönauer was an engineer and became a director of the Steyr works in 1896. Those who have researched deeper than I have dug out another employee of Steyr in 1900 and insisted that he, and not Schönauer, should really have the credit, but at this late date I am not about to argue with Steyr's decision. Similarly, there are those (Frank de Haas among them) who insist the action is not really Mannlicher's, but is really a modified Commission '88. However, since Mannlicher was a major contributor to the Commission '88, how does one differentiate?

The other rifle of the time that employed a rotary magazine was the Savage Model 1899, which was designed by Arthur Savage and first saw the light of day in 1895. Schönauer was known to have been working on rotary magazines as early as 1893, although it took some years to perfect it. The usual date given is 1900, with the introduction of the rifle that became the Greek Mannlicher. Frank de Haas believed that Ferdinand von Mannlicher devised the methods

Otto Schönauer's brilliant rotary magazine. It is believed that von Mannlicher designed the method by which it can be detached for cleaning. The cartridge shown is merely sitting in its cradle. It is not possible to load the magazine when it is out of the rifle.

The knurled button on the rail allows the rotary magazine to unspool, releasing the cartridges into the hand.

by which the rotary magazine could be easily detached from the rifle for cleaning, and that was a major accomplishment in itself. The lack of this feature is one of the drawbacks of the Savage 99, and one of several areas in which the Savage magazine is inferior to the Schönauer. We shall look at that more closely in a later chapter.

Another feature of the Mannlicher action worth noting is the means of unloading the magazine. A small knurled button on the right-hand rail of the action is depressed, allowing the magazine to unspool, releasing the cartridges conveniently into the hand. This is an improvement on virtually every other rifle in use at the time, except the British Lee-Enfield with its detachable box magazine. The cartridges do not need to be chambered before being ejected, as with lever actions, nor do they rattle to the ground like a Mauser when its floorplate is opened.

The Mannlicher 1903 became the foundation for a series of rifle models that lived on, ultimately, into the 1970s. If I were backed into a corner at gunpoint and forced to name the family of rifles I consider the best overall for big-game hunting, I would have to choose the Mannlicher-Schönauer. The Oberndorf Mauser sporting rifles are wonderful in many ways, as are the Savage 99 and the Winchester Model 70. Some of each of these families are great, but some are also downright lousy, and many, frankly, are mediocre. From all of those I have seen and handled, however, Mannlicher never made one model that was not at least good. They just never seemed to put a foot wrong.

This may elicit howls of rage from lovers of Oberndorf Mausers, Savage 99s, and Model 70s, and it is, admittedly, a subjective judgment. But I am speaking here of the overall quality of the entire family of rifles, and I do not know of a single Mannlicher model that was not good.

The first variation appeared in 1905. Called the Model 1905 (logically enough), it differed from the 1903 only in caliber (9x56 M-S) and barrel length (19.5 inches vs. 17.7). Three years later came the Model 1908 in 8x56 M-S, and finally the Model 1910 in 9.5x56 M-S. After the Great War, when Steyr resumed commercial production, it added a few different models, including a conventional rifle with a longer barrel and conventional sporter stock. Available chamberings were expanded to include a range of popular cartridges. Ultimately, if there were any lingering doubts about the action strength, some rifles in the 1950s were chambered for the .458 Winchester, as well as a number of other belted magnums. The Steyr production records were removed during the brief Soviet occupation of Austria after 1945, so exact numbers are impossible, but the Steyr factory estimates that about 185,000 Mannlicher-Schönauer sporting rifles were made during its seventy-year lifetime.

The Model 1908 was chambered for the new 8x56 M-S, and had a slightly longer barrel (19.5 inches) than the 1903.

Of them all, the one that stands out to me as perfect for its intended purpose is the original Model 1903, in 6.5x54 M-S. There is simply nothing about it I would change. We should keep in mind that, when it was introduced, riflescopes were not in common use for hunting, and so its adaptability to scopes, or lack thereof, was not a consideration and did not become so for at least twenty years. At that point, the split bridge and its high bolt handle presented serious obstacles, but we are not talking about those rifles.

My Model 1903, unloaded but with a sling, weighs 6 lbs. 11 oz. Although the barrel is short, the additional length of stock and the steel forend cap place a disproportionate number of ounces out beyond the leading hand, which contributes to steadiness and accurate shooting. It has none of the wavy-wand quality of more recent carbines and short rifles. Yet the rifle overall is less than thirty-nine inches long from muzzle to toe. This is shorter than the Winchester 92 (chapter II), or the Savage 99 we shall look at in chapter VIII. With a sling, a mountaineer could toss it on his back and be almost unaware of its presence, ducking under branches or negotiating overhanging ledges.

To contribute to accurate shooting, especially in thin air at high altitudes when the hunter might be panting and shaking, it is fitted with a double-set trigger. There is a fixed-blade front sight and an open sight on the barrel with a standing blade and one folding leaf marked "300." Metres, presumably.

* * *

The Mannlichers that followed the Model 1903 are all good in their own way. The models 1905 through 1910 had slightly longer barrels (20

Mannlicher-Schönauer Model 1956, in standard rifle configuration. The base of a Pachmayr Lo-Swing side mount is visible on the left side of the action. This is a .30-06.

inches, approximately, compared to 17.7) and their magazines were tailored to accommodate the three larger-caliber cartridges used (9x56 M-S, 8x56 M-S, and 9.5x56 M-S), so they are not interchangeable. Other than that, there was very little difference except for minor aesthetic changes, such as replacing the round-knob (Prince of Wales) grip with a conventional pistol grip and steel grip cap.

A major change was the development of a takedown model, in which the barreled action could be detached from the stock. This, of course, was a rifle model with a shorter forend, since such a modification would be pointless with a full-length stock. (See Introduction, page 3.) It appears that many of these barreled actions were sold separately to independent gunmakers for building custom rifles, and some have appeared with such London names on them as Boss & Co.

Over the seventy years of production that followed the Model 1903, Mannlicher-Schönauer hunting rifles appeared in many different calibers, in both rifle and carbine form, including the takedown. There were attempts to adapt the action to the use of riflescopes, which was difficult with the split bridge, and the most common type seen is the European claw mount, with the rear base affixed to the left side of the bridge. The action also proved adaptable to side mounts, like the Griffin & Howe or the later Pachmayr Lo-Swing. Both of these are detachable mounts, and the Lo-Swing can also be instantly rotated to the side to allow the use of the iron sights. Such dubious versatility is beloved of European hunters, but has never found the same favor in America.

Along with scope mounts, changes were made to the rifle's safety mechanism. In post-1945 models, a two-position side safety was added, but the original wing was left in place. The wing safety, by the way, physically resembled that on the Mauser 98, but was two-position instead of three. With the second safety in place, the wing could be left permanently in "Fire" position, and only the side safety used. Later still, in the early 1960s, the second safety was switched to the tang, like a shotgun. Stock shape was also an area of continuing evolution. It was gradually made more "modern," with the introduction of a Monte Carlo comb to raise the eye to scope level. In the Model 1956, Steyr made a concerted effort to solve the eye-height dilemma once and for all, with a unique roll-over comb that, from the side, looked like an exaggerated Monte Carlo. However, the cheek piece was dished (concave), allowing the cheek to be lower if iron sights were used, but to slide upward (while still supported) to use a scope. This stock was used on both carbines and rifles, and worked to perfection, but it was discontinued within a year or two. Presumably, it was too wild looking even for the 1950s, when extravagant tail fins on cars were the height of fashion.

Around 1970, a serious fire occurred in the Steyr factory, and some of the production equipment for the Mannlicher-Schönauer was damaged beyond repair. Reluctantly, but probably wisely, Steyr decided against replacing it. The final Mannlichers to leave the plant were assembled from existing parts, with the last one shipped in 1972.

* * *

During its lifetime, the Mannlicher—always affectionately known as "the little Mannlicher"—had a great influence on other hunting rifles. It had a feel to it the Mausers could only envy, and no Mauser action ever made can approach the silky feel of a Mannlicher. Also, by comparison, Mausers always seem a little heavy and mechan-

Model 1956 in traditional full-length stock, but incorporating the excellent cheekpiece that allowed the use of either open sights or a high-mounted scope. This rifle is fitted with an EAW side mount.

ical, whereas the Mannlicher is almost a living thing in your hands.

The Mannlicher's greatest contribution to the evolution of the hunting rifle was its stock, and even though it's dismissed by many because it adversely affects accuracy, for a rifle to be used in the mountains, the full-length stock is a valuable feature. I am not one to use a rifle as an alpenstock, but sometimes it can save your life, and the stock provides a secure grip as well as protection for the barrel.

The Mannlicher's rotary magazine also established a reputation for smooth, flawless operation, feeding cartridges effortlessly into the chamber. This is an area of continuing problems for Mausers and for all other rifles that employ Mauser-style box magazines with staggered rows of cartridges. Partly this is because of attempts to chamber many different cartridges, of various lengths and shapes, while keeping magazine modifications to a cost-saving minimum. The original Mauser 98 was carefully tailored to the 8x57 J, down to the angle of the guide rails and the taper of the magazine box. Rechambering one, and then expecting the unaltered magazine to function as well as it did with the original cartridge, is a forlorn hope. The Mannlicher-Schönauer did not have the versatility and potential for rechambering that the Mauser 98 has, but it never encountered the feeding difficulties, either.

Mannlicher-Schönauer rifles and carbines carry their pedigree on the action ring.

Weatherby Mark V Safari-grade .270 Weatherby. The Weatherby cartridges epitomized the quest for high velocity in the second half of the twentieth century.

CHAPTER VI

HIGH VELOCITY

HOLY GRAIL OR FALSE GOD?

London's Great Exhibition of 1851 set many things in motion. Although it cannot be proven definitively, one of these may have been the Great Quest for Velocity that continues to this day. Although James Purdey is credited with the original "express" rifles, which fired lighter bullets at higher velocities, he may have gleaned the idea from Lt. Col. David Davidson, who had an exhibit displaying his early telescopic sights and rifles specially engineered to fire smaller, lighter projectiles at higher velocities.

Lt. Col. Davidson was an officer of Scottish birth who served in the Bombay Army in India through the 1830s and '40s. While there, he pursued his ideas about velocity and long-range shooting. By the time of the Great Exhibition, he was retired and back living in Scotland, where he devoted his life to the development of rifles and telescopic sights.

The essence of the express rifle, as made by James Purdey, was not so much smaller calibers as it was lighter bullets and heavier powder charges. A bullet was reduced in weight by hollowing out the nose. This not only made it lighter, affording higher velocity, but also made the bullet prone to expand on impact, increasing its shocking power. Depending on the resistance it encountered, this expansion slowed the bullet's passage through the animal and reduced penetration, but it also produced some spectacular kills.

From the 1850s to the 1890s, a controversy raged in the sporting press over these occasional spectacular kills with express rifles, versus the equally frequent surface wounds, failure to strike a vital part, and animals escaping to die lingering deaths. If this sounds familiar, it's because the controversy has continued to this very day, throughout the development of self-contained cartridges, smokeless powder, and jacketed bullets. The debate has ebbed and flowed, but the same pattern seems to repeat itself with disquieting regularity, and always taking the same tone: someone will rise up and claim supernatural results for high velocity *in and of itself,* as if surpassing a certain velocity would somehow impart magical killing power to a bullet out of all reasonable proportion, ignoring dreary mathematical realities.

One such person was Major Sir Gerald Burrard, Bt., DSO, RFA (Ret'd), who was possibly the greatest authority on English shotguns of modern times as well as an expert on forensic ballistics. He wrote the definitive three-volume work *The Modern Shotgun* (1931), and was a pioneer in the field of forensic ballistics. *The Identification of Firearms and Forensic Ballistics* (1934) is recognized as a ground-breaking work. Sir Gerald was also an artillery officer and big-game hunter, so he came by his interest and knowledge of ballistics from several angles. In *Notes on Sporting Rifles,* which he wrote after 1918 when he was in hospital recovering from wounds sustained in the Great War, he states, "The shock given to an animal when hit by a bullet traveling with an initial velocity of about 3,000 ft. per second is enormous, and seems to have a paralyzing effect. I do not think the reasons for this are quite understood. I believe there is something in it more than mere bullet energy. When a velocity of 2,500 f.s. is exceeded the blow of the impact seems to have a different effect on the tissues struck to the effect obtained with a bullet traveling at a lower speed. It is this peculiar property of shock which makes the magnum small bore such a splendid killing weapon . . ."

Much of the material included in *Notes on Sporting Rifles* had already appeared in *The Field*, in feature-article form, so Sir Gerald (or Maj. Burrard, as he then was) carried a considerable reputation among the most respected of English sporting ballisticians. His favorite rifle for stalking was a .280 Ross, chambered in a Charles Lancaster double rifle, and he could not praise it highly enough—provided, he wrote, "It is not abused by being employed against very heavy dangerous game at close quarters." When he wrote that, he was undoubtedly thinking of the fate of George Grey, in Kenya in 1911, killed by a lion while armed with a Ross rifle. Maj. Burrard was assisted in compiling much of the ballistic data, trajectory tables, velocities, and so on, by F. W. Jones, a man of impeccable credentials both as a ballistician and a competition rifle shooter. We shall meet Mr. Jones again in the next chapter, wherein we study the checkered career of the .280 Ross. For his part, Maj. Burrard credited the .280 Ross with ushering in the modern era of high velocity.

* * *

In recent years, we have seen similar claims made for the .220 Swift, for the smaller Weatherby

cartridges, and even for the tiny bullets of the .17 HMR. An article in the 1951 *Gun Digest*, by Roy Weatherby, was the most egregious example I have seen, wherein Weatherby claimed that his .257 and .270, on an extended African safari, had proven to be better killers *on any animal* (my italics) than either the .375 H&H or .470 Nitro Express. Furthermore, he said, with ultra-velocity, an animal did not need to be hit in any vital area to die as if struck by lightning. It could be hit in the paunch, in the leg, anywhere—all that was necessary was a kiss from a bullet at high velocity, and that was the shuddering end. By comparison with this, Maj. Burrard was the soul of moderation and sober observation.

In retrospect, the astonishing thing to me is that *Gun Digest's* editor, John T. Amber, would print such hogwash, but that is somewhat

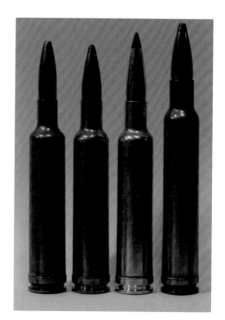

The major Weatherby high-velocity performers were, from left, the .257 Weatherby, .270 Weatherby, 7mm Weatherby, and .300 Weatherby. All are excellent long-range hunting cartridges, but they do not possess supernatural powers.

balanced by the fact that Weatherby's contribution was only one half of a two-part article, with the opposing view written by Elmer Keith. Keith, predictably, came down in favor of heavy bullets at reasonable velocities, and his contribution is by far the more plausible.

During the black-powder era, technology limited maximum possible velocity in a number of ways. One was the fact that bullets were made of pure lead, and when they were driven above 2,000 fps, lead fouling would gum up a barrel within a few shots. Another was simply the amount of powder that could be packed in, and this became even more of an issue after muzzleloaders gave way to self-contained cartridges. The arrival of smokeless powder, followed by jacketed bullets, changed all that. Suddenly, more velocity was possible with considerably less powder, and the original cupro-nickel jackets did not foul barrels to the same noticeable extent as lead. In later years, it was discovered that super-high velocities resulted in considerable cuprous fouling, but that was a separate issue.

Early military rifles that employed smokeless powder fired bullets that today we consider heavy for those calibers. The 7x57 bullet was 175 grains; the .30-40 Krag was 220; the .303 British was 215; and the 8x57 J was 226. Velocities were all in the 2,100–2,400 fps range. In 1905, the Germans switched to a 154-grain bullet with a spitzer tip, and a muzzle velocity of 2,880 fps (the 8x57 JS). This load, with its flatter trajectory and greater point-blank range, changed the game for everyone. The US responded by redesigning its .30-03, modifying the new Springfield rifle, and arriving at the .30-06 with its 150-grain bullet at 2,740 fps; the British abandoned their 215-grain bullet in favor of 174 grains, at 2,440 fps (the famous Mk. VII load). Comparing the 8x57 JS with the .30-06, the Germans were able to coax

This Montana elk was taken with a .270 Weatherby, firing a 150-grain Nosler Partition. The bull was hit squarely in the lungs at about 250 yards and died quickly, but he did not drop "as if pole-axed," as the literature would have it. High velocity is not a magic elixir.

more velocity, from a smaller case and with a heavier bullet, because they had the finest smokeless powders in the world at that time.

The British had learned a hard lesson about long-range shooting and ballistics during the South African War (1899–1902). It was not that their Lee-Enfields were terribly outclassed by the Boers using Mausers, because the ballistic differences were not that great. However, the English press used the perceived shortcomings of the Lee-Enfield as a bludgeon to use on the War Office and the Conservative government in power, and this caused a great scramble to improve upon, or even replace, the Lee-Enfield and the .303 British cartridge. More than that, it sparked an interest in rifle shooting, rifle clubs, and target shooting among all classes in England that bordered on frenzy. Suddenly, gunmakers were called upon to produce small-caliber, high-velocity rifles with elaborate long-range sights, for shooting at targets from 100 yards all the way out to 1,200.

This passion for rifle shooting lasted until 1914, with a tremendous number of significant developments. A key figure was a wealthy Scottish baronet, Sir Charles Ross, one of the most controversial and intriguing figures in rifle history. His work in rifle, cartridge, and bullet design, and the study of ballistics, was to have far-reaching consequences, on both sides of the Atlantic, that stretched into the 1930s. We will get to Sir Charles in the next chapter. However, one footnote is required to this short history of the pursuit of velocity.

Accounts of the development of the German 8x57 cartridge in its various guises, including reloading handbooks, the many editions of *Cartridges of the World,* and histories of the Mauser rifles themselves, describe the original 8x57 J, with its .318-inch, 226-grain bullet, and the switch in 1905 to the 8x57 JS, with its .323-inch, 154-grain bullet at higher velocity. Rarely is mention made of the fact that beginning around 1917 and extending into the 1930s, the Germans replaced the 154-grain JS load with a heavier bullet, of superior ballistic configuration, but (of necessity) at a lower velocity. This was for standard infantry use.

This load used a 198-grain bullet at a velocity of around 2,700 fps, although some references claim up to 2,850 fps. The bullet was an elongated spitzer with a boattail base, and it originated in 1917 as a cartridge for use in machine guns. The standard "S" load, with its flat-base, 154-grain bullet, did not give sufficient range and penetration for machine gun purposes. The heavier load (designated "sS," for *Schwerespitz*) gave the desired penetration, according to some accounts, all the way out to 4,200 yards.

American forces, which began arriving on the Western Front in early 1918, found that their standard .30-06 load gave the same problems in their machine guns as the Germans had experienced, and they requested development of a load comparable to the new German ammunition. This set off a long quest in America to solve the problem of mass-producing boattailed bullets.

When Germany began rearming in the mid-1930s, and resumed production of 8x57 JS ammunition (prohibited by the Treaty of Versailles), the load adopted by the army was the 198-grain boattail.

One vital fact that proponents of ultra-velocity tend to leave out when praising their babies is that a lighter bullet may start out faster, and get out to 300 yards more quickly (with a resulting flatter trajectory to that range), but around that point a heavier, slower bullet catches up, eventually passes the light bullet, and continues to lengthen its lead until both fall to earth, exhausted. The key to exploiting this ballistic fact is a heavy-for-caliber bullet, of superior ballistic form and coefficient. This concept originated with Sir Charles Ross around 1906. Whether it was Ross's own idea or not, he was the man who made it famous on the pre-1914 target ranges, and inspired a host of rifle developments, in America and Germany as well as in the United Kingdom.

The Germans put this to use in 1917 with their 198-grain sS, followed by the Americans with refinements to the .30-06 in the 1920s. In the modern era, these bullets, sporting names like "ultra-low-drag" and "extended ogive," have been used in specialized sniper rifles and for long-range target shooting, all to great effect. We should remember, however, that it's a concept that is now at least 110 years old. All the developments we have seen since the Gulf War in 1991, remarkable though they are, only build on the work of Sir Charles Ross and his associates, in the years before 1914.

* * *

Ross M-1910, chambered for the .280 Ross.

CHAPTER VII

WHAT PRICE GLORY? *SIR CHARLES ROSS AND THE FABULOUS .280*

AUTHOR'S NOTE AND GENERAL DISCLAIMER

This chapter was, by far, the most difficult to write in this entire book. Partly, this is because of all the disparate strands involved, including the life and career of Sir Charles Ross, the design and evolution of his rifles, and the development of his major cartridge. There is the performance of his military rifles compared to his target and hunting rifles. Finally, there is no happy ending, either for Ross or for his inventions. It all ended in a welter of confusion, with lawsuits, claims, counter-claims, hysterical magazine articles, unproven accusations that became articles of faith, and bizarre allegations about the faults of the Ross rifle that continue to this day.

Insofar as possible, we will try to deal with each of the major issues separately, but they are so intertwined that this is almost impossible. If repetition occurs in the recounting, I apologize in advance. Although this is a book about hunting rifles and their development, events that affected Sir Charles Ross's military rifles and their reputation had a direct impact on his hunting rifles as well. The general perception of failure of the military rifles caused the closing of his factory, and that ended production of what I consider to be one of the finest hunting rifles ever made, for its time and within certain limits.

The major obstacle was sorting out fact from fiction amid conflicting claims and accusations dating back more than a century. This was aggravated by the fact that accusations on both sides (pro and con the Ross) came from writers for whom I

have great respect. The most anti-Ross writer was Philip B. Sharpe, who became almost hysterical in his condemnation of rifle and cartridge, and Jack O'Connor, who was more measured; on the positive side were Frederick Courteney Selous, Major Sir Gerald Burrard, Bt., DSO, Capt. E. C. Crossman and, to a lesser extent, Col. Townsend Whelen. No less a personage than His Imperial Majesty, King George V, endorsed the .280 Ross cartridge (if not the rifle) after extensive use during his 1911 grand tour of India. The King used a Lancaster double in that caliber, similar to that used by Burrard. Ross's major biographers, Roger Phillips, François Dupuis, and John Chadwick, attempted to sort it all out, but even their exhaustive 1984 treatise on Ross and his rifles (The Ross Rifle Story) left questions hanging in the air.

It should be noted that, in logic, it is impossible to prove a negative, and this is a severe impediment to anyone who sets out to discredit the many claims of accidents, maimings, and even deaths resulting from Ross malfunctions. For example, one celebrated incident was the supposed death of one Louis LaVallee (spellings vary) in Keith, Alberta, in 1926. He was allegedly mortally injured when he took a shot at a coyote from an upstairs window, shooting from his left shoulder, and the bolt blew back into his head. He died five hours later, so the story goes. Phillips et al report that an account of the incident was published in the Calgary Herald, and the story reprinted in Outdoor Life. At least one pro-Ross (or anti-fiction) researcher wrote that his investigations had found no record of such a person living in Keith, Alberta, in 1926, and no such story carried in the Herald. *Assuming this researcher is telling the truth, what does that prove? Absolutely nothing. A quick search of the* Calgary Herald *archives on-line revealed nothing, but does that prove it never happened? No. Do I, personally, believe it happened? No comment.*

And so we begin—with the birth of Sir Charles Ross, one of the most fascinating, infuriating, swashbuckling, gifted, and tragically flawed characters in the history of riflemaking.

PRELUDE

Sir Charles Ross—his rifles, his cartridges, his life and career—constitute an historical Gordian knot. If we add the seemingly endless lawsuits, love affairs, and political machinations, we have a plot worthy of Dickens. Sir Charles can best be described as a driven man whose lofty ambitions and undoubted talents ran aground on a combination of bad luck and his own failings. The life of Sir Charles Ross was a Shakespearean tragedy.

Sir Charles Henry Augustus Frederick Lockhart Ross, Bt. (ninth baronet of Nova Scotia, and the Ross of Balnagowan), was a man several times larger than life whose monumental failings were easily a match for his prodigious talents. His astonishing combination of brilliance and arrogance produced an always volatile, and sometimes toxic, brew. Throughout his seventy years, controversy followed Sir Charles Ross like a faithful dog. The first recorded instance of what was to become the pattern of his life occurred when he was just six years old: To emphasize his status above his classmates in Inverness, he arrived at school with a chair from the family castle. It was taller than the school chairs and he perched himself, haughtily looking down on those around. The schoolmaster was not impressed, and ordered the chair—and young Charles—removed.

Descended from one of the oldest aristocratic families in Scotland, he was heir to the second-largest landholding in Britain and what should have been a substantial fortune. He was born in 1872 on the family estate at Balnagowan, near Inverness, and grew up in the most pampered of circumstances. His father died when he was eleven years old, removing any semblance of parental discipline, leaving him to be raised by an adoring mother who granted his every wish. His mother's indulgence exhausted most of the family's liquid assets, so that by the time he came into his inheritance at the age of twenty-one, he was land rich but cash poor. Sir Charles's response was to hire a lawyer and take his mother to court, alleging that, by indulging his whims, she had squandered the family fortune. That action, perhaps more than any other, illustrates the bad side of the character of Sir Charles Ross.

The estate at Balnagowan included a vast private game preserve, and young Charles grew up in an atmosphere of rifles and shotguns, shooting red grouse and stag stalking. An early childhood photograph shows him clutching a rifle taller than he is. He killed his first stag at the age of twelve, and rifles and stag stalking became his lifelong passions. The estate had an extensive armoury, and the Balnagowan gun room, according to a 1903 inventory, included guns by James Purdey, Holland & Holland, Charles Lancaster, Alexander Henry, Mannlicher, and Mauser, among others.

Sir Charles Ross was blessed with a brilliant mind—some said genius, others insanity—and a decided talent for mechanical things. By the age of twenty-two, he had taken out two patents for inventions (his first rifle and an arc lamp) and his goal was to design the finest hunting rifle of all time. His first rifle was designed while he was at Eton College and patented in 1894. It was a straight-pull mechanism that closely resembled Ferdinand von Mannlicher's Model 1890—so closely, in fact, that some writers of the day said it was a "direct copy." That's not true. There were differences, including a Winchester-style external hammer, but there is no doubt that Ross was attempting to emulate Mannlicher. Straight-pull rifles seemed, in that age, to be the design of the future. Austria-Hungary had already adopted Mannlicher's Model 1884 and would soon switch to the even better Model 1895; Switzerland adopted the Schmidt-Rubin in 1890, and in the US, Winchester used James Paris Lee's straight-pull action in its Lee-Navy rifle. Ross was farsighted, however, and envisioned a time when armies would be using semi- and even fully automatic rifles. By 1896, he had a semiauto design completed as well.

While rifle design may have been his main interest, he was also determined to recoup his financial fortunes. He took out loans against his landholdings and embarked on a number of business ventures around the world, one of which was a rifle factory in Hartford, Connecticut.

In 1900, there was a close relationship between the great London gunmakers and the British upper classes, so it's no surprise that Ross was able to interest Charles Lancaster & Co., one of London's premier gunmakers, in his rifle. He persuaded Lancaster to build rifles on his Connecticut-made actions using Lancaster's own, renowned, oval-bored barrels, and this relationship lasted for many years. Lancaster-Ross rifles were displayed at the Paris Exhibition in 1900, and at the British Military Exhibition in London the following year. Knowing how the world worked, at least at his own level, Ross commissioned presentation rifles which were then presented to the King, the Prince of Wales (later King George V), to Field Marshall Lord Roberts and, in America, Col. D. B. Wesson.

When the Boer War broke out in 1899, Sir Charles Ross hastened to South Africa where he commanded a machine gun battery, arming his men with rifles of his own design and manufacture. As an army officer, Ross was well aware of the controversies involving the relative merits and capabilities of the Boers with their assortment of Mausers, and the British and Imperial soldiers with their Lee-Enfields and the .303 British cartridge. Since Ross armed his machine gunners with auxiliary rifles of his own design, he obviously did not think very highly of the Lee-Enfield. He came back from South Africa determined to design both a better rifle and a better cartridge.

In 1902, Ross sold the Canadian government on his rifle and undertook to set up a factory in Canada. The country needed rifles, but Lee-Enfields were in short supply in England and the War Office would not allow any to be sold to the young dominion. For the Canadian government, Ross's proposition presented an opportunity not

The desire to see "Made in Canada" on their military rifles was a powerful incentive for Canadian politicians in their dealings with Sir Charles Ross.

only to fill an urgent military need but also to gain an industry. Ross began moving machinery from Connecticut to Quebec City; many of his employees also moved north, and Ross was soon deep into production of his first military rifles.

DEVELOPMENT OF THE .280 ROSS

While the new Ross Rifle Co. factory was getting into production in Quebec—and not without many hitches along the way—Sir Charles himself was back in England, in hot pursuit of the "ultimate" long-range, high-velocity cartridge. Being an inveterate stag stalker, it was natural that it would be a hunting cartridge, but he also perceived it as a target and—most important—a military round. With money always in the back of his mind, Sir Charles Ross knew that the real profits in gunmaking lay in military contracts.

It was the new age of smokeless powder and Sir Charles believed the cartridge of the future fired a small-bore bullet at high velocity. His experience in South Africa, and his study of von Mannlicher's work in Austria, convinced him the ideal bullet diameter was .280, with a 150-grain bullet. He wanted a muzzle velocity of 2,800 fps, and more if possible. No commercial cartridge had ever reached the magical plateau of 3,000 fps, and Sir Charles Ross set out to do just that. Recognizing the advantages of a rimless case, he began with a cartridge slightly larger than the military 7x57, and in 1906 unveiled what he called the .28/06. Some references assume this was the American military .30-06 necked down, and Ross's .28/06 was certainly similar, but there were dimensional differences. Also, it had what we would today call a semi-rimless case, although in England then it was simply called rimless. As we have seen, Ross was extremely well connected. He was able to call on friends in high places, not only politically, but in the firearms trades.

Given his impatience with detail, Ross needed specialists to help turn his ideas into reality. He hired Frederick W. Jones as a consultant to help with cartridge design, and prevailed upon Eley Brothers to produce .28/06 ammunition.

F. W. Jones was one of the world's foremost experts on rifle ammunition. Born in 1867, he entered the gunpowder business and, at the age of thirty-one, obtained a patent for coating smokeless powders to regulate burning rate. This prompted Captain Edward Schultze (of the Schultze Gunpowder Co.) to dub him "the father of smokeless powder." He wasn't, of course; he came along too late for that. But his coating process opened the door to all later developments, including one that made the .280 Ross possible. During his career, Jones variously worked for the New Explosives Company, Eley Brothers, Nobel, Imperial Chemical Industries, and the British government. For his later ballistics work during the Great War, he was awarded the Order of the British Empire. Sir Charles Ross could not have found a more qualified man.

But F. W. Jones was far more than just a technician. He was also a high-level competition rifle shooter and a member of the English Elcho Shield team from 1908 until his death in 1939. The Elcho Shield is an annual team competition shot at 1,000, 1,100, and 1,200 yards. By comparison, the famous Palma match is shot at 800, 900, and 1,000 yards.

Jones's initial testing of the .28/06 recorded a muzzle velocity of 2,735 fps with a bullet weight of 150 grains. This was good performance–certainly better than the .275 Rigby, as the 7x57 was known in England–but not good enough. Sir Charles refined the case, lengthening it and making it wider at the base. This gave it a pronounced taper, highly desirable with a straight-pull rifle, since they lack the camming power of

Kynoch produced .280 Ross ammunition until 1967.

The .280 Ross loaded with the famous 160-grain hollow-point bullet.

a turn-bolt to loosen stuck cartridges. In 1907, the .280 Ross-Eley was introduced to the world. This nomenclature was retained until 1912, when other companies began making .280 ammunition. Since that time, head stamps have read either .280 Ross, or simply .280.

Tested by F. W. Jones, the new cartridge delivered a velocity of 3,047 fps at the muzzle with a 140-grain bullet. It was loaded, not with Cordite, but with 58 grains of the New Explosives Company's Neonite powder, a coated guncotton-based propellant in the form of black flakes. The bullet, for reasons unexplained, was .288 diameter rather than the .284 of the 7x57. At least one modern authority believes that, while the groove diameter was .288, Ross intended the bullet itself to be .284. At the time, some ballisticians espoused the idea of bullets of bore diameter, while others believed they should be groove diameter. Almost every factory .280 Ross bullet I have measured has been .286, which is no help.

To say the .280 Ross-Eley exploded on the scene almost understates the case. From the moment of its debut, its influence spread in every direction: From target shooting at Bisley to big-game hunting in Scotland, Africa, and India; from

rifle design, to gunpowder development, to the construction of hunting bullets.

CONQUERING BISLEY

Over the years, Sir Charles Ross has had several biographers, but none more thorough than Roger F. Phillips, a Saskatchewan historian and gun collector. Phillips's 1984 book, *The Ross Rifle Story*, written in cooperation with Ross scholars François J. Dupuis and John Chadwick, is the bible on Ross, both positive *and* negative. Phillips was not concerned with condemning or exonerating Ross or his rifles, only with documenting the truth.

Too many Ross writers over the years have depended on contemporary newspaper reports, soldiers' letters home, politically motivated interviews, earlier magazine articles that were based on any or all of the above, and even openly biased newspaper editorials. The universal flaws with these renderings of the Ross saga are over-simplification and accepting early reports without question. This is compounded by the fact that many reporters had no familiarity with rifle mechanisms. They did not understand what they were being told, and had no basis on which to challenge questionable statements.

At this point, we could follow the Ross story down several paths, and trying to explain the .280 Ross cartridge and its career is like picking out the hoofprints of one particular horse and following them through a stampede. You pick up the trail, you lose it, you pick it up again.

In 1907, F. W. Jones took a prototype .280 Ross-Eley target rifle to the Bisley matches, not to compete, but just to see how it performed. *The Field* reported that Jones made "a number of possibles," and the Ross team went home and began building a real target rifle for the next year's matches.

The annual Bisley meet in England includes competitions for both service and match rifles. The .280 Ross was purely a match rifle, but Ross's service rifles, as used by the Canadian militia, were chambered in .303 British. Accordingly, Ross became involved in both types of shooting, as well as production of superb match ammunition in both .280 Ross and .303 British.

Between 1908 and 1913, Ross and his products competed in all and dominated most. Not surprisingly, there always seemed to be an element of controversy. This happens when one rifle or cartridge comes to dominate competition: Losers look for excuses and some of them even file protests. First, the .280 match rifle. According to Phillips, Ross's special match rifle had a heavy barrel with a unique lede. Instead of a tapered throat to guide the bullet into the lands, it had parallel sides and the cartridge was a "push fit," similar to that used by *schützen* competitors. The

Ross match ammunition, in .303 British (left) and .280 Ross. Even this was controversial. Both won their share of silverware, in both Ross rifles and those of other makes. The .303 bullet weighs 200 grains, while the .280 is 180 grains.

long bullet was then positioned to enter the bore precisely. The .280 Ross-Eley target ammunition was loaded with a 180-grain spitzer full-metal jacket bullet that we would now call "extra-low drag." This was just one of many ways in which Ross and Jones were ahead of their time. The muzzle velocity was 2,700 fps—not at all bad, even today.

In 1908, F. W. Jones all but swept the field, winning five individual and aggregate long-range matches. It was a phenomenal performance–at least until Britain's National Rifle Association (NRA) received a complaint and found that, although the rifle as a whole was within legal weight, the barrel itself was a couple of ounces too heavy. Jones returned the silverware, but the Ross retained the glory. Partly due to its performance and partly to Sir Charles Ross's abrasive manner, the rifle and cartridge made enemies. In 1909 and 1910, the Eley match ammunition was not as good as it had been. This led to conspiracy theories and prompted Sir Charles Ross to begin making his own. He added an ammunition production line at his factory in Quebec, using brass obtained from the U. S. Cartridge Co., and making such excellent match ammunition, in both .280 Ross and .303 British, that the Canadian service-rifle team dominated competition at Bisley between 1909 and 1913.

Roger Phillips: "In 1910 they won principally the Mackinnon Cup, the Daily Graphic Cup, and second place in the prestigious King's Prize match. In 1911 they did the ultimate, winning both the coveted King's Prize and the Prince of Wales Prize, an unprecedented achievement."

These two prizes were both won by Private W. J. Clifford, top shooter on the Canadian team, which won a host of other honors, and defeated the British team overall with 1,581 points to 1,569.

The .303 match ammunition used in 1911 was specially prepared by the U. S. Cartridge Co. to Ross's specifications. It fired a 174-grain hollow-point bullet, manufactured at his rifle plant in Quebec, using a machine of his own design. It had a soft iron jacket, was coated with a mixture of wax and graphite, and had a muzzle velocity of 2,638 fps. (It should be noted that Ross's .303 match ammunition used different weight bullets at different times, ranging from 174 to 215 grains.)

After the 1911 matches, there was the usual round of carping, sour grapes, and murmured innuendo from other teams, but nothing came of it. Then, in 1912, pitted against the very best

.303 match ammunition that could be made in the United Kingdom, shooters using Ross match rifles and ammunition won fifty of the ninety-four prizes. Many old records were shattered, including the 1,200-yard King's Norton match, where Canada's George Mortimer made a new world's record, scoring 73 out of a possible 75.

Phillips: "During the years 1911 and 1912 Ross was truly the master of Bisley. Never before in history had one man's name so dominated the scene there. The caliber .303 Ross Mark II** (the Canadian service rifle) was without peer among the service rifles of the Commonwealth and Ross .280 match ammunition proved beyond doubt that smaller caliber bullets driven at high speed had unsurpassed accuracy."

This was undoubtedly the high-water mark of Sir Charles Ross's career, not just at Bisley, but as a riflemaker. Alas, his less admirable personality traits had served to alienate too many, including his colleague, F. W. Jones. British gunmakers had begun barrelling Mausers and Mannlichers to shoot the .280 Ross, and Jones switched rifles. Competitors using Ross ammunition in non-Ross rifles were so successful that Ross ordered that his match rounds be sold only to competitors using Ross rifles. This in-fighting ended with the beginning of the Great War, and when it was over, the Ross Rifle Co. was out of business.

* * *

Although the .280 Ross was initially a target cartridge, its designer intended it also as a military and hunting round. After the 1908 Bisley triumph, gunmakers began chambering hunting rifles for it, as well as developing proprietary cartridges to compete with it. In Germany, Mauser's new magnum action suited the .280 Ross perfectly, and it became a standard Mauser chambering. Ross's friends at Charles Lancaster

& Co. chambered the .280 Ross in their bolt rifles, and also developed a flanged (rimmed) version for use in double rifles and single-shots.

The British War Office, impressed by both the cartridge and the Ross rifle's performance at Bisley, began development of an entirely new military rifle to replace the Lee-Enfield. This was the Enfield P-13. Its long Mauser-type action was intended to accommodate the new .276 Enfield cartridge, a round so similar to the .280 Ross that the source of inspiration is undeniable. With the outbreak of war in 1914, work on the new rifle/cartridge combination was halted, since the War Office quite rightly did not want to get into a changeover in the midst of a shooting war. The cartridge was abandoned but the rifle was not; it was subsequently adapted to the .303 British (P-14), and later the .30-06 (P-17).

The .280 Ross was as successful on big game as it was on targets. The 1914 Charles Lancaster & Co. catalogue contains fourteen pages of photographs, testimonials, and reprints of magazine articles praising the .280. Most are unsigned, since a gentleman of that time rarely wanted his name in the public prints. There was, however, one exception: Charles Lancaster had more royal warrants than any other London gunmaker, and in 1911, its most illustrious client was His Imperial Majesty, King George V. In that year, the King took his Lancaster .280s on his grand tour of India, and shot everything, including Indian rhinoceros and Bengal tigers. In a letter, he described his .280s as "a great success."

Most of these letters were dated 1911 or 1912, and 1911 was also the year of the .280 Ross's most notorious failure. George Grey, brother of the British foreign secretary, Sir Edward Grey, was killed by a lion in Kenya after shooting it five times with a .280 Ross. Dying in a Nairobi hospital, Grey admitted it was his own fault for riding too close to the lion. Ever since then, however, it has been held up as an example of the inadequacy of high-velocity bullets on dangerous game.

* * *

The .280 Ross long outlived both the rifle and its designer. Ammunition was manufactured until 1967, when Eley-Kynoch finally discontinued it, but during its sixty years it had enormous influence. In the United States, du Pont developed a new powder, #10, which made possible the .280 Ross's wondrous ballistics in American-made ammunition. Introduced in 1910, but not released for canister sale until 1912, it was discontinued in 1915. According to reports, until it was released to the public it was known as "Ross powder," and competitors obtained supplies by buying Ross ammunition and pulling the bullets. DuPont #10 made possible the high-velocity cartridges of Charles Newton, introduced around this time, and set the stage for a series of ever-slower burning powders in the IMR series.

On a less serious note, in the 1920s, the German-American ballistic fraudster, Hermann Gerlich, took the unaltered Ross case, renamed it the .280 Halger, and embarked on his comic-manic campaign to convince people he was getting unbelievable velocities.

In 1920, the irrepressible Sir Charles Ross, advised by his doctor to get a complete rest, complied by booking a long safari in East Africa with his extra-marital friend, the New York big-game-hunting socialite, Mrs. Emily Key Hoffman Daziel. The safari provided the second Lady Ross, the beautiful Kentucky heiress Patricia Ellison, with the ammunition for a lurid divorce suit. In the meantime, Sir Charles and Mrs. Daziel used the safari to demonstrate the effectiveness of the .280 Ross once and for all. On his return home, he commissioned a bust of himself, dressed in safari garb. His cartridge loops all contain the distinctively long, tapered .280 cartridge. The bust, in marble, now resides at Balnagowan.

It's only fair to give the last word to Sir Charles Ross. In a letter written in 1919 to a former Canadian infantry officer, in which he undertakes to explain everything that took place regarding his rifles between 1912 and 1916, Sir Charles rather plaintively states that "The true Ross rifle was my 'sporting rifle,' which I designed myself; the military rifles turned out at my factory were an official arm over whose structure I had no control . . ."

Self-serving as this might seem, the facts, as compiled by Roger Phillips, bear it out. And the "sporting rifle," of course, includes the .280 Ross cartridge. While his accomplishments have been almost obliterated by the "Ross rifle controversy," the .280 Ross was certainly the first, and one of the greatest, of all the 7mm magnums.

These were all straight-pull designs, and went through several models with alterations and improvements often being implemented in mid-production. Ross did not follow the practice of the British War Office in designating models and sub-models with numbers, marks, and asterisks, punctuated by formal periods of range, field, and troop trials along the way. Confusing and ponderous as that system might seem, it is vastly superior to Ross's "damn the torpedoes" attitude. Although Ross rifles today are denoted by numbers and marks, these were mostly determined long after the rifles themselves were manufactured and assigned retroactively in an effort to eliminate confusion.

Almost from the beginning, there were problems with Ross's straight-pull design. The most notorious instance involved an NCO of the Royal North-West Mounted Police (later the

A CAREER IN THE MILITARY

The controversy that sank the Ross rifle, the company that produced it, and the reputation of Sir Charles Ross himself, was rooted in Canadian politics as much as anything. Having sold the Canadian government on a Canadian-made rifle for its militia in 1902, Sir Charles built a factory near Quebec City, imported skilled machinists and craftsmen from the United States, and began to build his rifles.

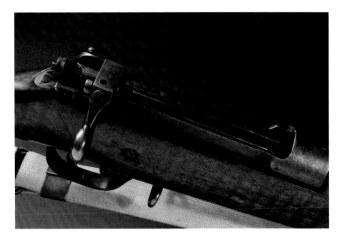

The Ross Model 1905 (or Mk. II), in .303 British, was dependable, accurate, and saw long service with many countries, including the USA. It has the most graceful action of any Ross rifle, and is beautifully made.

Royal Canadian Mounted Police) who was badly injured when a rifle self-destructed, for lack of a better term. That was in 1905. Ross corrected the faults, and what emerged was the rifle now known as the Mk. II, or 1905 Ross. Like both the Mannlicher and the Mauser, the Ross had twin opposing locking lugs that rotated into recesses in the receiver ring by the camming action of the bolt sleeve. The 1905 had solid lugs, was quite a good rifle, and later saw service with some units of the American military, among others. It also has the most graceful action of any Ross, and could be the basis of an interesting custom rifle.

It was followed by the Mark II**. During 1909–10, Ross made substantial changes to the

The interrupted-thread locking mechanism was immensely strong, as indicated by the proof levels. According to Roger Phillips, it withstood proof pressures of 150,000 psi.

*The bolt of the Mk. II** (or Mk. III) used interrupted-thread locking lugs, similar to an artillery piece or naval gun, rather than the usual dual opposing lugs of the Model 1905 (Mk. II).*

action, chief of which was switching from solid locking lugs to an interrupted-thread design similar to a big naval gun. Ross claimed as much as 50 percent more strength in this design, which was borne out by proof testing. Unfortunately, the rifle was not subjected to sufficient operational testing, under field conditions, before being put into production. It was made with a very tight (match quality) chamber, which later proved to be the main cause of its downfall, although there were other problems as well.

The Mark II** was also known as the Mark III, and a 1913 army manual refers to it as such. The same action was used for the Model 1910 (M-10) civilian hunting rifle. The M-10 was chambered for the new .280 Ross cartridge, which was intended as a military, target, and long-range hunting round, all in one.

The Mark II** was adopted by the Canadian militia (forerunner of the Canadian Army). The minister of militia in the federal government was Sam Hughes, a friend of Sir Charles Ross since Boer War days, and one of the least admirable characters in Canadian political history. Sam (later Sir Sam) Hughes was a tall, imposing, vain, overbearing, and blustering character who bullied everyone around him. From the beginning, his relationship with Ross, and his championing of the Ross rifles through thick and thin, gave rise to suspicions of nepotism and unethical dealings. Inevitably, the Ross rifle became linked with Sam Hughes, which made it a target for Hughes's political enemies—of whom there were many, and whose numbers increased steadily through the years.

When war broke out in 1914, Canada immediately declared war on Germany and pledged military and logistical support for Britain. Canadian soldiers went overseas armed with Ross rifles chambered for the standard .303 British. This was the rifle Ross all but disowned in the letter quoted above, and it certainly had problems. It was more a target rifle than a rough-and-tumble military arm like the Lee-Enfield. Undoubtedly accurate, it was also very finicky as to the ammunition it would accept. As long as Canadian troops were supplied with Canadian-made ammunition, everything was fine. In the chaos of war, however, this could not be guaranteed, nor could the uniformity of ammunition from a wide variety of factories in many different countries. The Lee-Enfield could accommodate these anomalies; the Ross could not.

Canadian troops went into battle for the first time in the spring of 1915, and problems with the

Ross were reported almost immediately. Mostly, these involved rifles jamming as a result of the varying ammunition, and the lack of camming power in the straight-pull action to break a stuck cartridge case free of the chamber. Another cause of jamming, which developed later, was the rearmost thread of the left locking lug striking the bolt stop. This caused peening, which resulted in the bolt sticking when it was slammed closed. The ammunition problem was resolved by recalling Ross rifles and opening up their chambers. The peening problem was solved by installing a wider bolt stop that would not hammer the thread enough to damage it. There was, however, a third problem, and this was the one that would bedevil Ross rifles, military and civilian, henceforth and to this day.

Accusations arose that it was possible to assemble the bolt incorrectly, in such a way that it would only appear to be closed, yet still fire a cartridge. Because it was not locked, it would then fly back and injure or kill the shooter. These accusations were seized on by Canada's political opposition party, and its allies in the press, in order to attack the government. The enmity that Sam Hughes had built up during his bullying, blustering career was coming home to roost, and his underhanded behavior in support of the Ross only made it worse. Eventually, in the spring of 1916, the British Commander-in-Chief, Field Marshall Sir Douglas Haig, ordered the Ross withdrawn from service completely, to be replaced by the Lee-Enfield. This was the rifle with which the Canadian Corps fought the rest of the war.

Although there are no recorded *and confirmed* instances of a Canadian soldier being killed by a bolt blown back, the accusation remains, more than a century later. Phillips et al do mention one case of a soldier allegedly being killed. It was described by a former Canadian Army armourer,

Lindsay C. Elliott. In a letter to H. V. Stent, a firearms writer with *Outdoor Life* in 1922, Elliott wrote that a soldier standing next to him in a trench was killed when the bolt blew back, and on examining the bolt, Elliott found it had been "misassembled." Furthermore, he stated, this was not the only instance he knew about. This is puzzling, not to say suspicious, for reasons we shall see shortly. No mention is made of that incident when, in 1938, the official history of the Canadian Army in the Great War was published. It included a separate appendix (Appendix III) dealing with the Ross rifle issue, which dealt at length with the ammunition problem as well as the peening of the locking lug. Nowhere, however, does it mention a single instance of a bolt blowing back and injuring a shooter. The official history was compiled and written with complete objectivity, twenty years after the Armistice, when the main characters were long out of public life. Its authors, and the Canadian Army itself, had no ax to grind, and no political considerations to worry about. Had the blow-back problem genuinely existed, it should certainly have been prominently mentioned. There is nothing.

However, such was the extent of the controversy, even this omission is subject to examination. Roger Phillips and his co-authors suggest that just because they are not documented in the public records does not mean they did not happen. They suggest that since most shots were taken with soldiers standing up in the trenches, bolts blown back would miss their heads and cause no injury. Well, not according to Lindsay C. Elliott, who claimed to have been standing beside the dead man in the trench when it happened. But, to continue.

In 1999, Canadian arms historian Clive Law undertook to reprint Appendix III, under the title "A Question of Confidence," to ensure that such an important historical document remain readily available to researchers. In the foreword, a professor from Canada's Royal Military College notes that Lt. Col. A. F. Duguid, lead author of the official history, obviously sided with the anti-Ross faction, yet he does not go out of his way to condemn the rifle for alleged blow-back incidents.

Toward the end of the war, amid a flurry of claims and counter-claims, and contracts unfulfilled, the Canadian government expropriated the Ross Rifle Co. factory in Quebec, and in 1920 paid Sir Charles Ross the then-immense sum of $2 million in compensation. He retired to Florida, where he lived out the rest of his life, a very wealthy man.

Over the next twenty years, a small growth industry sprang up within the legal community, suing Sir Charles Ross on behalf of shooters who had allegedly been injured by the infamous "deadly bolt" of Ross hunting rifles. To all appearances, rather than fight case after case, and probably just weary of it all, Sir Charles took to settling many of these out of court. He could well afford to do so, but such an approach did nothing for either his own reputation or that of his rifles. When one goes looking for actual instances of injuries, of incidents involving poorly assembled Ross bolts, they either cannot be found or are highly questionable. Undoubtedly there were genuine incidents, but equally undoubtedly, Sir Charles Ross found himself tagged by lawyers as an easy mark. In civilian circles, the Ross M-10 in .280 Ross acquired a reputation as being only slightly less dangerous than a black mamba.

Ever since, articles about Ross and his rifles tend to quote earlier articles, which in turn quote articles from earlier still. With each telling, the accounts of injuries become more serious but less specific. I saw one in which it was stated that "thousands of Canadian soldiers died" because of

Ross malfunctions. This is utter hogwash. The Canadian Corps established itself as the premier fighting unit on the Western Front, of any army on either side, beginning with its very first action in April 1915. For the next four years, it never retreated without orders, never failed to take an objective it was ordered to take, and never lost a position that was not quickly retaken. An army does not compile a record like that using a worthless rifle.

In his *Complete Book of Rifles and Shotguns* (1961), Jack O'Connor wrote that the Ross Model 1910, with the interrupted-screw locking system, "was a bad actor if the bolt was incorrectly assembled. It was possible to fire this model unlocked, and many people were maimed and even killed when the bolt blew back into their faces." As a professional journalist, he probably thought he was playing it safe with such a general statement. Even so, it's surprising O'Connor would write that.

Roger Phillips et al include a chapter, "Ross Rifle Accidents and Causes," in which they attempt to track down and evaluate specific incidents. They even go so far, when court records can be obtained, to name the lawyers and law firms who acted for the plaintiffs and the defendant, as well as damages claimed and damages paid. While including considerable detail, this chapter in some ways is as infuriating as other accounts, where the issue becomes a will-o'-the-wisp, with the real cause always flitting just out of reach. For example, there was the case of Louis LaVallee (or LaValley) mentioned earlier. Conversely, the most recent incident reported occurred in Deep River, Ontario, in 1965, and the authors not only spoke to the victim, but knew the location and current owner of the rifle in question. That is difficult to dispute.

One disturbing thread that runs through most of the accidents reported in that chapter is that they involve borrowed rifles. The victims usually (though not always) were unfamiliar with the Ross and its operation. This does not excuse anything, of course, but it does suggest that it is not a rifle you want to lend to a friend to take hunting, especially if he's the kind of guy who will want to take everything apart to see how it works. Experienced soldiers and riflemen, who knew the rifle intimately, used them without a problem, often under the worst conditions, and admired them for their accuracy.

Philip B. Sharpe became a very vocal critic of the Ross rifles, although his attitude is somewhat contradictory. In both of his books he becomes almost hysterical in insisting that no Ross rifle with an interrupted-thread bolt should ever be fired, under any circumstances; elsewhere, he tells of buying a half-dozen Ross rifles when the US government disposed of its remaining stock, then "shooting them to pieces." He writes that he attempted to assemble a bolt incorrectly and make it fire, but while he could do this to a point, the firing pin could not reach the primer. He was working with primed cases only (not live ammunition) but never succeeded in igniting a primer. This only adds to the mystery. During the Great War, in urgent need of small arms of all kinds, the US government purchased twenty thousand Ross Mark II rifles (Model 1905) and presumably these are what Sharpe obtained. Since the 1905 has solid lugs and was never accused of any of the faults of the Mark II**, it's hard to see exactly what Sharpe thought he was proving.

We will return to this issue, but first, a look at the Ross M-10 hunting rifle. As a child, Sir Charles Ross stated his ambition to design "the greatest hunting rifle the world has ever known." When the Ross M-10 (.280 Ross) sprang upon the world, he had done exactly that, at least in terms of range, accuracy, and killing power. It was also a beautifully made and finished, well-balanced rifle with a superb hunting stock. Being made in Canada, it was available to big-game hunters on both sides of the Atlantic, and it quickly got a lot of attention. In America, one of the most prominent and influential gun writers of the day was Capt. E. C. (Ned) Crossman. He was sent one to try and famously called it "the rifle of my dreams" in a 1910 article of the same name that appeared in the NRA publication *Arms and the Man* (forerunner of *The American Rifleman*.)

By the time the Ross Rifle Co.'s 1914 catalogue was released, Ross had gleaned a raft of glowing reports on his rifle. Some were tales of spectacular long-range kills; others praised the speed of the action (three black bears dead in twenty-three seconds, and that kind of thing.)

The catalogue itself, which is available in reprint from Cornell Publications, makes very valuable reading for anyone with an interest in ballistics and rifle performance. It examines in detail every aspect of the M-10 Ross sporting rifle, its cartridge, the bullets available for hunting, the proven accuracy, the function and strength of the action. No possible question is left unanswered, yet it's all couched in very reasonable tones— neither strident nor excessive. In fact, it exudes an air of quiet confidence—certainly well-deserved in light of the rifle and cartridge's performance at Bisley, and the reports then coming in from the big-game countries of the world. It reads very much like one of the London gunmakers' catalogues of the era, such as Holland & Holland's.

THE ROSS .280 M-10 SPORTING RIFLE

The M-10 sporting rifle, based on the Mark III (or Mark II**) action, is the most famous of the Ross big-game rifles, but by no means the only one. An earlier sporter, the Model E, was based on the predecessor Mark II, or Model 1905, action.

That rifle had exceedingly pleasing lines, abetted by the streamlined shape of the action, and was available in either .303 British or .35 Winchester.

This was followed in 1907 by the Ross High Velocity Scotch (*sic*) Deer Stalking rifle, the first to employ Ross's new interrupted-thread locking lugs. By the time the 1914 catalogue appeared, this had evolved into the M-10 sporting rifle, the flagship in the Ross line. There was also the Model R, a civilian version of the military Mark II** with the extended box magazine, chambered for the .303 British and rated at a weight of just 6 lbs.12 oz. The Model E-10 was similar, but with a more refined stock, better finish, and checkering. For the record, the M-10 listed at $55.00, the E-10 at $42.50, and the Model R for $33.00. By comparison, the Haenel-Mannlicher New Model we looked at in an earlier chapter was available at the same time for about $26.00.

Personality aside, Sir Charles Ross was the perfect person to design a hunting rifle: He was a dedicated and experienced hunter who grew up stalking stags in the Highlands, and he knew the qualities a fine hunting rifle required. His mechanical aptitude allowed him to project how a rifle should operate best, and then turn it into reality. Having grown up with Purdeys and Holland & Hollands, he recognized quality and fine workmanship, and his long association with Charles Lancaster gave him an understanding of what was meant by building London quality into a rifle of his own design.

The Ross sporting rifles were built to the highest London standards of fit and finish. Even the military Model 1905 actions are sleek, smooth, and beautifully finished. Their military stocks leave something to be desired, but then, all military stocks did. When it came to the M-10, Sir Charles Ross put all his expertise into fashioning a rifle that was far ahead of its time in every way. The finish of action and barrel was every bit the equal of London magazine rifles from Lancaster or H&H. The stock on the M-10 is as good as anything from that era, and vastly better than most. It is slim, graceful, handles like a fine shotgun, and comes up to the shoulder with the eye perfectly aligned with the sights. Both wrist and forend are slim by any standard, and it had extensive, well-executed, wrap-around checkering.

According to the Ross catalogue, all sporting models were stocked in Italian walnut. The contoured steel buttplate is checkered, the grip cap is horn, the forend has a delicate *Schnäbel*. As with most rifles of the time, makers believed there should be a forend screw to attach it to the barrel, and this belief did not die quietly. (This somewhat archaic feature lasted on the Winchester Model 70 until 1963.) On the Ross, this screw goes through the wood into a barrel band. On my rifle, the forend screw itself is the forward sling eye but, inexplicably, it has no rear sling swivel as shown in the catalogue. However, Ross sporting rifles were a semi-custom proposition, so the original buyer may have specified this for whatever reason.

The rifle has a box magazine flush with the stock. Like the Mauser, the floorplate is removable with the nose of a bullet or similar tool. Otherwise, cartridges must be unloaded by working them partly into the chamber, also the same

as with a Mauser. The barrel is carbon steel, 28 inches long, although it could be ordered with a 26-inch barrel. The rate of twist was advertised as 1:8.66 inches, more than sufficient to stabilize the heaviest bullet at Ross velocities.

One of the most interesting features about this rifle is its sights. As it came standard from the factory, it had a fine bead front sight on a barrel band, and a single-blade rear sight, also on a barrel band. The blade has one number on it: 500. This blade could be either fixed or folding. It was possible to order the rifle with a telescopic sight; unlike the Model 1905, the "Ross Model of 1910 Action," as it was formally known, had a receiver bridge to accommodate a peep sight, if desired. According to the catalogue, which is replete with charts, graphs, and explanations, the trajectory of the .280 Ross was so flat that the single blade served for all distances out to 500 yards simply by the accepted expedient of taking a fine or a full bead.

Major Sir Gerald Burrard (mentioned in the previous chapter) was one expert who greatly admired the .280 Ross cartridge, but did not agree with the principle of "fine or full" beads, and questioned the performance claimed for the cartridge. Sir Gerald believed that an experienced hunter should acquire the same sight picture each time, and then either hold high or low, depending on the range. Testing a Ross rifle with the 500-yard sight, he found that holding dead on

Sir Charles Ross set out to design "the greatest hunting rifle the world has ever known." With the Model 1910, he came very close indeed. It is a beautifully made and finished, well balanced rifle with a superb hunting stock.

at 100 yards placed the bullet eighteen inches high. Keeping in mind his aversion to "fine or full," however, these two statements more or less cancel each other out.

Not surprisingly, given its record on the target ranges of the world, the Ross company placed great emphasis on the accuracy of its rifles and cartridges. Captain Crossman, who was at one time high-power rifle-shooting champion of California, claimed to have shot groups at 500 yards that measured four to seven inches. His rifle was fitted with a 3.5X Pernox riflescope. Townsend Whelen, on the other hand, reported that he took six rifles from a dealer's stock, spent a day shooting them at 200 yards, and averaged ten-shot groups of about eight inches. Some writers backed Crossman, others supported Whelen.

In spite of this, Whelen stated in print that the Ross M-10 "just might be the kingpin of all rifles."

* * *

The M-10 bolt has controlled-round feed, like the Mauser 98, with the extractor picking up the case as it is pushed forward out of the magazine. The ejector is a spring-loaded triangular projection, unobtrusively low on the left side, just forward of the bridge. The M-10 safety catch is a small wing on the bolt handle that locks the striker, is easily manipulated by thumb alone, on or off, and can be absolutely silent.

The Ross trigger is the standard (for the time) two-stage military-type, with a reasonably light, crisp release. It was designed in such a way that, if the action is not completely locked up when the trigger is pulled, the force of the striker spring serves only to push it closed the rest of the way. When the safety is on, the trigger moves easily. The trigger is not blocked by the safety; instead, the safety pulls the striker back from any contact with the sear.

The receiver bridge houses the bolt stop, which is a knurled catch. The 1914 catalogue states bluntly that the bolt stop is copied from the 1906 Springfield, but then makes the startling statement that Ross sporting rifles have "no magazine cut-off," and goes into some detail as to why the company believed magazine cut-offs were a mistake on hunting rifles. And yet, the bolt stop on my M-10 has three positions, and in its third (up) position it does act as a magazine cut-off. Down all the way, operation is normal; at mid-position, the bolt can be removed; up all the way, it projects slightly forward, blocking the bolt from coming completely to the rear. This ejects the empty case, but prevents the bolt from picking up a round from the magazine. In this way, the rifle can be used as a single-shot, while keeping the entire magazine in reserve, or in order to switch to different ammunition quickly, without emptying the magazine. One more contradiction, as if there were not enough already.

Sir Charles Ross, and of course his collaborator, F. W. Jones, were as interested in bullet design as they were in every other aspect of shooting. Their work with long-for-caliber bullets, and extra-low drag bullets, especially for long-range target shooting, was hugely influential, and bullet designers are building on that foundation to this day. Ross also designed hunting bullets that were revolutionary. Among the hunting bullets with which the .280 Ross was loaded, two stand out. One was a jacketed hollow point, the other was his famous "copper-tube" bullet that employed a spitzer tip of copper that, on impact, drove down into the lead core and caused the bullet to open up. This was not a new idea even then, Westley Richards having used the concept with bullets for black-powder cartridges. The Ross, however, was a streamlined, deadly, ultra-modern bullet that would not look out of place in a bullet catalogue

.280 Ross cartridges, from left: 145-grain "copper tube" hunting bullet, 160-grain hollow point, and 180-grain match.

of today. The idea was adopted in the 1960s by Canada's Dominion Cartridge Co., and marketed as the Sabre-Tip, as well as by Remington (Bronze-Point), Nosler (Ballistic Tip), and dozens of others in recent years. More bullet makers are adapting the design all the time.

The cartridge itself was the most influential ballistic development of its day. Sir Gerald Burrard considered it to be a watershed. When it appeared, he stated, it "changed everything." He himself used the .280 almost exclusively in the Himalayas, but did so in a Charles Lancaster double rifle with oval-bore rifling because he vastly preferred the advantages of a double. As well, the oval bore minimized the effects of "nickelling"—fouling resulting from firing cupro-nickel jacketed bullets at high velocity.

The interrupted-thread locking lugs which caused problems in the Ross Mk. II** were undoubtedly every bit as strong as Ross claimed.

They withstood proof pressures up to 150,000 psi, according to Roger Phillips, and when Charles Newton designed his own rifle in 1915, he employed the same principle. In fact, Phillips states that the Newton bolt head was a "direct copy" of the Ross. Since then, it has been used on various semiautos. The Weatherby Mark V's nine-locking-lug configuration, introduced in 1958, is a variation on the theme of the interrupted thread, and is acknowledged to be extremely strong.

Even after its replacement by the Lee-Enfield in 1916, the Ross continued to be used by Canadian soldiers, and especially snipers, in the trenches. It was the most accurate rifle employed by any nation in that war, and if you looked after it, knew how to use it, had the alteration made to the bolt stop to avoid peening, and were careful about ammunition, a sniper such as Herbert W. McBride (*A Rifleman Went To War*) could use it to devastating effect.

After the war, Ross rifles found their way to the four corners of the earth, usually as small lots of surplus military rifles bought by desperate countries or paramilitary forces. When the Canadian Army switched to the Lee-Enfield in 1916, its Ross rifles were given to Britain in a "straight swap." With several hundred thousand Ross rifles in storage, Britain gave some to the Royal Navy, armed some home-defense units with them, and hauled them out in 1940 in preparation for an anticipated German invasion. Between the wars, the Baltic states (Latvia, Estonia, and Lithuania) were supplied with Ross rifles, while others went to Russia in the 1920s and were used in the long post-Revolution civil war. Years later, these resurfaced—reworked, restocked, and with new sights—and were used by the Russian shooting team to win the international running-deer competition in Caracas, Venezuela, in 1954.

* * *

Here is an interesting point that jumps out from all the accounts of Ross sporting rifles and their mishaps: None that I can find were reported before 1914, when the war began. All of the civilian claims date from *after* 1918, *after* the widely publicized controversy over the performance of the military rifles. This is very strange, not to say suspicious, given the fact that the sporting Ross M-10 was in use, all over the world, from 1910 onwards with, to all appearances, nary a misstep. Before 1914, it was all glowing accounts of great successes, from three grizzlies downed in less than a minute to an elephant dropped at 400 yards with a 180-grain solid. After 1918, it's all injury claims and lawsuits.

In 2002, *Gun Digest* published one of the best-balanced articles about the Ross, written by Jim Foral. Foral spent an entire summer shooting Ross rifles and loading ammunition for them. He is a diligent researcher who makes a specialty of delving into what appeared in print a century ago, in such publications as *Outdoor Life* and *Arms and the Man*.

Among the writers quoted by Foral from original publications are Capt. Crossman, Capt. (as he then was) Townsend Whelen, and Maj. Charles Askins Sr. He also quotes a "Canadian gun writer" by the name of Linsey (or sometimes Lindsey) Elliot (one "t")—presumably the same Lindsay C. Elliott mentioned by Roger Phillips, whose letter to H. V. Stent at *Outdoor Life* described the death of a Canadian soldier in the trenches. Since Phillips identifies Elliott in some detail, we can assume his full, correct name was Lindsay Clinton Elliott. Incidentally, one more minor mystery: if H. V. Stent was writing for *Outdoor Life* in 1922, he must have been a writer of extraordinary longevity. His byline appears in *Gun Digest* as late as 1980, and *Rifle* Magazine as

late as 1986. Or, perhaps there was more than one firearms writer named H. V. Stent.

Elliott first appears in print as a resident of Carbon, Alberta, who describes his Ross rifle in glowing terms. Foral quotes him as saying the stocking and checkering were "of the very best," while the stock shape was excellent for managing recoil and "the balance of the rifle is perfect." Elliott tests some soft Dominion Cartridge Co. ammunition, which also gave Crossman fits on a hunting trip. The brass was soft, stuck in the chamber, and was extracted only with great difficulty. Elliott reported the same experience, but says that overall he liked the rifle "a whole lot, and hated it just a little." All he had "agin' it," he wrote, was the sticking bolt.

According to Phillips, Lindsay Clinton Elliott served in the Royal Canadian Ordnance Corps (RCOC) as an armourer-sergeant from 1915 to 1919. Elliott claimed to have originated the practice of putting a rivet in the Ross bolt housing, to prevent the kind of misassembly that resulted in accidents. At the time, he was said to have been serving with the 6th Canadian Infantry Brigade under Brigadier A. C. Macdonnell. However, Brig. Macdonnell commanded the 7th Brigade, not the 6th, so where did Elliott serve? Brig. Macdonnell and his officers were the most vociferous in condemning the Ross, leading up to its replacement in 1916. After the war, Elliott went to work for Canadian Industries Ltd. (CIL), which manufactured ammunition under the Dominion brand for the next sixty-five years. Elliott was employed by CIL for twenty-five years, giving sales demonstrations.

The thorniest issue involving Ross rifles, both military and civilian, is the claim that the bolt could be misassembled in such a way that it could be put back into the rifle, chamber a round, appear to be locked when it was not, and then blow back out of the rifle, injuring or killing the shooter.

It has been demonstrated that this can be done, but it is not easy to do, and the bolt does not slip readily back into the action. Even this controversy has survived for a century, with some authorities in the 1940s claiming to have done it, while others denied it was possible. A few years ago, a short video appeared on the internet showing a man accomplishing it with a military Ross, albeit with considerable difficulty.

It is usually described much as O'Connor wrote: "The bolt can be incorrectly assembled . . ." as if this were as easy as putting your shirt buttons in the wrong holes. It is anything but. Disassembling a Ross bolt in the first place is far from simple, and soldiers in the trenches were expressly forbidden to strip their rifles beyond a certain point, after which they were to be handed over to the armourer for repair. Supposedly, in the mud of the trenches, soldiers disobeyed this in a desperate effort to get their rifles working when they were choked with mud.

The Ross bolt operates inside a sleeve, rotated the way a ratchet screwdriver rotates its head. When the bolt mechanism is removed from the rifle, the bolt is all the way forward and protrudes from the housing by .93 inches. When replaced in the rifle, the bolt lugs come in contact with the barrel, and are then rotated into the locked position as the bolt housing continues forward. With the mechanism out of the rifle, however, the bolt can be rotated by hand, and is then drawn back into the housing by the striker spring. As long as the extractor remains in its groove forward of the lugs, all will be well. The bolt can be moved in and out at will. However, the extractor functions in a manner very similar to the extractor on a Mauser 98, and like the Mauser, it can be rotated out of its groove, allowing the bolt to retract slightly, then rotated back into its groove. Now the bolt is too short, and will not close properly. Is this confusing enough for you?

Actually accomplishing this is not nearly as easy as it sounds, and if you do manage it, the bolt does not slip effortlessly into the rifle. It binds, jams, and needs to be forced in. Jim Foral quotes Herbert Cox of Wilmington, Delaware, who, in a letter to the "Dope Bag" section of the *Rifleman* in 1945, stated he had mastered the technique, but not without considerable difficulty getting the bolt into the rifle, and then getting it back out only with the aid of a screwdriver and both hands, with the rifle locked between his knees. Roger Phillips confirms that Cox was one of America's foremost authorities on Ross rifles until his death in 1964, and that he had pinpointed several ways in which the bolt could be altered to prevent misassembly.

Keeping the bolt correctly and permanently aligned in its sleeve was relatively easily done, with a rivet or screw in the right spot. All of this, of course, is the kind of teething problem that arose with the Lee-Enfield in its formative years, and was corrected through various marks and asterisks as a result of troop trials. As Lt. Gen. Edwin Alderson, then commanding the Canadian Corps, wrote in a letter in early 1916, "The Lee-Enfield is an old experienced man as a service rifle, while the Ross is a baby." Lt. Gen. Alderson was, indisputably, treated very unfairly by the Canadian government, and removed from command shortly after he wrote that. It is probably unwise to comment on what appears on the internet, in such places as Wikipedia, since it could disappear tomorrow or be radically changed, but an entry devoted to Lt. Gen. Alderson refers to the Ross as "useless in the trenches." It certainly had its faults, but it was far from useless, and when Field Marshall Haig ordered it replaced in early 1916, it was mostly because Canadian troops had lost confidence in it; the mechanical problems themselves had already been largely corrected.

This is a good place to insert the fact that, were I to find myself in the trenches of Flanders in 1915 and had a choice, I would take a Lee-Enfield No. 1, Mk. III over the Ross with no hesitation whatever. The Lee-Enfield was unquestionably one of the finest battle rifles of the twentieth century.

* * *

Jim Foral also quotes a Canadian firearms authority from the 1940s, C. C. Meredith, as saying, "As to the safety of the Ross action, more nonsense has been written than you can shake a stick at." After exhaustive research that would have driven lesser men to the bottle, Roger Phillips and his co-authors concluded that:

"Generally speaking, a Ross rifle with the 1905, 1905 modified, and 1910 actions are safe to use if they have not been tampered with after leaving the factory, are used with ammunition designed for them, and are in the hands of users who actually know the rifle."

I cannot claim to know the Ross as well as I would like to. I still struggle every time I try to deliberately misassemble the bolt and get it back into the rifle. I still wince inwardly when I pull the trigger on a live round, even though I know—*know*—that the bolt cannot just "slip" into a misassembled and dangerous state.

But pick up the M-10, look at its checkering, put it to the shoulder, work the bolt back and forth a few times, dry-fire it once or twice, heft it in your hands, and you know you're handling a thoroughbred. As a hunting rifle, it was well thought out from stem to stern. Those careful thoughts were then transformed into walnut and

steel to the best standards of the London gun trade, by craftsmen who really knew their work. It is beautifully balanced and fits every bit as well as other rifles mentioned in this book—and it preceded most of them, and set an example for others to follow. Stocks on American custom rifles did not catch up to the Ross M-10 for twenty years, and to this day, most are still not as good.

It's impossible to consider any of Ross's accomplishments separately from his failures, but we can say for certain that in the .280 Ross cartridge, Sir Charles created the first and one of the finest of the 7mm magnums, and that he set in motion a train of events that led to

The .280 Ross (extreme left) inspired a host of similar 7mm cartridges, including (from second left) the .280 Magnum (Rimmed Ross), .275 H&H, and .275 H&H Rimmed, also known as Holland's .275 Magnum. There was also the short-lived military .276 Enfield and, later, the .280 Halger, 7mm Mashburn, 7x61 Sharpe & Hart and, finally, the 7mm Remington Magnum.

Charles Newton, Roy Weatherby, and the modern high-velocity hunting cartridge. As it nears 110 years old, however, the .280 Ross is more than merely a cartridge. It's part legend, part hero, part villain. As a designer of both rifles and cartridges, Sir Charles Ross, Bt., deserves more credit than he receives. Brilliant, erratic, talented, impatient—he was, to put it bluntly, a spoiled brat who grew up sublimely intolerant of others. To Sir Charles, ironing out bugs was detail, and he had no time for detail.

One can hardly write about the .280 Ross and not get lured into Sir Charles Ross's life, loves, character, and accomplishments. It's easy to be distracted by the Ross rifles and their record on the target ranges of the world, or in the trenches of the Great War. One could also look at Ross's work in bullet development, the evolution of smokeless powders, and the search for higher velocities. He was an original and, even among the British aristocracy, wherein there has never been a shortage of eccentrics, he cut a swath at which we can only marvel.

No history of great hunting rifles can possibly ignore either the .280 Ross or the M-10 sporting rifle. They were too revolutionary, and too influential, for too long. Is it really a "great" hunting rifle? In the right hands, yes. But there is always that caveat. To be on the safe side, we'll say yes, and put an asterisk beside it. Which seems appropriate.

In a bizarre sort of the way, the Ross M-10 rifle and the .280 Ross cartridge are inanimate reflections of the man himself: brilliant, contradictory, controversial—but fascinating.

During his last illness, aged seventy, at his home in St. Petersburg, Florida, Sir Charles Ross's last words were addressed to the nurse who was attending him. He opened his eyes, muttered "Get the hell out of here," and died.

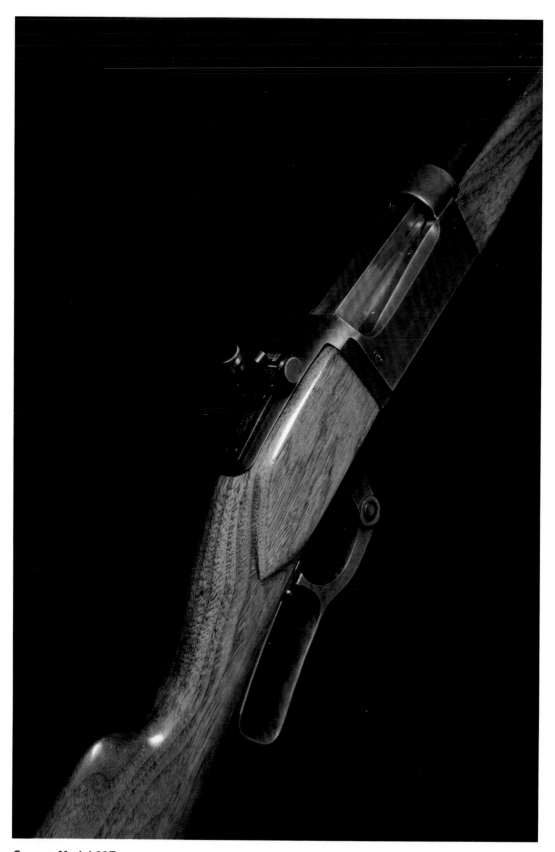

Savage Model 99E.

CHAPTER VIII

THE .250-3000—SAVAGE'S VELOCITY KING

PROLOGUE

In 1914, Savage Arms unveiled its own latest entry in the high-velocity sweepstakes: The .250-3000. It earned its name because it promised a muzzle velocity of 3,000 fps. Over the years, many writers have stated that it was the first commercial cartridge to reach that height—taking Savage's word for it, presumably—but of course it was not. That honor belongs to the .280 Ross, by almost a decade.

For Savage Arms, the .250-3000 (known more commonly today as the .250 Savage) was but the latest in a line of proprietary cartridges that delivered velocities higher than was normal at the time. Arthur W. Savage, designer of the Model 1899 lever action and founder of the company, learned early, as did P. T. Barnum, that there is no substitute for publicity. One area in which Arthur Savage truly deserves credit as a pioneer is in his use of advertising and bluster to sell rifles and ammunition.

Savage's first effort was the .303 Savage, a cartridge that is a ballistic twin of the .30 WCF (.30-30) and which may actually have preceded the .30-30 as the first commercial smokeless cartridge in America. The two appeared within months of each other, and it has never been definitively proven which was first. In a David-and-Goliath battle against Winchester Repeating Arms, Arthur Savage turned to the power of the printed word. Shortly after the .303 Savage's unveiling, ads began appearing with testimonials

to its unprecedented killing power, not just in the US, but in Africa and Asia as well. From the sound of it, everything from tigers to elephants gave up the ghost at the mere sight of a .303 Savage.

The .303 Savage was the cartridge that really put both the Savage Model 1899 and Arthur Savage himself on the gunmaking map. With the 99 (as it became known) firmly established as the heretic's favorite lever action, Savage decided to trump himself with an even newer, smaller, and faster cartridge. He turned to Charles Newton, a Buffalo, New York lawyer, ballistician, inventor, and writer, who was the first really serious wild-catter of the smokeless-powder era.

Newton is often called "the father of high velocity," and that is actually the subtitle of Bruce Jennings's 1985 biography, but Newton was at least third generation in the quest for speed. Lt. Col. David Davidson, James Purdey, and Sir Charles Ross had more valid claims to paternity, at least in terms of chronology. But Charles Newton was the first American to make velocity his life's work, and he was unquestionably the most influential. When Roy Weatherby came along a half-century later, he was building on Newton's foundation. Some call Weatherby the "*modern* father of high velocity," and that's fair enough. Although Newton's real work in the field came later than Ross's, they were contemporaries. Newton was four years older than Ross, and died a decade earlier—1932 versus 1942. The two

Savage's ground-breaking cartridges. From left, the .303 Savage (1895), .22 High Power (1912), and .250-3000 (1914). All seem diminutive compared with the .30-06.

men bore a remarkable physical resemblance to one another, and sharing a Christian name as they did, Phil Sharpe often referred to Newton jokingly as "Sir Charles." There are other eerie parallels between them, too, as if the pursuit of velocity carried its own demons to torment disciples.

At this late date, it's impossible to say exactly how much Sir Charles Ross's work directly influenced Charles Newton, but given the publicity the .280 Ross received on both sides of the Atlantic, to say nothing of the attention given to the Ross sporting rifle, it must have been considerable. Throughout this period, if Newton was competing with anyone, it was with Sir Charles Ross. Around 1915, when Newton designed his own bolt-action rifle, one particularly noteworthy feature was its locking lugs: Rather than using solid lugs like the Mauser, Newton employed an interrupted thread, copying the Ross Model 1910.

Newton's various biographers list a dozen different wildcat cartridges developed between 1902 and 1914, all but a handful of which are long-forgotten. In 1905, however, he took the .25-35 Winchester case, necked it down to .228, and created the .22 High Power (also called the Hi-Power, or "Imp."). It fired a 70-grain bullet at 2,800 fps. The very next year, Newton began submitting articles to *Outdoor Life*, and in the next few years created his 7mm Special and .25 Newton Special. These were both created by necking down the .30-06, making them precursors to the later .280 Remington and .25-06. Newton's first commercial breakthrough came in 1912, when Savage Arms picked up the .22 High Power and chambered it in their lightweight Model H takedown rifle.

The .22 High Power's moment of glory was brief but vivid. Savage's publicity department went into high gear, promoting the .22 High Power just as it had the .303 Savage, and suggesting it could handle virtually any game animal on earth. Adventurers were found to carry the rifle to the far corners, and report back on its devastating performance. One who became famous was a missionary doctor named Harry Caldwell. In China, he reportedly killed "many tigers" and other game with a .22 High Power. Not everyone was convinced of the .22 High Power's prowess, however, even on deer. One of the skeptics was Charles Newton himself.

Savage, however, was so impressed with Newton's work that it commissioned him to design a new cartridge just for the Model 1899 which, with its short action, could not handle cartridges the length of the .30-06. Newton took his .25 Newton Special, shortened it to fit, and created what came to be known as the .250-3000—one of the great hunting cartridges of all time.

Texas gunmaker Todd Johnson with a superbly restored Savage Model 1899 takedown rifle, chambered for the .22 High Power. The .22 High Power (or "Imp") was the second in the line of the high-velocity cartridges that built Savage's reputation, and the 99 was the epitome of lever-rifle sophistication.

in those days, but certainly someone made the fateful decision. After witnessing the career of Sir Charles Ross, and the splash that his .280 made from the Himalayas to the Rockies, the idea of a bullet reaching the magic plateau of 3,000 fps was on every riflemaker's mind.

It was possible to reach this goal—just—with Newton's .250, but only by reducing bullet weight to 87 grains. This allowed Savage to build an ad right into the cartridge's nomenclature: The .250-3000 proclaimed its prowess on every box of ammunition, engraved on every barrel, and reinforced every time someone mentioned its name. There is no denying it was brilliant marketing. From that moment, the .250-3000 defined the Savage 99 rifle, and did so for the next fifty years.

There are photographs from the 1920s, showing groups of deer hunters with a dozen or more deer hanging up on meat poles, and I have even seen some in which every single man was carrying a Savage 99. In the usual crowd of Winchester 94s and a scattering of single-shots, however, the graceful, deadly 99 fairly leaps out at you. According to those who were there, it was even possible, out in the woods, to tell whether a distant shot came from a .250 or from one of the bigger bores. The .250-3000 has a sharp *"crack,"* like a whip, and, so the stories go, there was usually just one shot. The 99 in .250-3000 became the deer rifle of the serious hunter, the *cognoscenti,* the sophisticate.

And it was not just a rifle for whitetails. As with the .303 Savage and .22 High Power, the Savage publicity department pulled out the stops. Probably the most famous appearance of the .250-3000 was in the hands of Roy Chapman Andrews, who hunted and explored the Gobi Desert for the American Museum of Natural History and collected Mongolian sheep and various other game. Again, there were reports of large animals that

SAVAGE AND THE .250

When Newton designed the .250, what he had in mind was a deer rifle firing a 100-grain bullet at 2,800 fps—a step up from the .22 High Power, which he considered marginal. Alas, the Savage company had other ideas. Traditionally, the blame for what happened subsequently is laid on the advertising department. It's hard to imagine an advertising copy writer having such influence dropped "as if pole-axed." Presumably, people in those days knew what a pole ax was. The focus of the cult of high velocity, initiated by James Purdey and perpetuated by devotees of the .280 Ross, was now transferred to the .250-3000, the latest *wunderkind*.

It was fortunate for Savage that, in those days, chronographs were few. Nor had hunters adopted riflescopes wholesale and begun devoting their lives to shooting smaller and smaller groups. In its determination to have that magic "3,000" associated with its new baby, Savage committed a couple of errors. With a cartridge of less intrinsic worth, or subject to closer scrutiny via chronograph and riflescope, these errors would probably have been fatal. The fact that the .250-3000 was able to soldier on and prosper in spite of them tells us just how good it was.

The two problems were related: Barrel length, and the rate of twist of the rifling. In 1914, many of the mysteries of twist rate and bullet stabilization had been solved, and formulae for determining the correct rifling twist for a given cartridge were well established. It was well known that the faster the bullet, the slower the rifling twist required. However, when velocity dropped, or the bullet lengthened, a faster twist was required to compensate and stabilize it, and a properly stabilized bullet was essential to accuracy. An added consideration was the belief at that time that a bullet could be over-stabilized—that is, if the twist rate was too fast, the bullet would have too much rotation, and become erratic. Riflemakers were just as cautious about *over-* as *under-*stabilization. In recent years, this factor has been discounted to a great degree, but in 1914 it was a major consideration.

The twist rate decreed for the .250-3000 was one revolution in fourteen inches (1:14). This would nicely stabilize an 87-grain bullet at 3,000

fps. With a 24-inch barrel, the cartridge delivered the advertised 3,000 fps (3,030 fps, to be precise), and the whole package worked well.

There is some disagreement as to the original twist rate. Philip B. Sharpe, in *Complete Guide to Handloading*, states that the original twist rate was 1:12, but that 1:10 would have been better, offering good accuracy in all bullet weights. All 99s in .250-3000 that I have measured, however, have had 1:14 twists, and most authorities agree that the standard twist originally decreed for the .250-3000 was 1:14.

After the .250-3000's debut, Savage began making a wide variety of rifles for it, with barrel lengths as short as 18 inches. This included some takedown models, which were very popular at that time. Naturally, the shorter the barrel, the more loss of muzzle velocity. As velocity fell, the twist rate became too slow to stabilize the bullet, and accuracy suffered. Most writers blame accuracy problems in the takedown models on the barrel connection wearing loose, but I suspect it was due to velocity loss and consequent bullet instability.

Sharpe, who knew Charles Newton personally, stated that, in a conversation with Newton shortly before his death, he was told the original design for the .250 called for a 100-grain bullet at 2,800 fps, and the twist rate was to be 1:10. Newton said Savage made a "grave error" in altering his design, and added that he'd been trying for twenty years to interest different companies in making ammunition to the original specifications, but without success. According to Sharpe, Newton died two months later, and a month after that, the Peters Cartridge Company finally came out with a 100-grain load at 2,850 fps. Other companies followed, although most loaded the bullet to a velocity of around 2,700. With the rifles then in use, and their 1:14 twist rate, this

Comparing weights and lengths: From left, the Sierra 90-grain hollow point, Sierra 100-grain spitzer boattail, 100-grain Nosler Ballistic Tip, and the 117-grain Speer. The Speer is considerably heavier, but actually slightly shorter than the Ballistic Tip. Assuming equal velocity, the Speer bullet could be stabilized with a slightly slower twist rate.

only aggravated the situation. Using a 100-grain bullet at that velocity, a twist rate of 1:10 is critical for accuracy.

Determining the minimum twist required for bullet stabilization depends on several factors, including bullet length, caliber, specific gravity (SG), and velocity. Specific gravity is required because it affects the spinning inertia of a bullet, and must be allowed for. Lead has a high specific gravity (11.3) while copper is 8.9 and steel just 7.8. A bullet combining lead with a copper alloy jacket has a specific gravity of about 10.9.

The first method of determining twist was the English Greenhill formula, devised in 1879, and it's still the basis of twist-rate calculations. However, it was formulated for artillery, and above a velocity of 1,800 fps, requires some modification. Another modern development that affects twist rates is the boattail found on many bullets, making them longer for weight. Rifling

that stabilizes a 100-grain round-nosed flat-base bullet, and is very accurate, might not stabilize a spitzer boattail of the same weight, and accuracy would suffer.

It is good to remember, too, that twist rates are relative, not absolute. A rate of 1:10 is fast for a .308, but moderate for a .257. Instead of thinking in terms of one revolution in ten inches (1:10), it's better to think in terms of calibers. As a very broad rule of a very broad thumb, a twist rate of 32.5 calibers will usually provide a reasonable rate of twist for a particular cartridge. By that rule, a .257 needs a twist rate of 1:8.35. That is very fast, and unheard of in .257-caliber rifles.

In the 1962 *Gun Digest*, John Maynard published an article on determining twist rates, and included a chart that allowed the user to apply those factors and arrive at a specific number. Today, several websites on the internet allow a user to input some data and get a read-out. These are vastly simpler, although Maynard's chart is still useful because it allows one to see how twist rates change as factors vary up and down. In effect, it imparts some understanding, whereas the internet formulae simply provide information.

To give some comparison figures, a 100-grain .257 bullet (Nosler Ballistic Tip) is 1.11 inches long. At a velocity of 2,700 fps, it requires a minimum twist rate of 1:10.9. A 117-grain bullet (Speer spitzer) at 1.084 is actually slightly *shorter* than the Nosler 100-grain, because it lacks a boattail and does not have a polymer tip. Being heavier, however, it will have lower velocity. Assuming we get 2,500 fps, it requires a twist rate of 1:10.7 inches. The Sierra .257-caliber, 90-grain boattail hollow-point is .900 inches long, and a 1:14 twist will stabilize it provided it reaches a velocity of 2,950 fps. As you can see, it is possible to get good accuracy from a short-barreled .250-3000 provided it does not lose too much velocity.

* * *

Savage had introduced a ground-breaking cartridge and then inadvertently hung several millstones around its neck. In spite of this, the .250-3000 racked up a very impressive record and established a reputation as a spectacular killer on deer. Sometimes this was attributed to the sheer velocity of the bullet, but the fact that it was a cartridge of moderate recoil, and easy to shoot accurately, was also a factor. As well, many users of .250-3000s were more serious hunters and shooters, the kind of guys who liked to shoot and practiced a lot, and could put the bullet where it belonged when the time came. That undoubtedly helped.

Some of the stories of its prowess on larger game may have been apocryphal, but not all. Jack O'Connor reported that the Yukon outfitter, Jean Jacquot, habitually carried a .250-3000, and had killed many grizzlies with it at a time when grizzlies were considered a nuisance and shot on sight.

Jim Carmichel, O'Connor's successor as shooting editor of *Outdoor Life,* commented on the .250-3000 in his 1975 book, *The Modern Rifle.* "I wouldn't consider (the .250-3000) a very good choice for elk," he wrote, "But I have to point out that the 'quickest deadest' I ever saw a bull elk dropped was with none other than a Model 99 in .250-3000 caliber."

One thing that is under-reported, either because of embarrassment or because the evidence disappears, is the number of times an animal is hit and does *not* do the vaunted pole-ax routine. If there is no evidence of a hit, and no blood trail, a hunter would assume he'd missed and go about his business, while the animal might die several terrible hours or days later. With a heavily furred animal like a grizzly, this could happen more often than not. The anti-high-velocity crowd was always eager to report instances of bullets "blowing up"

and leaving horrendous surface wounds without killing cleanly. It would seem likely, to me at least, that for every one of those horrifying examples there might be several more where the bullet wounded an animal but did not kill it, yet showed no indication of a hit and was counted a miss.

The reason this debate has raged for 150 years, beginning with James Purdey's express rifles and continuing on through the .280 Ross, the .250-3000, and later the Weatherby cartridges, is because there are genuine solid examples on both sides. Neither argument is clearly and conclusively right, but neither is clearly and conclusively wrong, either.

Savage chambered the .250-3000 in the 99 for about forty-five years, discontinued it briefly in the early 1960s, then brought it back in 1973. It remained in the line until the mid-1980s.

Over that long period, the company made the 99 in a dazzling array of models, variations, and grades. The differences were mostly in stock design and barrel length, but it also changed from the original rotary magazine to a detachable box, and was adapted to riflescopes. During the course of its life, the Model 1899 progressed from the old, crescent-shaped, sharp-cornered "rifle" buttplate of the 1890s to the flatter, more moderate shotgun- or carbine-style buttplate, and finally to recoil pads. The rifle began with a straight stock and slim *Schnäbel* forend, and ended with a pistol grip and a bulky, blocky forend more suited to a benchrest rifle. In some later models, its sleek, almost reptilian lines, were obscured by Monte Carlos, pistol grips, and beavertails. As you might expect, some of these rifles were better than others, and one or two could even be called downright bad.

My own search for the perfect Savage 99 .250-3000 began around the rifle's one-hundredth anniversary, and did not end for a dozen years.

During that time, I owned several .250-3000s. One was a late-production solid-frame rifle with a 24-inch barrel; another was an early takedown, which was in bad shape, but I had it restored; today, I own only two .250s. One is a Model EG from around 1949. It has a pistol grip, *Schnäbel* forend, 24-inch barrel, and a scope. It was owned originally by a rifle nut who obviously admired and cared for it.

The second rifle is what I consider to be the epitome of Savage 99s, as defined by G. T. Garwood and his theories of eumatics, and by my own idea of the perfect rifle for still-hunting and prowling creek bottoms and wooded ridges in search of whitetails. It is, quite simply, a wonderful hunting rifle.

SAVAGE MODEL 99 E

Savage Arms introduced its first "Featherweight" models in its 1904 catalogue. The company may not have been the first to use that term, but it was certainly the one that made it famous, and lightweight rifles stayed in the Savage line until 1973. At the time, Savage claimed its Featherweights were the lightest big-game repeating rifles in existence, with some examples weighing as little as six pounds. That is a light rifle even today, never mind in 1904.

Various means were used to reduce weight. Stocks were slimmed down to the maximum degree, and even hollowed out. Barrels were shortened and given the narrowest profile possible. The barrels were so thin, it was impossible to cut a dovetail for the front sight, so in the earliest models sights were brazed on. Later barrels had an integral lug—the first use of this feature by Savage Arms. The first Featherweights were available in .25-35, .30-30 Winchester, and .303 Savage. Two years later, they were made available in a takedown model as well.

In 1920, the entire line was revamped and renamed. The Featherweight became the Model E, and the takedown version the Model F. Logically, perhaps, it should have been the other way around. The Model E was available in five calibers: .22 High Power, .30-30, .303 Savage, .250-3000, and the new .300 Savage. The first three calibers were given 20-inch barrels; the .250-3000 had a 22-inch barrel, and the .300 Savage was 24 inches.

Whether by accident or design, Savage had, in its Model E .250-3000 Featherweight, created almost the perfect stalking rifle.

It had a straight stock with no pistol grip and with no trace of the perch-belly lines of early 99s. The forend was a short, slim *Schnäbel*. There was no checkering, but that was hardly necessary anyway, and no sling swivels. The front sight was a blade in an integral lug, held in place by a cross pin. As it came from the factory, it was fitted with

In .250-3000, fitted with a Lyman 56S receiver sight, the Savage 99 E is a near-perfect stalking rifle.

The Model 99 E's lines are graceful, economical, and deadly.

the usual open sight on the barrel. The buttplate was steel, gently rounded with horizontal grooves for stability. My rifle, unloaded but fitted with a Lyman Model 56S receiver sight, weighs 6 pounds 10 ounces.

In my opinion, 22 inches is the ideal barrel length for a .250-3000 *provided* you intend to use 87-grain bullets. For 100-grain bullets, only a 24-inch barrel can deliver the velocity required by the 1:14 twist. Alas, factory ammunition of any sort for the .250-3000 is nigh impossible to come by today, which makes shooting any .250-3000 largely a handloading proposition. This is no problem, since Sierra makes a 90-grain hollow-point bullet intended specifically to be tougher than the average 87-grain, which these days are usually intended as varmint bullets for use in more powerful cartridges like the .25-06 and .257 Weatherby. As mentioned above, the 90-grain Sierra HP requires only 2,950 fps to stabilize with a 1:14 twist, and it can easily be loaded to reach that velocity in a 22-inch barrel.

It has the usual Savage rotary magazine, similar in operation to that designed by Otto Schönauer, but not quite as refined. The cartridges do not press down into it quite as effortlessly, and if you don't get the angle right, can actually be annoyingly difficult. In operation, however, it works very well. One drawback is that, unlike the Schönauer, it is not in any way detachable. If you get dirt, moisture, and debris down in the

magazine well, it is difficult to clean. Also, the only way of unloading is to partially run each cartridge into the chamber and eject. Still, compared to the tubular magazines commonly found on lever rifles at that time, it allows the use of ballistically better hunting bullets, and it does not worry about cartridge length provided they are short enough to fit. Because of the expense, presumably, rotary magazines have never been widely used, although in recent years, Sturm, Ruger & Co. produced a series of scaled-down bolt rifles, chambered for cartridges like the .22 Hornet and .44 Magnum. These use detachable rotary magazines, and work beautifully.

I think of the Model E as primarily a rifle for woods prowling, carried as Theodore Van

The Savage rotary magazine is well-designed and beautifully made. Each cartridge is cradled in place and prevents bullet deformation under recoil. Feeding is smooth and reliable.

Dyke decreed for the still-hunter, in one hand at the trail, or in both hands like a bird hunter walking in on a point. I would not want to take a shot with it beyond 250 yards, and in that situation the vast majority of opportunities will be at considerably shorter range anyway. For this purpose, the Lyman sight is more than adequate, and with no scope to get in the way, the rifle is as comfortable to carry as the Winchester Model 92 covered earlier.

With its light weight, straight stock, and short barrel, the Model E is as quick to mount and shoot as a London game gun (well, almost), and lends itself to instinctive shooting at short range. Recoil and muzzle blast are moderate, and the rifle is simply fun to shoot. This leads to a lot of practice, which in turn leads to proficiency.

My rifle was manufactured in 1922, shortly after the model was introduced. Many of the early weight-saving measures had been scrapped with the changeover in 1920. In the 1932 catalogue, Savage listed average weights at around seven pounds—still very light for a big-game rifle. The next year, the Model E was discontinued, although the takedown Model F remained in the line until 1940. In 1935, Savage combined some of the features of the Model E with those of the Model G (pistol grip and more substantial forend, although still a *Schnäbel*) to create the Model EG, which became one of the most popular 99s ever made. It was suspended with all other civilian rifles during the war, but production was resumed after 1945—a measure of its popularity, when so many rifles and shotguns disappeared for good.

In 1955, Savage introduced another rifle with the Model F designation. This time it did stand for Featherweight, which leads to some confusion with the earlier Model E. Fortunately, the new Model F was the first Savage rifle to have the full model designation stamped on the barrel, which makes it easy to differentiate from the original Model E of 1920. It included various "refinements" that served only to water down the virtues of its forerunner, and it displayed many post-war "improvements" such as impressed checkering. The new-series F was dropped completely in 1973.

There was also a new Model E, and it stayed in the line through the 1970s and into the '80s. When Savage reintroduced the .250-3000 around 1973, it was in the Model A, a plain rifle that resembled the original Model E Featherweight, with its straight stock and *Schnäbel* forend. The Model A had only a 20-inch barrel, but with 1:12 twist it should work well even with heavier bullets at lower velocities.

Jim Carmichel, in *The Modern Rifle*: "Interestingly, both the .250 Savage chambering and the prewar straight-stock "A" model styling seemed a dead and forgotten issue only a few years ago, but just to satisfy some remote clamourings, the Savage people made a limited run of 99s in this combination. The item proved such a big seller that it's now (1975) a standard Savage

Jim Carmichel: "The .250 Savage is one of the best possible choices for deer-sized game in all sorts of hunting conditions."

catalog item. I'm not surprised at this success, because the .250 Savage is one of the best possible choices for deer-size game in all sorts of hunting conditions."

Having owned nine Savage 99s over the years, ranging in vintage from 1912 to the 1970s, in six different chamberings, four of which were .250-3000s, I have come to several conclusions about them. One is that Savage consistently missed opportunities to turn a fine rifle into a truly great one. My Model E is the exception that proves the rule. During the course of almost a century of production of the 99, and more than sixty years of the .250-3000, one would think they could have made many that would qualify as great; instead, there are only one or two, and then for very short periods.

I now have only one other .250-3000, a Model EG from around 1949. It has a 24-inch barrel, a pistol grip, longer forend (though still a *Schnäbel*), and was fitted by a previous owner with both a sling and scope. The twist is 1:14. As

outfitted, but unloaded, the rifle weighs 8 pounds 10 ounces—exactly two pounds more than the Model E. The addition of the scope and sling render it almost impossible as a still-hunting rifle, never mind the additional two pounds. Here is an interesting point about the sling. When prowling the woods, still-hunting, one would tighten the sling to the "parade" position, to keep it from flopping around, making noise, or catching on branches. When you do that, however, it gets in the way of operating the lever. Definitely non-eu, as Gough Thomas would have it (see chapter 12).

One of the traits of a really good still-hunting rifle is that you can hold it by the grip with one hand while using the other to part branches, and have the rifle ready to come into action in an instant. I can do that hour after hour with the Model E, but, because of the extra weight, not with the EG.

I do admire the EG—it's a nice rifle—but I dearly *love* the Model E.

* * *

Savage Model 99 EG in .250-3000, manufactured around 1949. With its 24-inch barrel, Leupold scope, and sling, this is a rifle more than a carbine, for careful, deliberate shooting rather than stalking and fast action.

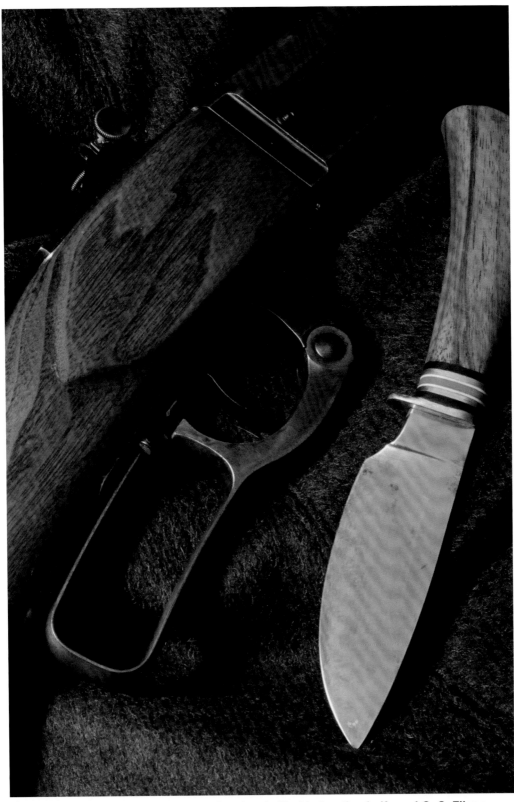

The Savage Model 99 E, along with the classic Marble hunting knife and C. C. Filson wool, were emblematic of an age when beauty and craftsmanship were married to utility.

New Winchester Model 70 Featherweight.

CHAPTER IX

FEATHERWEIGHTS: DEVELOPMENT OF A CONCEPT

If the "featherweight" concept in rifles began with the Savage 99 in 1905, it was not a word coined by Savage. It was borrowed from boxing, where the term was used as early as 1860. A featherweight boxer weighs a maximum of 126 pounds—heavy enough to do serious damage, yet light enough for speed and agility. The first formal featherweight boxing championship was held in 1889. With the widespread popularity and publicity given to boxing in those years, it was only natural that a gunmaker would pick up the term and apply it to a light rifle.

Unfortunately for Savage, it stopped using descriptive names in 1920 and switched to designating models by letters such as A, E, and F. It's interesting, though, that Sir Gerald Burrard, in his 1925 book *Notes on Sporting Rifles,* used the term "featherweight" as if it was a common generic term for any light rifle. After Savage abandoned it, the term fell into disuse in America until 1952, when Winchester began a minor rifle revolution with the unveiling of its Model 70 bolt-action "Featherweight." Ever since, the term has been associated with the Model 70, even though it has come and gone and come again as Winchester (and its successor, U. S. Repeating Arms) revamped their lineup.

The original Winchester Model 70 was introduced in early 1937. It was a complete redesign of the Model 54, Winchester's first attempt at a bolt-action rifle. The Model 70 was a superbly made rifle in its many sub-models and configurations, which included a heavy "bull" gun, super grade, standard, and National Match. It was produced for about five years before the US entered the second world war and all civilian production was suspended. After 1945, when production resumed, Winchester (along with every other rifle maker) had not only learned how to cut corners and reduce costs, it had also learned what it could get away with.

In the years immediately following the war, there was a huge upsurge in demand for hunting rifles and shotguns, much of it from men whose only experience with rifles had been the Springfield or the M1 Garand. Admirable though those rifles might be in other ways, neither of them is likely to impart a feel for what a rifle should be like for hunting.

Collectors of Model 70s (of whom there are many) now feel the post-war rifles were decidedly not up to the production standards of those made between 1937 and 1941. These standards included the polishing and finishing of metal parts, stock inletting and checkering, and the smoothness of the bolt, safety catch, and trigger. This lowering of standards was not peculiar to Winchester. All rifle companies came in for criticism about this from gun writers, including Jack O'Connor in *Outdoor Life*. One area about which O'Connor was particularly vocal was weight. By his own later account, he wrote a column in 1946 in which he criticized the extra pound or two that every factory rifle seemed burdened with.

This Savage Model 99 takedown, made in 1913 and chambered for the new .22 High Power, is a Featherweight, and was even called that in the catalogue of the time. The receiver sight is a Redfield Model 80L.

He had done a lot of mountain hunting, both before and during the war, and had experimented with custom rifles. His ideas about proper rifles for hunting in the mountains undoubtedly had a serious influence.

Over the years, some have credited O'Connor with being the prime mover behind the Model 70 Featherweight, but he himself wrote that he did not delude himself that rifle companies hung on his every word. However, that 1946 column did generate considerable mail, both to *Outdoor Life* and the rifle companies, and this provoked still more articles in the shooting press. Regardless of how it all came about, the Featherweight made its debut in 1952 and exerted a strong influence on every other rifle maker. From that point on, a general trend developed toward reducing weight.

At the time, it was not unusual for a standard factory rifle such as the Model 70 to weigh eight or nine pounds, minus scope and sling, and go more than ten pounds fully loaded and ready to hunt. That's a fair burden, and seems considerably heavier at the end of a long day of climbing, with the snow coming down and five hard miles back to camp. For example, one Model 70 standard grade, made in 1952 in .300 H&H, with a sling, weighs 8 pounds 5 ounces. Add a scope, mounts, and five rounds of ammunition, and you've easily topped ten pounds.

The Model 70 Featherweight was formally announced in August, 1952, coinciding with the new .308 Winchester cartridge. The announcement was too late to make the 1953 *Gun Digest* (which came out in the summer of 1952) and so the full-page announcement appeared the following summer, in the 1954 edition. This has given rise to some confusion since then, but in fact the Featherweight and the new .308 were made for each other, and sprang upon the world at the same time.

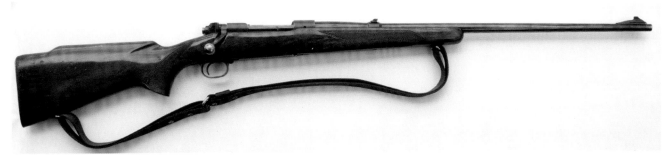

Standard-grade pre-'64 Winchester Model 70, in .300 H&H. Unloaded and without a riflescope, it weighs 8 pounds 5 ounces. Ready to hunt, it weighs more than ten pounds.

The Featherweight incorporated radical changes from the standard-grade Model 70. Winchester said it had been "re-engineered," and that was no exaggeration. The barrel was shortened to 22 inches, ideal for the .308, and given a slimmer profile. The integral flange on the barrel, which accommodated both the rear sight and the forend screw, was eliminated. This screw allowed the shooter to increase or decrease tension on the barrel, an important factor in tuning for accuracy. Eliminating it completely allowed the barrel to be "free floated," a term that was to come into common use in the next few years. Replacing the steel floorplate, trigger guard, and buttplate with an aluminum alloy (duraluminum, or "dural") pared still more weight. Shortening the forend by an inch to give it the right proportions with the shorter barrel saved a fraction of an ounce, and also gave the rifle an appearance of balance and cohesion—of all parts combining in harmony.

Altogether, the Model 70 had been carefully re-thought to accommodate an entirely new cartridge, just as the Savage 99 had been forty years earlier for the .250-3000. Winchester, however, learned from Savage's mistakes. In designing its new cartridge, it also drew on its own war experience.

The .308 Winchester (a.k.a., T-65, or 7.62x51mm NATO) was a near-perfect match

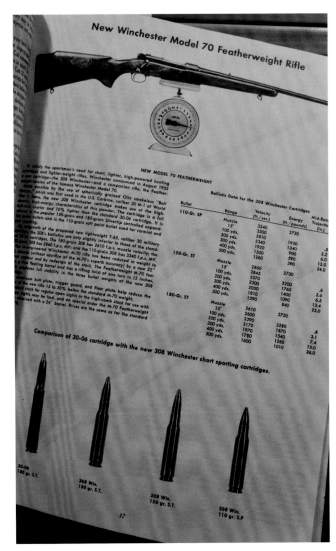

The new Winchester Model 70 Featherweight, and its running mate, the .308 Winchester, were announced in the 1954 Gun Digest. Actually, both were released in mid-1952.

with the new Featherweight. It was shorter than the .30-06 it replaced, yet delivered ballistic performance superior to that which made the .30-06's fortune in 1906. Where the .30-06 then fired a 150-grain bullet at 2,700 fps., the .308 got 2,860 fps. This improvement was credited to a new ball powder developed by Olin-Winchester for the .30 M1 Carbine during the war. Granted, in 1952 the .30-06 was also much better than it had been in 1906, and could comfortably outperform the upstart .308 with the newer powders, but that's not the point. Its original ballistic performance was an enduring benchmark, and the new Featherweight .308 gave a hunter better performance, in a shorter, lighter rifle, than had the Springfield that sent writers into ecstasy before 1914.

Winchester offered .308 ammunition in three bullet weights: 110, 150, and 180 grains. Rifling twist was 1:12, and Winchester assured shooters that it would comfortably stabilize all three bullet weights.

Initially, only two options were offered with the Featherweight. One was a 24-inch barrel, the other a modified Monte Carlo (high comb) stock for use with a scope. Within two years, Winchester had expanded the available chamberings to include the .270 Winchester and .30-06, and even offered a "super grade" of the Featherweight. After that, additional chamberings came thick and fast. In 1955, when Winchester unveiled the .243, one of its greatest cartridge success stories, it was a natural for the Featherweight. The .358 Winchester was also added, which probably had a bit too much muscle for a rifle that weight, but even worse was to come. The Featherweight's low point occurred in 1961, when Winchester chambered it for the .264 Winchester Magnum. That cartridge, in a 6½-pound rifle with a 22-inch barrel, was an

Major players in the saga of the Winchester Model 70 Featherweight, from left: .30-06, .270 Winchester, .308 Winchester, and the .264 Winchester Magnum. Chambering the huge .264 in the Featherweight created a monster, whereas the .270 was fine and the .308 ideal.

abomination: vicious recoil, ferocious muzzle blast, a flame out the muzzle that would clear a bunker, and less velocity, if anything, than the old .270.

In reviewing the new Featherweight rifle and cartridge in 1954, Maj. Gen. Julian S. Hatcher devoted more space to the cartridge and its development as the military replacement for the .30-06 than he did to the Featherweight itself. He states that Winchester asked permission of the military to introduce a civilian version specifically for its proposed light-weight rifle. He also notes that, though the rifle was advertised at six and a half pounds, the examples he had handled all ran slightly heavier.

The debut of the Featherweight in 1952 was as much a watershed for hunting rifles in America as Savage's .250-3000 had been in 1914, and the Springfield before that. It changed everything. In the years that followed, all factory rifles grew gradually lighter, and light weight became an end in itself for many riflemakers. This trend continued right into the 1980s, when small companies competed to see who could trim their rifles by another ounce, or half-ounce, or gram. As with most such trends, it went much too far in some instances, with the shooting qualities of a rifle completely ignored in the race to produce one that weighed a smidgen less. Certainly, a rifle can be too heavy, but it can also be too light. Through the 1950s and '60s, however, this particular problem lay well in the future.

The Winchester Model 70 Featherweight exerted an enormous influence on both rifle and cartridge design, and also on rifle aesthetics. One example was Browning, whose Belgian-made, Mauser-actioned High Power came in variations as light as 6¼ pounds. In a not-so-happy emulation of Winchester, its .264 Winchester Magnum weighed 7 lbs. 2 oz., with a 22-inch barrel. At the time, I was going through a brief, unrequited love affair with the .264, and the Browning was the object of my boyish affections. Fortunately for me, in 1965 I did not have the necessary $199.50 to inflict one on myself.

Given the influence it was undoubtedly having, what happened next is all the more baffling. In 1964, the Winchester Model 70 was completely redesigned, and the Featherweight disappeared from the line. Gone, completely, as if it had never existed. Or had it?

It's worth taking a moment to look at the sequence of events since the introduction of the Featherweight. It was greeted with a standing ovation in 1954, yet in reviewing the post-'64 Model 70s in the 1965 *Gun Digest,* Ken Waters made the startling comment that the Featherweight had "happily been abandoned." Happily? What was there to be happy about? The answer lies, I believe, in the distortions and excesses which Winchester had applied to the Featherweight in the eleven years since its birth, culminating in the addition of the .264 Winchester to the available chamberings, and the creation thereby of a true monster.

The move had been announced by Winchester at a writers' conference in 1961, along with an announcement that it was adopting a new barrelmaking process, pioneered in Europe, called "hammer forging." The first hammer-forged barrel to come from New Haven would be a 22-inch .264 in stainless steel, destined for the new .264 Featherweight. The first rifles appeared shortly after, and one went to *Gun Digest* Editor John Amber. He checked it out with handloads, then took it elk hunting in Montana. He reported that, as measured by an Avtron chronograph, his 140-grain Nosler Partitions left the muzzle at 3,050 fps—150 fps shy of the touted muzzle velocity. Amber suggested that an elk would not know the difference.

Reading reports from around this time by several other well-respected writers, including Bob Hagel, Ken Waters, and Pete Kuhlhoff, gun editor of *Argosy,* and reading between the lines, one comes to a conclusion or two.

One is that when the .264 Winchester was unveiled in 1958, it was available only with a 26-inch barrel—completely appropriate, and the only length with which it could realize its advertised ballistics. This did not sit well with all writers, however, some of whom complained that it was too long and cumbersome to carry in the mountains. Three years later, when Winchester put it into the Featherweight with a 22-inch barrel, and the velocity dropped dramatically at the same time as muzzle blast, flame, and recoil became extreme, these same writers hardly felt they could then complain that the barrel was too short.

One of these writers was John Amber himself, who admitted as much in print. Confronted with the result, he could do little except gulp, live with it, and try to make out that the velocity loss was no big deal. But was it? Consider that a .270 Winchester with a 130-grain bullet was rated—*from a 22-inch barrel*—with delivering 3,130 fps with a 130-grain bullet, and you see that Winchester had, in effect, reduced its new, world-beating, small-bore belted magnum to little more than a reflection of its older, smaller brother. With the addition of the .264 Winchester chambering, the Featherweight had become a monster. This may well account for Ken Waters's obvious satisfaction that the whole concept had been dropped—or so it appeared.

Studying the Model 70 lineup unveiled in 1964 reveals a different story. The Featherweight may not have been there in name, but it was certainly there in fact—in the form of the redesigned standard grade. The post-'64 Model 70 Standard resembled the pre-'64 Featherweight far more than it did the old Standard; it weighed just seven pounds, sported a 22-inch free-floating barrel, and its chamberings were the old standbys—.308, .30-06, .270 et al—with big bangers like the .264 relegated to more seemly rifles, like the 26-inch barreled Model 70 Westerner. In the end, the rifle on which the Featherweight exercised the most influence was its own parent.

For the next fifteen years, Winchester struggled to overcome the adverse publicity generated by the Model-70 redesign, offering this change and that one, and watching as the pre-'64 became a cult object, the darling of collectors, and the action most desired for rebuilding into a gilt-edged custom job.

Then, in 1981, the Featherweight returned in the form of the Model 70 XTR Featherweight. Gone were some post-'64 features, replaced by a stylish rifle with a classic-style stock, graceful *Schnäbel* forend, and ribbon-pattern checkering copied from an early Winchester custom design. The weight was 6¾ pounds (compared to the 7½ pounds of the Standard Grade). It was offered in the original calibers, as well as in 7x57 and .257 Roberts.

In its own way, if anything, this latter-generation Featherweight was more influential than the original. It came just as the push for lighter and lighter rifles really gained momentum, and it caused other riflemakers to offer comparable models.

One company to jump on the second coming of the Featherweight bandwagon was Parker-Hale of Birmingham, England, a venerable name in rifles, sights, and target shooting. For some years, Parker-Hale had been manufacturing a line of rifles on Mauser 98 actions. In 1984, it introduced its Model 1100 Lightweight, using a Santa Barbara Mauser action. It looked like the new Winchester Featherweight in much the same way that first cousins occasionally bear an uncanny resemblance to one another. This was mostly because of its *Schnäbel* forend. It weighed 6½ pounds. I mention it here because I owned one in 6.5x55, and used it in 1990, backpacking for Dall sheep in Alaska. By that time, it was just one of many such on the market, but it was an excellent rifle.

In 1993, U. S. Repeating Arms introduced what it called the "classic" Model 70 action. Whether this was due to public pressure, to the demand for pre '64 actions for custom rifles, or simply a desire for something new to market, is

The author in the Chugach Mountains of Alaska, backpacking with a Parker-Hale Model 1100 Lightweight in 6.5x55 Swedish. The Parker-Hale closely resembled the Model 70 Featherweight.

impossible to say. Having adopted CNC machinery and other advanced manufacturing methods, the company was able to produce small lots of special designs without major retooling. The "post-'93 pre-'64" Model 70 action reincorporated one of the most lamented losses from the 1963 redesign: controlled-round feeding. At first, the new action was used only on higher-grade models, but it gradually spread throughout the line. Finally, the post-'64 action was relegated to the cheaper models only.

Between 1990 and 2017, the entire Winchester line underwent drastic and life-threatening change. The Winchester name was still owned by Olin Corporation and used under license by U. S.

Repeating Arms. When that company closed its doors in 2006, shutting down the historic New Haven factory where Winchester firearms had been built for 130 years, it seemed it would be the end of the line. Instead, in an odd reversal of fate, the line was taken over by Browning Arms, which is owned by FN and is part of a worldwide weapons conglomerate. John Browning had done so much to make the Winchester company in the first place, and now the Browning company saved both the Model 70 and the Browning-designed lever-action Model 94.

Since then, the Featherweight has undergone some serious changes along with the other Model 70s. Mainly, it is no longer completely

The author with a fine Dall sheep, taken in the Chugach in 1990. The rifle was the aforementioned Parker-Hale, an excellent mountain rifle.

manufactured in one place; instead, production is spread over several facilities, and not all are in the US. FN and Browning are ultra-modern and globalistic in their approach, with manufacturing and assembly operations all over the place: barrels hammer-forged at a new plant in South Carolina, actions built by an American subcontractor, and stocks originating in several locations. In 2001, I ran into an acquaintance from Browning in the Basque gunmaking town of Eibar, where he was paying a flying visit to oversee production of walnut stocks on a mass-production pantograph-type machine. This monster was installed on the second floor of a seemingly ramshackle industrial building, overflowing with walnut chips and shavings, just down the winding street from the old Ugartechea factory. Such is globalization.

The venerable Model 70 trigger, admired by all, envied by most, but copied by few, was replaced by a modern trigger designed for the Browning bolt rifles and unveiled in 2007. It's an admirable trigger, with a light, crisp pull as it comes from the factory. With the stock removed, it can be adjusted by two tiny screws in the trigger housing, but not to a pull lighter than three pounds. Presumably, with this limitation, the hoi-poloi won't hurt themselves and sue the company.

The Winchester Model 70 Featherweight that is sold today is, in my opinion—after handling many but, alas, never the 1952 original—the best it has ever been. It's a global product, and engraved on the barrel are the words "Made in Portugal by Browning Viana," not the trusted old "MADE IN NEW HAVEN, CONN. U. S. OF AMERICA." In .270 Winchester, fitted with a Leupold scope and mounts (unloaded, no sling)

it weighs 7 lbs. 14 oz. The barrel is 22 inches. The trigger guard is alloy, but the floorplate is steel. It retains some of the post-'64 touches, such as a jeweled bolt, but the stock is walnut, pleasing but not gaudy, with a subdued oil finish. The *Schnäbel* forend is graceful. Its ribbon-pattern checkering may have been done by a machine, but it's beautifully cut nonetheless. There is no Monte Carlo or cheekpiece, and the recoil pad is black, elegant, and devoid of white-line spacers.

Altogether, the new Browning-made, European-assembled Winchester Model 70 Featherweight looks exactly like the American Classic it has become. If, taken overall, the Model 70 Featherweight is not the finest American factory hunting rifle of the past sixty-five years, then what is?

* * *

The new Winchester Model 70 Featherweight, chambered in .270 Winchester and wearing a Leupold VX-III 2.5-8x36 scope. As is, it weighs 7 lbs. 14 oz.

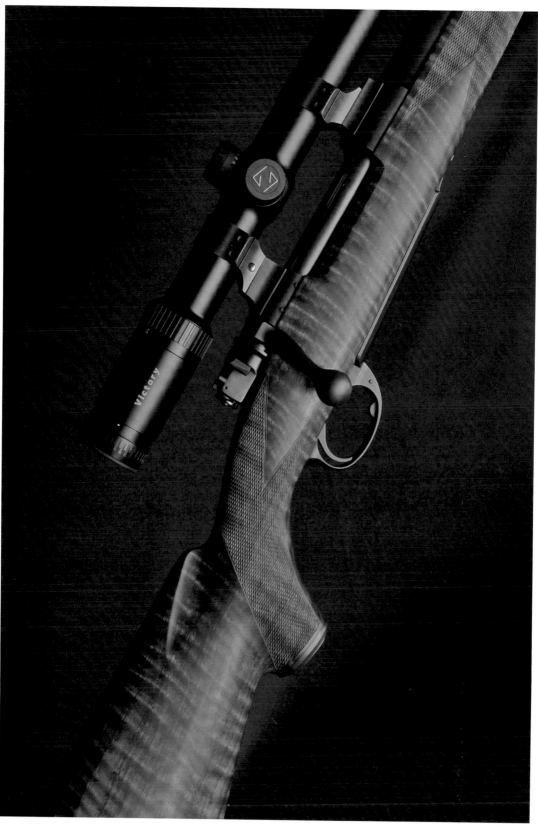

A .375 H&H, built on an FN Supreme action by Texas gunmaker Todd Johnson. The detachable scope mounts are by Joe Smithson.

CHAPTER X

ELUSIVE PERFECTION: THE CUSTOM RIFLE

On the surface, it would seem that the answer to getting your perfect big-game rifle is to find a good custom gunmaker and have one made to your exact specifications, tastes, and idiosyncrasies. This has been the answer for many hunters since as far back as 1850. In fact, at various times, in various countries, custom riflemaking has been the *only* answer.

In his 1952 book *The Big-Game Rifle*, Jack O'Connor began his chapter on having a custom rifle made with the words "Getting a custom rifle made up is beset with many pitfalls which the beginner can avoid if he exercises care and takes advice, but most of us learn the hard way." In the sixty-five years since that was written, this has become ever more true. The pitfalls are even greater today than they were then. And, most of us still learn the hard way—if we learn at all.

The modern era of custom riflemaking in the United States began with the first sporterizing of the Springfield military rifle, shortly after it was adopted in its final form in 1906. The business really took off in the 1920s. That was almost a century ago, and since then there have been entire books devoted to the subject, as well as innumerable magazine articles. The standards of craftsmanship have risen, as have the costs, but if you compare today's prices with those of the 1950s, taking into account the effects of inflation, there is not a vast difference between prices then and prices now.

One great truth stands out today, just as O'Connor wrote in 1952: "Hand labor is expensive, and no one ever became rich making custom rifles." No fine gunmaker is ever fully compensated for his time, effort, and skill—not when compared to a trained man, paid by the hour, in a union shop, with vacations and overtime.

Our subject here is not just custom rifles, but custom big-game rifles, and there is a huge difference between the two. Some custom rifles today are not intended for hunting or, in some cases, even to be shot at a target. It's not unusual to hear numbers like $50,000 as a base price for a bolt-action rifle, or $100,000. At one point, a few years ago, I heard of an American riflemaker who was planning to build the ultimate bolt-action big-game rifle, perfect in every way, a true "best" gun, and the asking price was to be, if memory serves, $180,000. This, you should know, would not have been a rifle built to your specifications, but to his. Not as a hunting rifle for you, but as a demonstration of how he thought a rifle should be built, incorporating his ideas of what constituted a proper stock, carved from an ideal piece of walnut, and his ideas of what sights and trigger a hunting rifle required. You, the lucky purchaser, might have found that the rifle suited you or not. It might have fit you, it might have the right weight and balance, the trigger might feel good. Or, all of the above might not. In fact, *probably* not.

Undoubtedly, the rifle would have sported an indescribable piece of walnut, cut from a five-hundred-year-old tree on a north-facing slope in the potassium-rich soil of the south Caucasus, or some such blather. It would have had an action milled from a grade of steel alloy costing three times the usual, and requiring machining costing five times the usual, and even requiring the making of special engraving tools by the last remaining specialty tool maker in a remote village in the Swiss Alps. The checkering would have been exquisitely cut at thirty-two lines per inch, with the diamonds at the precise angle which, after lengthy analysis, had been found to be the optimum for gripping the rifle while wearing mink-lined gloves. We could go on, becoming ever more fanciful, but you get the idea. And, in the end, the one thing I believe I can say for certain is that it would not have been a very good hunting rifle. If it had turned out to be a good hunting rifle, it would be pure unadulterated luck.

When Jack O'Connor was writing about custom rifles, and igniting every boy's dreams in the 1960s, legendary names in stockmaking were Alvin Linden, Tom Shelhamer, and Adolph Minar. Barrelmakers were Bill Sukalle and John Buhmiller. The metal men were A. O. Niedner and Emil Koshollek. Many of these greats were dead even then, but up-and-comers strove to be mentioned in the same breath. As custom gunmaking evolved through the 1980s, with the establishment of the American Custom Gunmakers Guild (ACGG), and its "peer review" panels to determine who qualified for membership and who did not, the panoramic view of the forest was discarded in favor of microscopic examination of the trees, branch by branch.

Let's face it: Checkering is put on a rifle to help the shooter grip it solidly. Polished walnut is slick, so it's checkered. When you think of it,

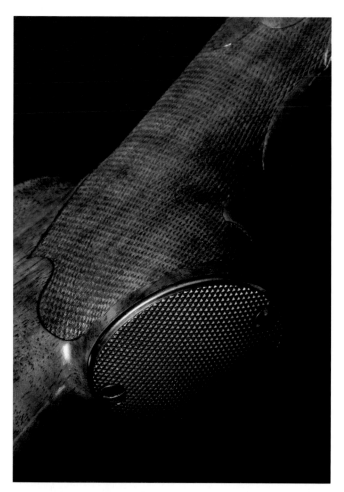

This checkering on a rifle made by Al Biesen is superbly done, as is the knurling on the custom-made steel grip cap. Biesen was an all-around man—equally good at working with wood and metal.

extensive checkering is not required. Just in two spots, really: the grip, and a small part of the forend. For a good grip and durability, you need something between eighteen and twenty-six lines per inch. Anything greater, like thirty-two lines per inch, does not provide much of a grip and gets very smooth, very quickly, with any real use.

Checkering is not an art, it's a craft. Classical music, sculpture, and landscape painting are art forms, and have no useful purpose except to be art. Checkering, on the other hand, is an industrial process applied to a tool in order to make it a more useful tool. The same is true of engraving.

On a rifle, it serves the purpose of breaking up reflective surfaces, of retaining oil to prevent rust, and in some applications to make a slippery surface less so. Although it is not often admitted, engraving can also be employed to cover up mistakes or poor workmanship, which is not exactly noble. All of this could be accomplished just as effectively, and much more easily, with random file cuts or sandblasting. Admittedly, professional engraving approaches an art form more than checkering does, but at its roots it's still an industrial craft. Blueing also serves a purpose, as does stock finishing. Both have protective value, and while there is good blueing and stock finishing as well as bad, they are not art forms in and of themselves.

To clarify, as mentioned earlier, beauty in a rifle does serve a valuable purpose: A rifle that looks good, and looks expensive, is more likely to be well cared for than one that resembles a grimy old car jack. That's why more high-quality rifles have survived through the ages in fine condition than utilitarian ones sold at the corner hardware store. Too much beauty, however, can cause its owner to be more worried about scratching his rifle than he is about creeping up on that big six-pointer. The rifle becomes, through excessive adornment, unsuitable for hunting. One definition of decadence is an object so refined that it cannot be used for its original purpose, which is why many of the so-called custom hunting rifles, turned out at great expense by the Guild-certified *artistes,* are decadent.

This decadence evinces itself in many forms. For example, it has been well known for a century that the best shape for a forend, in cross-section, is either round, slightly pear-shaped, or a slim (!) horizontal oval. Any of these allow the fingers to wrap around and get a solid grip without having to white-knuckle the checkering. On most custom rifles today, however, the forends are vertical ovals with flat sides. Why? Because they are easier to checker, on the one hand, and allow the checkerer a proper "canvas" to really show what he can do. Personally, I don't much care what heights the checkerer is capable of; I do care what the rifle can do, and how well I can use it.

Since the vast majority of so-called custom stocks today are turned out to standard patterns on pantograph machines, the vertical oval has become the most common forend shape. Trying to get anything different is like pulling teeth.

Two superb custom rifles that were built for hunting. Top is a new (2009) .505 Gibbs. The magnum Mauser action was made by Fred Wells. Bottom is a John Rigby & Co. rising-bite double, in .450/.400 (3 1/4"). Every feature on this double rifle—including the engraving—serves the purpose of making it a perfect hunting rifle.

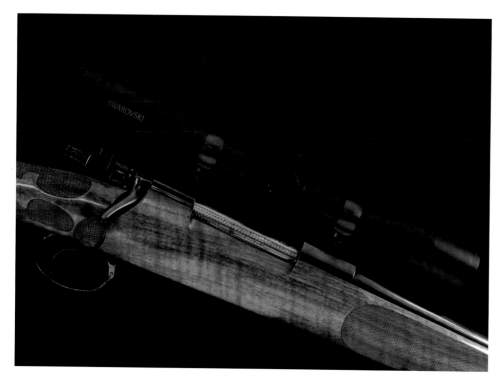

A beautifully crafted hunting rifle by Al Biesen, exhibiting most of the fine touches found on a top-notch custom rifle. Biesen refashioned an FN Mauser Deluxe action, reshaped the bolt, made a new shroud with a three-position wing safety, jeweled the bolt, knurled the bolt handle, and fitted the floorplate with an Oberndorf-style release. He carved the stock from a blank and applied his own style of inletted fleur-de-lis *checkering.*

Since the average "stockmaker" starts with one of these pre-shaped stocks, and has no real idea how to carve a stock from a blank, you are presenting him with a major problem.

This leads into the second trend which has been evident in custom gunmaking for several decades, and that is increasing specialization. These days, some stockmakers don't checker; a checkering specialist does no inletting; a metal man won't touch wood; the engraver leads his own life, off in the woods somewhere; somebody else is brought in to put custom scope mounts on the rifle. In the end, the rifle is the product of a committee, and like most committee products, it turns out to be a camel when you hoped you were buying a racehorse.

There have always been specialists, of course. Alvin Linden did very little metal work, but he collaborated with his neighbor, Emil Koshollek, who was a superb metal man, and the two worked so closely for so long they might as well

have been one person. Al Biesen, the "genius of Spokane" who became Jack O'Connor's favorite gunmaker, was an all-around man. He was equally good on wood or metal, excellent at stock shaping, inletting, and checkering, but could also overhaul an action and even make a completely new bolt shroud with a three-position safety. Over and above all of that, however, Al Biesen was a hunter and shooter who knew what a good hunting rifle should feel like. Since he was the man making the entire rifle, he knew where he could shave extra ounces, or where they should be left on in order to make the balance right. Feeling the rifle develop in his hands as he completed it, it could be made absolutely perfect.

Some custom-rifle buyers feel they can deliver minute specifications in order to get exactly what they want: "Well, I want a maximum weight of 7.25 pounds with the scope, so the stock cannot be more than such and such a weight, and the barreled action can't weigh more than whatever, which leaves 1.4 pounds for the scope and mounts." The craftsmen in question may in fact deliver exactly what you ordered, but if it balances properly, it will be wholly by chance.

As a magazine shooting editor, I have received letters, usually from teenagers, outlining the rifle they intend to order someday. They are always very specific. The barrel will be 23.25 inches long, with a rifling twist of one in 9.75 inches; there will be .425 inches of freebore, and so on. One of the lessons I have learned in having a custom rifle made is that if you are too exact, and shackle your gunmaker to a list of specifications, chances are you will get exactly what you asked for, but it will not be what you wanted.

One of the most common alterations to a Mauser 98 is the addition of a replacement bolt shroud with a Model 70-style three-position wing safety. Several fine metalsmiths specialized in producing such shrouds for sale to the trade. This is a Granite Mountain action.

* * *

When Jack O'Connor was writing about custom gunmaking in the 1950s, there were relatively few really fine riflemakers around. There were two or three barrelmakers, for example; today there are at least a dozen, maybe more. It's hard to keep count, and even harder to remember who is on top today and who is yesterday's man. When O'Connor was writing, there were four main actions to choose from in building a custom rifle: the Mauser 98, Springfield 1903A3, Enfield P-17, and the Winchester Model 70. Today, with CNC machinery, there are many more actions, but none that I have seen are any better than three of those four. (I am not a fan of the Springfield, and it has all but disappeared anyway.)

New actions to come along include the Weatherby Mark V, and that company builds custom rifles in its own shop. Various small companies tried to design specialty actions that would improve on what was available, usually by going to three locking lugs and a low bolt lift, or making them magnum-sized to accom-modate huge cartridges. A few names spring to mind, such as Wichita and Champlin. None of them went anywhere, and custom rifles built on them are now little more than curiosities. They certainly don't command high prices in the used-gun market.

The all-time classic is the Mauser 98, and this includes a plethora of variations: Military K98s made in Germany, Austria, Czechoslovakia, Belgium, and Poland; commercial actions made at Oberndorf (Germany), FN (Belgium), Santa Barbara (Spain), and Zastava (Yugoslavia, now Serbia); and American versions like the Granite Mountain and its commercial German equivalent, Prechtl. At this writing, the Mauser company itself has reentered the lists, with both a magnum and standard Model 98 action, modern in every way but authentically Mauser. These actions come in so many shapes, sizes, and levels of quality that entire books could be written on this subject alone. In a way, however, condition hardly matters if the action was well-made in the first place, as the majority were. In the hands of a good custom gunsmith, even a rough military

The author in Botswana with a red lechwe. The rifle is a Dakota Arms .30-06, built on the Dakota 76 action. American classic stocks do not come much more classic than this.

98 can be turned into a masterpiece if the quality is basically good.

The only action that really competes with the Mauser 98 is the pre-'64 Model 70, but these have now become scarce, and pristine specimens are high-priced collectors' items in their own right. In the 1970s, as the cheap pre-'64 market dried up, a couple of custom gunmakers got together and designed an updated version of the pre-'64 called the Dakota 76. It was the brainchild of Don Allen, Pete Grisel, and Ken Howell, and Allen founded Dakota Arms to build entire custom rifles on it. As well, for many years, the action alone was sold, in the white, by Brownells. It was expensive even then, running around $1,500 when you could buy a Zastava Mark X Mauser (admittedly of inconsistent quality) for a quarter of that price. Around that time, you could still buy a pre-'64 for less than $500; military Mausers

(depending on the vintage and sub-model) were even cheaper.

Don Allen's Dakota rifles were beautifully made. He was one of the masters of the "American classic" stock style, which eschewed Monte Carlo combs and extravagant features. American classic was the style developed by Alvin Linden and Griffin & Howe, and which became *de rigueur* on custom rifles in the 1990s. In many ways, however, Dakota Arms found itself facing the same problems that sank earlier companies like Niedner and Hoffman. This is exactly the problem Jack O'Connor laid out: Skilled hand labor is expensive, and no custom riflemaker is ever truly compensated for the work he puts in. Customers want the best, but insist that "the best" is overpriced. This is bad enough to deal with when you are working on your own, and you just hope your wife keeps her good job with its steady income and health benefits. For the owner-manager of a company, with a payroll to meet, it is something else again.

In California, Weatherby has encountered some of the same problems. The much older Pachmayr company survived by gradually moving out of custom guns into manufacturing scope mounts, recoil pads, and other accoutrements that riflemakers need. These can be mass produced and sold at a profit, with the Pachmayr name lending them cachet.

There are fads and fashions in rifles, and several small companies arose to fill the demand for specific types of rifles. A couple spring to mind.

As accuracy became more and more of a critical issue with custom rifles, Kenny Jarrett of South Carolina, a top-notch benchrest competitor, began building his "beanfield" rifles, intended for shooting whitetails across the soybean fields of the south out to four or five hundred yards. Initially, they were built on modified Remington 700 actions, which were noted for being inherently accurate, with Jarrett making his own barrels. For years, a Jarrett rifle was the last word in accuracy.

Another trend of the '90s was toward ever-lighter rifles, eventually reaching the ridiculous. Still, there is a lot to be said for a light rifle for the mountains, or for hunting whitetails in the woods, and Melvin Forbes set up his Ultra Light Arms company in West Virginia to make "ultra-light" rifles. Forbes modified the basic Remington 700 action to shave weight, along with developing his own line of composite stocks designed for light weight combined with strength. He eventually sold the company to Colt, then went back into business for himself several years later, producing essentially the same rifles.

Eventually, it seemed as if every barrel company wanted to be a rifle company, as did every maker of actions. Many of the allegedly accurate rifles that were offered in competition with Jarrett's proven product were based on Remington 700s. I say allegedly because claims are easy to make but hard to prove. For some reason, they are much easier to disprove. Funny thing, that. Having shot a good number of these rifles over the years, I find my dominant memory is that the vast majority were surprisingly unmemorable.

Kenny Jarrett originated the guarantee of rifles that would shoot half-inch groups, and his rifles lived up to that. The condition was that Jarrett would do the load development for whatever cartridge you chose. When he arrived at the half-inch goal, he would provide you with loaded ammunition. The guarantee applied only to his rifle, his load, his ammunition—which is fair enough. By the late '90s, Remington 700 actions were becoming rather ramshackle, so Kenny invested in a massive CNC machine, designed his own action, and began making them himself. He also branched out from beanfield rifles to dangerous-game rifles, stalking rifles, and rifles with wooden stocks rather than his usual composites.

Dakota, Jarrett, and Ultra Light typify the more expensive specialty rifles that came onto the market through the 1980s and '90s, taking the place of the traditional custom rifle as those became more and more expensive—and also as they moved away from being hunting rifles, toward being merely show pieces. All three of these companies produced some fine rifles for their intended purposes. But all, I found, also had some shortcomings. In the case of the Jarrett and Ultra Light rifles, I have never been an admirer of composite (i.e., fiberglass, kevlar, carbon fiber, and so on) and am becoming less so as I get older. This is not merely a matter of taste or aesthetics. Composite stocks are certainly stable, and not prone to absorbing water, or drying out and

This walnut stock was cut on a duplicating machine, using a pattern drawn from a hand-carved stock made by Siegfried Trillus. It was then inletted, checkered, and finished by Todd Johnson.

warping. They are also strong, and don't crack or break. Right there, however, you have exhausted their virtues. They were right for Kenny Jarrett, in seeking maximum accuracy, and also for Melvin Forbes, in reducing weight to the absolute minimum. But this is the reason you will find neither a Jarrett nor an Ultra Light in this book. They simply don't *feel* right.

Also—and this is my major complaint about composite stocks—no one has managed to produce one that has exactly the right dimensions in every respect, from length of pull to grip circumference to the cross-sectional shape of the forend. Those that don't look and feel like they came from a discount toy shop are usually oversized, clubby, and unergonomic to an astonishing degree.

The overwhelming virtue of walnut is that it can be shaped to exactly what you want in every respect, which means it can be made to fit like a tailored suit. Composite stocks, conversely, are made in moulds, and what comes out of the mould is all you are going to get. Because most are hollow inside or honeycombed, they can't be

shortened, lengthened, bent, shaved, or trimmed to fit. And for reasons that completely escape me, no maker of composite stocks has seen fit to find a really good rifle stock to use as a pattern, even in order to arrive at a one-size-almost-fits-all standard.

A decade or so ago I got two H-S Precision rifles to test, and even took one to Africa. They were okay—I wouldn't give them any more than that—but my particular complaint was their stocks, which were composites. The forends were too big around, as were the pistol grips. Fine for shooting off a bench, maybe, if that's your taste, but barely adequate for hunting.

The stock of a good hunting rifle should never get in the way of the shooter, and stocks can intrude in several ways: by positioning your trigger hand in the wrong place, by forcing you to stretch your finger to reach the trigger, by preventing you getting a firm grip on an oversized forend, or forcing you to raise your head to see the sights. When a stock really fits you, you pick up the rifle, everything is immediately in place, and you are hardly aware the stock is even there.

* * *

In the 1960s, during the heyday of custom rifle-making, when every corner gunsmith fancied himself a riflemaker, and surplus Mauser 98 actions were dirt-cheap and readily available, an astonishing number of custom rifles were produced. As Jack O'Connor noted, the term "custom rifle" covers a mulititude of sins and, were the truth known, probably 95 percent of those rifles ranged from merely mediocre to absolutely dreadful.

Some were aesthetically so bad they defy description, and you wonder if they were cobbled together by a troll under a bridge. Others functioned, but only barely, and if you hit something you were aiming at, it was purely by accident. However, what concerns us here is not the sad majority but the remaining—and surprisingly good—five percent. Not every corner gunsmith was a cretin or a "bodger," to use the English term. Many were, in fact, knowledgeable riflemen and hunters, and knew what a good hunting rifle should feel like. As well, they did not need to be stockmakers because, in those halcyon days, there existed two companies that could supply very nice semi-finished wooden stocks to fit just about any rifle you could name. These were E. C. Bishop & Sons, and Reinhart Fajen, both of Warsaw, Missouri, in the heart of the Ozarks and the largest concentration of black walnut trees in America.

Reinhart Fajen, in particular, supplied a wide range of styles, from American classic, to Weatherby-style California, to wilder-than-wild thumbhole stocks. These were semi-finished, not drop-in, and required final inletting, checkering, and finishing. But if you wanted a nice,

This is Ted Blackburn's replacement bottom metal for the Mauser 98. Blackburn was an excellent metalsmith who produced components for custom gunmakers. His bottom metal included a floorplate with an Oberndorf-style release inside a graceful trigger bow. Blackburn Custom Gun Metal is now a division of Swift Bullet Company.

usable stock in a design that wouldn't frighten the horses, they were available.

Another source of semi-finished stocks was Herter's, of Waseca, Minnesota, and the Herter's catalogue provided me with many long hours on many cold winter evenings, admiring the color photos of stocks and exotic woods. I don't know anyone who ever actually bought a Herter's stock, or had one installed on a rifle, but I do know a few who had Bishop and Fajen stocks. Fajen also provided a custom service, using either its own semi-finished stocks or, so I understand, starting from a blank of your choosing. It's safe to say that the custom-rifle industry of the 1960s and later could not have existed without Fajen and Bishop. After years of studying Fajen catalogues, I think I could pick out a Fajen stock on a gun rack at thirty paces, and if I was forced to voice an opinion, I would say they were surprisingly good even by modern custom-rifle standards. The men who worked for Reinhart Fajen seemed to understand what a good hunting rifle stock should be (as well as target stocks, which they also offered) and this benefited several generations of hunters and buyers of economy custom rifles.

Out of all this emerged the occasional rifle you stumble across at a gun show, or on the rack at an out-of-the-way gunshop, or in someone's garage. It's like finding a champion show jumper pulling a milk wagon. Every so often, that unknown, unsung corner gunsmith would put together a rifle that was just right. I mean, *just right*. It doesn't happen often, and you need luck to find one, but pick up such a rifle, put it to your shoulder, and you will immediately know—sort of like that setter puppy that leapt into your arms and demanded, with a great deal of face-licking, to be taken home. You may end up kissing an awful lot of frogs before you find a princess, but they are out there.

There have been several trends over the past twenty to thirty years which have had dramatic effects on the custom-rifle business, over and above the influence of the American Custom Gunmakers Guild and the ascendance of the *artistes*. One was the Gulf War of 1991. It marked a turning point in the attitude of Americans to the military and, by extension, military weapons. After Viet Nam, the military was not widely respected. Those who were interested in military rifles were viewed with some suspicion, if not downright hostility. After the Gulf War, the US Army was once again an institution to be respected, and this only increased after September 11, 2001, the invasions of Afghanistan and Iraq, and the other conflicts in the Middle East. Out of this came two particular trends: one was a fascination with rifles like the AR series and other military semiautos; the other was the cult of the sniper.

Snipers are now admired like Hollywood celebrities. Movies are made about them. Overweight wannabes dress like them. Guys

The forend of a stock hand-carved from American black walnut by gunmaker Siegfried Trillus. Trillus cut the tree down himself, sawed it into blanks, and seasoned it before making the blanks into rifle stocks. Trillus's forends tapered into a horizontal oval that was slim and comfortable to grip. It is one of the best shapes for the forend of a hunting rifle. This one is a .450 Ackley built on an FN Supreme action.

who have never hit a target farther than fifty yards are buying sniper rifles and taking shooting courses, dreaming of decking an elk at 1,200 yards. Such long-range shooting at any legitimate game animal is unethical, and cannot be made so by any amount of expensive equipment. It violates the fundamental rule of fair chase, which is to get as close as possible, in order to place your first shot where it needs to go in order to effect a clean, quick kill with no unnecessary suffering. As long as the wind blows and the sun causes heat mirage, this is simply not possible at long range. The answer is not to buy a bigger rifle or more powerful scope, it's to creep closer. Stalking is most of the fun of hunting anyway, unless you are someone who simply likes to kill things.

Another trend which has affected both riflemakers and rifle buyers has been the influence of benchrest shooting and the worship of pin-point accuracy at all costs—sacrificing weight and handling characteristics in favor of shaving an eighth of an inch off a three-shot group. Benchrest shooting as we now know it really took off in the late 1940s (although it originated much earlier) and it became the big non-traditional shooting game of the next thirty years. Theirs is a search for pure accuracy, and nothing else matters. Rifles used in benchrest are absolutely useless for anything else, but that doesn't matter, because they are not required for anything else. The one-hole group became the Holy Grail for several generations of shooters. As one who admires accuracy in any rifle, I would be among the last to denigrate benchrest or belittle the contribution that benchrest shooters have made to the game, including improvements in factory hunting rifles. One can, however, go too far.

Benchrest shooters learned a lot about proper bedding of rifles, and that benefited everyone. They discovered things heretofore unsuspected about bullet construction and methods of manufacture, and that was also good. Makers of both bullets and primers strove to improve, and these improvements trickled down to us peasants out hunting deer. Two benchrest discoveries did not help, however. First, benchrest shooters discovered that big, heavy, awkward stocks made of fiberglass gave them a firmer foundation, along with such refinements as pillar bedding, and soon hunting rifles were being made with stocks with wide, flat forends, fat buttstocks, and beefy, steeply radiused pistol grips. These were more stable when shooting off sandbags, but were a serious hindrance in the field. The second discovery was the improved ignition qualities to be found in short, fat cartridges like the 6 PPC, with near parallel walls and steep shoulders. After the 6 PPC dislodged the .222 Remington as king of the benchrest game, it was only a matter of time until there emerged a family of hunting cartridges with the same shape and general characteristics. Rick Jamison, then of *Shooting Times*, originated the line that later became the seemingly unending parade of Winchester Short Magnums (WSM). The original short magnums were belted cases such as the .308 Norma, .338 Winchester, and 7mm Remington, in the early '60s, but no matter. The new ones became *the* short magnums, and the claims that were made for them were many—some barely credible and others ballistically impossible.

The one thing that can be said for them, without fear of contradiction, is that they do not feed easily from a conventional staggered magazine. Logically enough, the longer a cartridge, and the more pronounced its taper, the more easily it will feed, and the great .375 H&H is a classic example. Short, fat, and parallel, however, is a recipe for noisy, difficult feeding. Sales of most of the short magnums either started slow and tapered off, or never went anywhere at all, and the majority have fallen by the wayside with few manufacturers chambering them, and even fewer making ammunition or brass.

The combination of benchrest stocks and pseudo-benchrest cartridges, along with general adulation accorded to sub-minute of angle (MOA) accuracy, led to a broad trend toward heavier, more awkward, less ergonomic rifles. At the same time, German and central European optics makers, catering to the desire for sniper-type riflescopes, gradually persuaded American hunters that if a scope did not have a 30mm tube it was virtually useless. Since 2005, big European scopes with 30mm tubes and high magnification ratios have dominated the high-end scope market, and that includes custom big-game rifles.

* * *

Much as it pains me to write this, I believe the great age of the custom hunting rifle is over. Neither the demand nor the supply is what it once was. On the demand side, there is increasing focus on semiauto rifles of the AR class, and military-style sniper or long-range rifles. More and more deer hunters hunt from stands, and do as little walking as possible. In other kinds of big-game hunting, there is more driving in vehicles than there is walking or climbing, and very little hunting is now done on horseback.

Whether some young people will grow into an appreciation of traditional hunting rifles is another question, and one that no one can answer. Even if they do, there will never be the mass interest that existed with the post-war generation of hunters in the 1960s. The basic materiel required to build a mid-quality rifle (functionally good, but modest in appearance) is no longer there. Fajen and Bishop are long-since out of business, the supply of good military Mauser 98s has dried

up, and while there are more barrel makers than ever, you need an action on which to put a barrel.

Finally, while there are a number of top-notch riflemakers in the mould of the old custom guys, they are so expensive as to preclude any but the wealthy. The last time I looked, you could still get a rifle from the David Miller Co. in Tucson for $50,000, but how many of us can do that? Not many. There used to be a large number of gunsmiths around the country who could do basic gunsmithing, but who were also quite good at putting together a decent custom rifle for a reasonable price. Many had emigrated from Germany or England after the war, and from other parts of Europe in the 1950s. These men are dead and gone. While a few Americans learned from them, and carry on the trade, they are few in number compared to the old days. Graduates from gunsmithing schools today favor careers either making sniper rifles or accurizing and customizing Colt 1911s and AR-15s. And the skills

This Al Biesen .270, built on an FN Deluxe action, was made for a client sometime in the 1980s. The author bought it in 2016 for considerably less than its original price. Such rifles are out there, and they are worth searching for.

they acquire at most gunsmithing schools are not the skills of a real gunmaker anyway.

Suppliers of gunsmithing tools and raw materials, like Brownells, publish massive catalogues every year, but more and more these are directed at drop-in and bolt-on parts for 1911s, ARs, Ruger .22s, and Mini-14s. Anyone who knows a good riflemaker who can fashion a great stock from a walnut blank, or barrel an action and fit it with a claw mount, keeps it a secret because they don't want them overworked, with lengthening delivery times.

There is, however, a major silver lining to this cloud, and that is that if the gunmakers are fading away, so are their old clientele. As the owners of custom rifles die off, their heirs are putting their collections on the market. And, since many young shooters have little interest in bolt-action rifles, some custom Mausers (even made by big names of the past) sell for a fraction of what they cost originally, never mind what it would cost you to duplicate the rifle today, starting from scratch.

If the golden age of custom-riflemaking is past, the golden age of used-custom-rifle buying is upon us.

Dakota Model 10 single-shot rifle, custom stocked by James Flynn.

CHAPTER XI

WALNUT: THE WOOD OF KINGS

For centuries, gunmakers and shooters alike recognized that the finest material on earth for fashioning a gunstock was wood from the walnut tree. Originally, it came from Europe, and is known today as English, French, or Circassian walnut; two world wars and countless lesser conflicts reduced the supply of walnut in Europe, where it was needed for military rifles, but the same tree is found farther afield in the Caucasus, which is the origin of Circassian or Turkish walnut, and even as far east as Kashmir and the Himalayas.

Thin-shelled walnuts were transplanted in North America, which already had the tree known as American black walnut. California English is known as "claro" walnut. Eventually, the two species were crossed to produce bastogne walnut, which has some of the characteristics of both.

The most common designation for thin-shelled walnut is English; other names, like French, Spanish, or Circassian, usually refer to its country of origin. So from here on out, we will simply refer to it all as English walnut. What are its virtues? Aside from its sometimes breathtaking beauty, English walnut is light for its strength—or strong for its weight, whichever you prefer. It's a stable wood that resists warping, especially if a stock is cut correctly with proper grain structure. It is tough and resists breaking. At its best, it cuts "like cheese," with no splintering, which makes it easier than other woods for both inletting and checkering. If necessary, a stock can be bent, using steam and pressure, and take and hold its new shape with no tendency to rebound or return to its original form. This is of more value in shotguns than rifle stocks, but it's a useful trait nonetheless.

American black walnut, which is the traditional wood seen on old Winchester, Savage, and Marlin lever actions, is not quite as dense, will not take checkering as fine, and rarely has anything approaching the beauty of a really top-notch blank of English walnut. Beauty in a blank is really of secondary interest here, but it's a significant factor in both custom and factory riflemaking. As the really great blanks increase in price, the lesser blanks below get pulled along in their slipstream. Eventually, their cost becomes a factor that rifle company accountants have to deal with. Often, this means turning to either another type of wood entirely or, most recently, to the use of synthetic and composite stocks.

In spite of the tidal wave of synthetics over the past twenty years, during which they have progressed from being a curiosity to a standard factory product, English walnut is still the best material available for making a stock for any big-game hunting rifle.

Aside from the virtues listed above, why do I say that? Why is a cheap walnut stock with little or no color or attractive grain still a better choice for a serious hunting rifle than any synthetic stock ever made? That can best be answered with

American black walnut at its best, on a Savage Model 1899.

that certainly look cutting-edge, especially combined with their thumbhole design. We were, of course, hunting from stands, and it was December, with a dusting of snow, occasional rain, and constant chill. In driven hunting, it behooves one to always have the rifle in his hands, ready for a quick and sudden shot at a disappearing target. That rifle was impossible to hold for long, even wearing gloves. The carbon fiber worked like a heat sink, sucking the warmth out of your hands, and no matter how long you held it, it never got warm. I took to gripping it with one hand for a few minutes, then switching while the other warmed up.

Synthetic stocks become very cold in the cold, and very hot in the heat. A black synthetic stock under the Botswana sun can become almost too hot to touch, much less shoot. Wood of any kind never gets that cold or that hot, and quickly adjusts to your hand temperature. That's one point. Another is noise. Wood stocks, moving through brush, rubbing up against leaves and twigs, are almost silent, and what little noise they do make sounds natural. Synthetics will give off a twangy or scratching sound that animals find alarming. Bump a tree with a synthetic stock and it sounds like a tin drum. This noise is also noticeable when you work the bolt quickly, and hear an echoing "*thwang*" as the stock reverberates. It sounds hollow because it usually is hollow.

Synthetic stocks come out of a mould, and what you get is all you will ever have, period. They cannot be altered in any significant way. They can't be bent, or shaved down to custom dimensions. You cannot prescribe less checkering, or more, or get a different pattern.

In theory, because they are made in a mould, and a mould is made from a pattern, there is no reason a company could not obtain a really fine

an example. In 2016, I was hunting in Germany, and we were all using the new Sauer 404 rifle. These were fitted with sexy carbon fiber stocks

There is no reason a company could not obtain a really fine hunting stock, like this one made by Al Biesen, and copy it in a mould. That way, a synthetic stock might at least approximate one that feels and handles well. Alas, no one ever has.

hunting stock, such as those made by Al Biesen or Alvin Linden, and simply copy it. But no one ever has. Virtually every synthetic stock I have ever handled has not felt right. Some were too bulky, others the wrong shape. One exception is the synthetic stocks on the Ruger 77/44 and 77/357 series (see chapter XVIII.) Other than those, the closest I've seen to a stock I would like to hunt with is the factory-issue stock on the Ruger Hawkeye FTW Hunter, a rifle that came out in early 2016. Even that stock, however, doesn't feel exactly right. Moulded-in checkering is not checkering at all, in the sense of providing a better and more secure grip. It's just a slippery rough spot, nothing more, and usually looks like it belongs on a toy gun.

Some makers of synthetic stocks have tried alternate approaches, substituting a kind of stippling. Others have splattered the slick surface with droplets of goo that dry into a rough surface, like molten chocolate dribbled onto a plate. Usually, this is more aesthetics than utility, and like everything else, we have gone through fads of colors, designs, camouflage, spattering like modern art, and even an after-coat applied to the stock to make the whole thing rough. This does no favors to the shooter when the cheekpiece on a hard-kicking rifle is like coarse sandpaper. If anything will induce a flinch, that will. You

would think the riflemaker might realize the problem, but apparently not.

If I had to pinpoint my major complaint about synthetic stocks, it would be the fact that they are completely lifeless—machine-made, with no semblance of individuality or character. You cannot imagine the hands of a skilled craftsman cutting the checkering or inletting a skeleton buttplate. There is nothing about them to admire. They don't get better with age, like fine walnut. You cannot steam out any scratches and restore them to their original lustre. As with any plastic item, they are mass-produced and disposable, to be tossed aside and replaced by something newer, when something newer comes along.

This complaint is largely a matter of taste, but the other virtues of walnut are very real. For anyone serious about getting the perfect hunting rifle for himself, and having it fit him exactly the way it should, and the way he wants it to, there is little alternative to wood of some kind. Any synthetic stock will always be a compromise, with no way of correcting its inevitable imperfections.

Related to this is the question of getting a new stock for a rare or obscure rifle. By their nature, synthetic stocks are mass-production items. To be economical, they need to be produced in great numbers of identical stocks, which means they need a large market to justify production and

make it profitable. This is why you see synthetic stocks available for the most common rifles, such as Remington 700s and Winchester Model 70s, but not for Schultz & Larsens or Sako FinnBears. Stocks break, they get damaged, or a new owner needs or wants a stock of different dimensions. Without wooden stock blanks and craftsmen with the skill to make a new stock, they are out of luck.

* * *

Walnut is not the only wood used for gunstocks. Through the centuries, almost everything has been tried and some have been found to work quite well. Beech is the usual alternative when walnut is scarce or expensive, and birch has also been used, notably in northern Europe, on military and low-priced civilian rifles. How closely they resemble walnut in their working qualities, I do not know. Beech or birch stocks are white or yellow, devoid of figure, so they are usually stained a dark brown or "walnut" color. About the best one can say of beech or birch is that they are not synthetic. The ones I have seen have usually been bulkier than a walnut stock would be, but whether that is deliberately to enhance strength, or just the lack of refinement found in mass production, is impossible to say.

The traditional wood for American Pennsylvania or Kentucky long rifles was maple, either bird's-eye or fiddleback. Maple is heavier than walnut and more difficult to work, but it is undoubtedly strong, and has been used as a wood for custom riflestocks for a century. In theory, it should be good for hard-kicking rifles, or dangerous-game rifles where a little more weight is not a bad thing.

For a while, the Weatherby rifles from California were stocked with screwbean mesquite as an alternative to their usual claro walnut, and

A skilled stockmaker can fashion a piece of walnut with any shape of forend or cheekpiece you might desire, creating a rifle that fits you, and your preferences, exactly.

A Schultz & Larsen Model 65 DL. Early S&L rifles had stocks similar in style to the Weatherby, in walnut that ranged from plain to quite nice. Having such a rifle restocked today would be very difficult and very expensive.

in its wilder forms it went quite well with the over-the-top California styling that Weatherby made popular. Mesquite has its own problems and idiosyncrasies, but functionally it worked quite well. Weatherby rifles are not pussycats when it comes to recoil. Mesquite's blonde-and-black, zig-zag grain complemented the angular California style of Weatherby stocks. I found them intriguing as a teenager, grew to admire them for shooting as an adult (I had a .300 Weatherby, one of the last made in Germany, with a rather wild piece of claro), and still find the Weatherby style quite attractive. Part of that attraction is knowing that, in spite of appearances, the older, slimmer Weatherby stocks worked every bit as well as a good American classic stock.

Another wood that enjoyed its moment in the sun fifty years ago was myrtlewood, from Oregon. Myrtle stocks were displayed in glorious color in the Herter's catalogue, and that probably had something to do with it. Jack O'Connor had one rifle stocked with myrtle and discussed its shortcomings at length. After picking through about two hundred blanks, he found one with good grain and color. Apparently after cutting, myrtle blanks need to be stored underwater for several years before being dried. Even after all that, most have no grain and nothing, really, to recommend them. O'Connor concluded that English walnut is better in every way, so why bother with myrtlewood?

At various times, there have been fads for using different types of wood. In the 1980s, I recall reading about a citizen who, presumably to give his life meaning, decided to have a complete room full of Browning BBR rifles custom-stocked. They were all in .300 Winchester Magnum, identical in all respects except they were stocked with every different wood he could find, and according to the article, he had "scoured the world." The gun rack along his wall made an interesting photograph, but the entire concept makes me break out in hives.

For anyone interested in every wood that might possibly be used, Dick Simmons's book *Custom Built Rifles* (1949) covers it as well as I have ever seen. He discusses scores of different stock woods, from Africa, Australia, Central America, Burma, and Indonesia, among others, as well as the more familiar ones. Most of these woods would never be seen today, either because they are rare or considered endangered if not extinct. Still, it makes interesting reading. Having studied the book, the thing that struck me at the end was that, regardless of price, there was not one that could be considered better, in any meaningful way, than a good blank of seasoned English walnut. The best any of them could hope to be was "as good as" walnut.

One reason for the great interest in these different woods during the Cold War was the dearth of walnut from the Soviet areas in the Caucasus Mountains and farther east. For many years,

there was an export ban. With the break-up of the Soviet Union in the early 1990s, these areas became independent and opened up to trade with the West. Since then, it has been increasingly difficult for rapacious wood dealers to claim that such and such a tree was "the last one known to exist," and try to peddle the blanks for outrageous sums. There is no shortage of walnut, including some breathtaking pieces. Instead, what there is today is a shortage of buyers for full-length rifle blanks, to be used for stocking custom rifles.

After the Iron Curtain came down, Bill Dowtin, a stockmaker and walnut dealer from Great Falls, Montana, explored many of these newly opened regions, and began importing

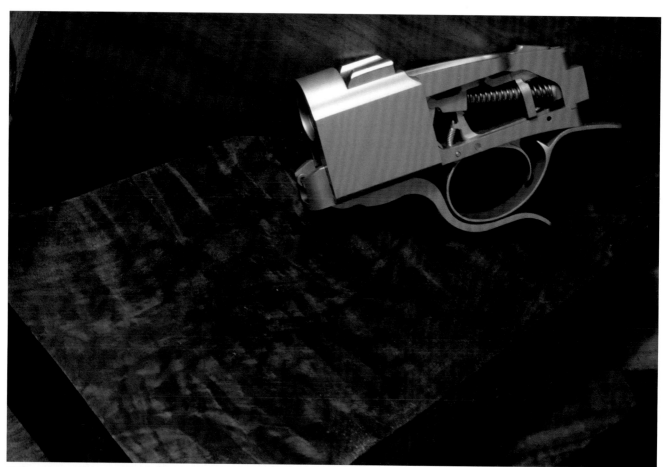

This extraordinary walnut blank came from a tree cut in the foothills of the Himalayas, and was used to stock the Dakota Model 10 single-shot rifle at the beginning of this chapter. The stock was made by James Flynn of Alexandria, Louisiana.

some spectacular walnut. His accounts of being in partnership with the local warlords makes reading worthy of Ian Fleming—a strange mix of blood feuds, mobile phones, and AK-47s worn as a fashion statement. All of that, with a dash of the Taliban thrown in. Eventually, Bill settled on Armenia as the most reliable source for fine walnut. Dowtin is not very popular with other wood dealers or importers because he does not pretend there is a shortage—that we are down to our last few "good" blanks, and people should buy them as investments and squirrel them away. He says there are many, many of those fine, five-hundred-year-old trees, growing on the higher slopes of various mountain ranges. The only problem is getting in, and getting out with some blanks, without getting your throat cut. Added to this is the fact that, to make a good blank, a tree must be cut down properly, sawn into appropriate pieces the correct way, and then seasoned and dried. This takes time, skill, and knowledge—none of which can be added to the local skill set with a three-week night-school course. In some areas, during the Soviet ban, cutting fine walnut for gunstocks was an underground activity, and smuggling them out was a local black-market industry, so such knowledge does exist in some areas.

The term "Circassian" is thrown around pretty freely, as is "Turkish." Turkey was a source of walnut for many years, but according to my best information, the really good trees are long gone. Turkish wood dealers buy their blanks from surrounding countries, like Armenia and Tajikistan, and the phrase "Turkish walnut" is almost a generic designation, like jeep or aspirin. Circassia is an ancient territory that lies along the northeast coast of the Black Sea, but it, too, no longer refers to a specific geographical region. Circassia today is more a state of mind, provided the mind in question belongs to a walnut-loving reprobate. Not unlike myself.

The stock-blank business in many ways resembles the high-end, used-gun business. When serious money begins to change hands, expect to see an influx of loud talkers, with big claims and little real knowledge. The unsuspecting can find themselves holding the bag, along with a much lighter bank account. They may then find that the blank they bought is unsuitable for anything except firewood, or maybe a lamp stand. Or—more likely—it may be perfectly fine, but their gunmaker will try to convince them that it's not. Why? Gather round, children, and hear my tale.

Walnut being a living thing, at least originally, grading stock blanks combines knowledge of proper grain and stockmaking with an appreciation for color, texture, grain pattern, and overall beauty. Over the last twenty years, there has been a general trend toward grade inflation, as dealers run out of superlatives. At one time, there was X, XX, and XXX blanks. Then came XXXX and XXXX-plus. Then "exhibition" grade, whatever that is, and "museum quality," or "investment quality." These terms have little grounding in any real benchmark. How could they? No two stock blanks are exactly alike, including those sold at a premium for matched pairs. Such terms as deluxe, grande deluxe, and super deluxe are equally meaningless.

But back to fraud and deception. Quite often, a gunmaker will select a half-dozen blanks which he keeps on hand to sell to clients who order a rifle. Maybe he pays $200 to $500 apiece, then sells them for $1000 to $2000 each. Such a profit is a nice bit of icing on the gunmaking cake. If, however, a client comes along with a blank under his arm that he has already picked out and paid for, that's a blank on which the gunmaker can't make a profit. What does he do? He looks the blank over, shakes his head ruefully, and says, "Sorry, we can't use this." It's too thin, he says, or the grain pattern is wrong, or it wasn't seasoned correctly. The poor benighted client doesn't know any better, but what can he do? If the gunmaker flatly refuses to use his precious blank, he's out of luck. As this practice has become more common, or at least more commonly known, a buyer will make his offer for a blank conditional on the approval of his stockmaker. Most dealers, knowing the way the world works, will not send out a blank on approval when that condition is attached. Who can blame them? It's probably a waste of time and money.

Another pitfall of riflemaking, from the client's point of view, is that any attempt to keep costs down is often doomed by human nature. Consider this: You are ordering a rifle, and you want it to be your ideal hunting rifle, as we have already discussed. You are not looking for "exhibition" grade walnut. In fact, you just want a nice piece with attractive color but perfect grain structure, and nothing else matters much. Such a blank can be had for $500. But the making of the stock itself is going to cost you at least $5,000 in skilled labor, even though the stockmaker may begin by shipping the blank off to a colleague who owns a pantograph machine, to have it pre-shaped or "turned." Any self-respecting stockmaker wants his work to look as impressive as possible, to enhance his reputation and attract potential clients, so he wants you to start with the most elaborate blank possible. And really, who wants to pay $5,000 to shape a $500 blank? So you move up a grade, or two, or three. It's only money.

* * *

There is an alternative to both walnut and synthetics that dates back three-quarters of a century.

Stocks made from laminated wood were first used by the Germans during the Second World War, as an alternative to solid wood. They had a variety of reasons for this, but the laminated stocks they used on Mauser K98k rifles, usually post-1942, were anything but second rate. In fact, if we went back in history and found some engineer arguing to his production manager that such stocks would be both better and cheaper, he would not be far wrong.

The original German stocks used very thin sheets of wood, almost veneer thickness, glued together under pressure with the grain all running in one direction—unlike plywood, where the grain alternates with one sheet lengthwise, the next cross-wise, and so on. With thin laminates, the finished stock has a very even, but not unnatural-looking, grain pattern, and you need to look closely at the underside of the stock (where the laminate edges lie) to see that it is, in fact, a laminate. This can be made even more difficult by grime and discoloration.

The addition of the glue makes such a stock slightly heavier than one made of a single blank (depending, of course, on its density), but it is considerably stronger and more stable, able to resist both breakage and warping. Possibly, laminated wooden stocks would have become the military standard except that synthetics came along so quickly, replacing wood on many of the post-war military semiautos.

My first encounter with laminated stocks for civilian use was the outlandish Remington Model 600 Magnum carbine that appeared in 1965. This was a variation on the original Model 600, which had a standard stock but was chambered for such mild cartridges as the .222 and .35 Remington. The 600 Magnum was chambered for the new 6.5mm and .350 Remington Magnums. With the .350, recoil was pretty vicious, and a laminated stock was used for strength. Combined with the carbine's full-length ventilated rib, shark-fin front sight, nylon trigger guard, and a bolt handle that angled to the front in two right angles, the Model 600 Magnum was one of the more remarkable rifle creations of a curiously tasteless decade. Maybe Remington felt that with a rifle that was already so far-out, the addition of a laminated stock could not make it any worse.

Unlike the Germans, Remington used thicker layers and alternated walnut (brown) with birch (white). This was cheaper, but gave the stock a distinctly odd appearance that turned an entire generation of riflemen against laminates. That was unfortunate, because for certain purposes there is no better material. On the positive side, a laminated stock is very strong and extremely stable—perfect for a rifle that will spend its life in wet conditions, as in coastal Alaska. It will withstand recoil, so it is also good for a large-caliber dangerous-game rifle. Even on a mountain rifle, which may take a battering from rocks, they work very well.

I have had two rifles with laminated stocks. One was a .338 Winchester Magnum, built on a Mauser Mark X action, and stocked by Fred Wenig, formerly of Reinhart Fajen. It was conceived after spending three weeks in pouring rain, hunting brown bears in Prince William Sound. The other was a .458 Lott, built on a Dakota magnum action. The stock was provided by David Miller, who had been experimenting with laminates looking for a more durable, lower priced alternative for his extraordinary custom rifles. Both rifles did what was expected of them. The .338 was a wet-weather beast, and the .458 Lott went to Africa and killed a Cape buffalo. While I liked both rifles well enough, when someone came along that liked them better than I did, I was not hesitant in taking the money.

What both lacked was that "part of me" feel of a rifle that handled like an extension of my arms. So down the road they went.

The negative side of laminates is their additional weight, and the fact that they are difficult to work using traditional stockmaking tools. The resin dries as hard as a rock, and is just about as easy to carve, while non-matching grain can throw a tool off track. This makes inletting them tricky and difficult, but with a laminated stock it only makes sense to hog them out and glass-bed them anyway. The ideal of a superb inletting job, without the slightest gap, is rarely a goal with a laminated stock.

If a laminated stock gives the rifleman in some ways the best qualities of both wood and synthetics, they give the rifle company the worst qualities of both. They're difficult to work on the one hand, not very attractive on the other, and, from what I understand, give no cost advantage over a standard-quality solid walnut stock. Undoubtedly, laminated stocks are more difficult, time consuming, and expensive to make—both blank and finished stock—so there is likely a cost disadvantage compared to synthetics.

Various rifle companies have offered laminated stocks in the half-century since the Remington 600 Magnum, including Ruger and Winchester, but they have never stayed in the line very long. It seems those who prefer wood want real walnut, and those who don't want walnut prefer synthetics.

* * *

The simple answer to the problem of the high cost of modern custom stockmaking is to go looking for one that is already made. The greatest bargain in a custom rifle is buying a used one. A rule of thumb is that a rifle that cost $10,000 new will bring no more than $5,000 if you try

There is no substitute for the seductive appeal of lovely walnut.

to sell it. There are exceptions, of course. There is a small coterie of collectors and aficionados who try to find rifles stocked by Alvin Linden or Seymour Griffin, or with a genuine Bill Sukalle barrel, and anything that can be proven to be a Linden, Griffin, or Sukalle commands more money. There are other names on that list, too, but we won't go into the custom-rifle collecting market in detail.

One of the major problems with this market, however, is that collectors demand provenance—proof that Linden made that stock, or Bob Owen or Tom Shelhamer. Most such craftsmen never signed their work anywhere. Even riflemakers who put together entire guns did not usually mark them as such. One gunmaker told me he didn't do it because he "wanted his work to speak for itself." Well, that may or may not be a laudable sentiment, but it pretty much sinks the chances of his work becoming seriously collectable. These rifles are, by definition, one of a

kind. It is too easy to copy a style, or a trademark feature, and then claim the rifle was made by someone it wasn't.

One exception to this rule, and a name that does have value in itself, is Al Biesen. Jack O'Connor's favorite riflemaker always put on the barrel: **AL BIESEN GUNMAKER SPOKANE WN**. This feature of certifiability, plus the obvious quality of Biesen's rifles and the name connection with O'Connor, all combine to put a used Al Biesen rifle in an entirely separate category from a run-of-the-mill custom rifle from years past.

Not surprisingly, gun dealers are quick to try to cash in, trying to convince the unwary that a stock is by Linden, Shelhamer, or Biesen, and insisting that any knowledgeable person can tell by the styling or the checkering pattern. Unless there is a name on there somewhere, I tend to disbelieve the blather unless it is something I can recognize for myself. However, and it is a very large however, what really counts with me, with a custom rifle from the old days, is how it feels in my hands. If it's heavy and awkward, and handles like a barge pole, I don't want it no matter who made it. But if it's a gem, who really cares who the gunmaker was?

The way to find the elusive but seductive no-name custom rifle of your dreams is to haunt gun shows, roam the internet, look at listings in gun magazines, and talk with high-end gun dealers like Puglisi's in Duluth, George Caswell at Champlin Arms, or Willoughby McCabe in Dallas. None of these dealers is likely to under-price a fine rifle, but none is going to try to lie to you about who made what. If you come across as sincere and honest, they may even give you a call when a nice rifle comes in that may fit your requirements. Better still, they may know where a rifle is lurking, with an aging owner who might allow it to go to a good home.

Custom .250-3000, built on an "intermediate" Mauser 98 action by an anonymous riflemaker. It has been extensively remodeled, with an Oberndorf-style hinged floorplate, custom bolt shroud with three-position wing safety, and custom bolt handle.

CHAPTER XII

THE MAUSER 98

The Mauser 98 is one of very few serious contenders for the title of "greatest rifle of all time." Not merely the greatest military rifle, or sporting rifle, or bolt-action, but the *greatest*—period. Anyone who disputes this is invited to nominate an alternative. Judged by every logical standard, including widespread use, total number manufactured, longevity, and versatility, as well as the usual yardsticks of strength, dependability, and accuracy, there really is no other rifle that compares. The Mauser 98 is a masterpiece.

The best estimate for the total number of Mauser 98 rifles produced, both military and sporting, in every country where it was made over the course of 120 years, is 14 to 15 million. Some of these rifles were excellent in every way; others were rough and badly finished, with poorly hardened actions. Not every Mauser 98 was created equal, so not every Mauser 98 is a great rifle.

One quality that sets the Mauser 98 apart from any of its rivals is that, assuming it began as a *good* rifle, made from high-quality steel, properly finished and heat treated, it can be transformed into a *great* rifle. This applies to military 98s produced at Oberndorf, in Germany; in Brno, Czechoslovakia; or in Radom, Poland. It applies to commercial 98s, produced in Liège, Belgium, in Santa Barbara, Spain, or at Zastava, in Yugoslavia (now Serbia). Like thoroughbred horses, lineage and ancestry count with Mauser

98s, and where a rifle began life often dictates how it will be valued, regardless of whether it is intrinsically good. A commercial action from Oberndorf commands big money, while an equally fine action from FN is priced lower. Yet some FN actions have been built into custom rifles that are absolute masterpieces of gunmaking, while some Oberndorf actions have been condemned to mediocrity.

However—and this is a very important "however"—any Mauser 98 action that has not been hopelessly mutilated can be rescued from mediocrity and given new life in the hands of a real gunmaker. After fifty-plus years of trying to analyze exactly what it is about the Mauser 98 that sets it apart from actions like the Springfield, Enfield P-17, or even the pre-64 Winchester Model 70, I have concluded that the Mauser's magical quality is the fact that its design is mechanically perfect. Over the twenty years of design evolution that led to the Model 98, Paul Mauser refined it in every detail—and simplified it in many ways—to the point where, even if a feature is later found wanting by a technological development not even imagined in 1898, it can be modified to accommodate it, and do so with the maximum degree of engineering elegance.

Engineering schools probably have a term for this. I would call it "economy of design." A minimum number of parts perform the maximum number of functions, and it all goes together with an essential "rightness" that either prompts the comment "Well, of course it should be like that. It's so obvious," or, more likely, "Why didn't I think of that?" The great English shotgun writer, G. T. (Gough Thomas) Garwood, who was a professional engineer as well as a shooter, coined a term for a certain quality in a firearm: *eumatic*. This word appears in no dictionary, nor has it gained the currency of ergonomics, although the two are certainly related. Garwood defined "eumatic" as follows:

(It) expresses that quality in a manually operated device whereby it is totally correlated to the human being that has to use it. This means that parts requiring to be handled shall be fully conformable to the hands or fingers, as the case may be, and shall be placed so that they are accessible, and can be worked without assuming any forced or unnatural postures. Further, that the direction and range of motion, and the resistance to be overcome, shall be such as to employ to best advantage those muscles which the operating posture brings most naturally into readiness and play. Lastly, that the quality of the motion shall be in conformity with the operator's expectations, free from all harshness and from any sudden changes in resistance or direction.

Garwood abbreviated his term into "eu" and "non-eu," a clever play on the "U" and "non-U" debate in the '50s over the vocabularies of the upper and middle classes in England. As an example of a non-eu device, he offered one where "a strong initial resistance suddenly collapses, so that the motion continues headlong, until brought up with a jerk."

I can give a specific instance of such a non-eu mechanism: Joe Smithson's quick-detachable scope mount, as used on some of the very finest custom bolt actions of recent memory. The last I looked, a Smithson mount cost about $2,000 and involved a one- to two-year waiting period for

Smithson himself to modify an action and install it. I had one on a .375 H&H custom rifle, and it was one of the reasons I parted with it. It was such a close fit (a "sucking" fit, gunmakers call it) that one had to overcome the resistance of the suction, which suddenly lets go, and your hand and scope career to the rear, probably scraping your knuckles on the safety lever.

Compare that with the classic, old, and still the best-ever detachable mount, the German claw. Everything about it is eumatic, from the motion to release it, to detaching the scope, to reinstalling the scope and snapping it into place. We shall look at the claw mount in greater detail in a later chapter. The Smithson mount is extraordinarily precise, elegant to look at, and beautifully made, and the friend who bought my rifle quite likes it. I, however, did not. And by G. T. Garwood's definition, it is definitely non-eu.

We can use "eu" and "non-eu" to grade the various features of the Mauser 98 as originally designed, or as modified to suit later use. We can also use it as a yardstick for the so-called improvements to the 98 that resulted in the Springfield, Enfield P-17, or Winchester Model 70. In every case that I can think of, the "improvements" were nothing of the sort. Where the 98 was non-eu in its original form, it could easily be made eumatic by a modification.

For example, the original bolt handle on the Gewehr 98 used in the Great War protruded straight out from the action at a right angle. It was easy to grasp even wearing thick mittens, but it did get in the way—when the rifle was slung, for example, or placed in a rack. Worse, when scopes came into general use, the bolt handle precluded mounting them where they should be. The answer to the first question was easy and, on the later K98 used in the Second World War, the bolt handle was simply turned down to the side.

Problem solved. For civilian use with a scope, the bolt handle could be cut off, reshaped, and welded back on at a lower angle, or replaced by one of the various after-market handles offered by gunsmith supply houses like Brownells.

The original three-position safety on the 98 had every virtue except one: It is somewhat non-eu, in the sense that it requires the use of thumb and forefinger to move it readily between some of its positions. It also interfered with scope mounting. It does have one overwhelming virtue in its original configuration, and that is, it's impossible for it to move from "safe" to "fire" accidentally, although if left in the center position (straight up) it could be accidentally knocked either way.

The great advantage of a three-position safety is that, in this center position, it positively locks the striker but allows the bolt to be cycled to eject a cartridge from the chamber. This may not seem like much, but it's a priceless asset. The alternative two-position, which most of the so-called solutions were, either forces the shooter to move the safety to "fire" before unloading, or allows the bolt to open while on "safe," which means there is no way to lock the bolt closed. Any backpack

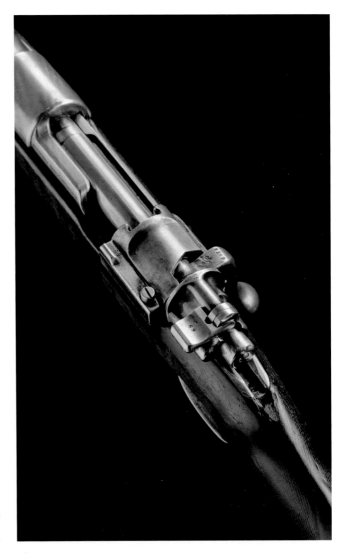

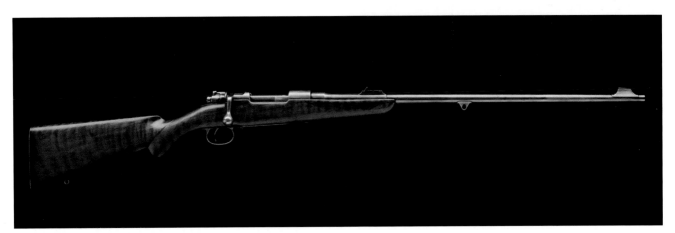

This is a 7x57 (.275 Rigby) made by John Rigby & Co. of London, and owned by the famous hunter of man-eating tigers, Jim Corbett. It is built on an Oberndorf Mauser action and has both the original Mauser three-position safety and turned-down bolt handle. Corbett carried it in the foothills of the Himalayas the way other men carry a walking stick. Photos courtesy John Rigby & Co., London.

hunter will tell you this is anathema, and I, for one, refuse to carry any rifle that allows the bolt to pop open when it catches on a branch or on my belt as I'm climbing hand over hand up a snowy mountainside.

The current prevalence of the two-position safety supports my suspicion that most rifle designers are not serious hunters. The last time I hunted with a Remington Model 700 with such a two-position safety, a dozen years ago, I was climbing the mountain on Admiralty Island, through mud and wet snow. There was a round in the chamber because a Sitka deer might pop out at any moment (or, less welcome, a brown bear) and three times—*three times*—the bolt handle snagged, popped open, and tossed the round into the snow. By the time I reached the top, I'd sworn never to use a Model 700 again, or any other rifle with such a safety.

Of all the solutions for replacing the Mauser's military over-the-top wing, the best *by far* was the Winchester Model 70's three-position wing that moves forward and back rather than up and over. Not only does it allow unimpeded use of any scope you care to mount, it can be operated by the thumb alone. When customizing Mauser 98s became an industry in itself, a thriving sub-industry arose producing replacement bolt shrouds with such a safety. It is standard equipment on such high-quality civilian 98s as the Granite Mountain, as well as the new Mauser 98 rifles made by Mauser in Germany and introduced in 2017.

Another shortcoming of the military Mauser 98 for civilian use is the floorplate. It's opened by using the tip of a cartridge to depress a spring-loaded latch, allowing the floorplate to be removed for cleaning. For military purposes this is fine, but not for a hunter who might need

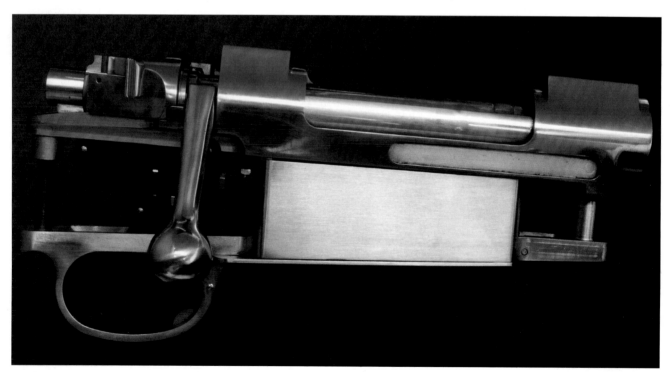

Granite Mountain Mauser action, in the white. It has a modern bolt handle as well as a three-position horizontal (forward and back) wing safety. The hinged floorplate is released via an Oberndorf-style catch inside the trigger guard.

to load and unload his rifle several times a day, climbing in and out of vehicles or returning to camp. One does not always want to run every round through the chamber to unload although, with the three-position safety, this can be done safely and was probably one of the applications Paul Mauser envisaged when he designed the safety that way. The solution, beginning with Oberndorf Mauser sporters and continued on most rifles to this day, is a hinged floorplate released by a lever or button. The Oberndorf sporters used a lever with the release button inside the trigger guard.

The Winchester Model 70, an unapologetic grandson of the Mauser 98, tried to improve on its ancestor in several ways. First, Winchester replaced the multi-part bolt-stop mechanism with a simpler one of pressed metal that can best be described as chintzy. This was replaced in turn with something better when Don Allen and company designed the Dakota action, which was based on the pre-'64 Model 70. The second change was a simple button ahead of the trigger guard to release the floorplate. This is definitely non-eu, because if you use your fingertip to release the floorplate, as you need to do, the plate springs open and catches the cuticle of your finger—not life-threatening, but painful enough, especially if it happens several times a day. With the Mauser system, on the other hand, you press the button with your thumb and position the forefinger ahead of the trigger guard to keep the floorplate from flying all the way open and dumping the cartridges on the ground. To accomplish this with the Model 70, you need to use both hands. Incidentally, the Dakota action stayed with the Model 70-style release, which is definitely non-eu.

In custom circles, when working with a Mauser 98 military action, the answer to all of the above was to replace the entire floorplate and trigger guard with a single, self-contained mechanism. This bottom metal included the trigger guard, floorplate, and sometimes a magazine box.

The Mauser 98 trigger is another good example of the action's superior design. It's an extremely simple three-piece mechanism attached to the underside of the action body by a single cross-pin. In its original form, it is a two-stage trigger, but this can be altered to one-stage. Either way, it's a good trigger as is, and can be adjusted and stoned to give a crisp, light, trigger pull. Alternatively, it can be replaced by any of a dozen different designs. The Canjar, Dayton-Traister, and Timney triggers were excellent for this purpose. If desired, you could even install a single- or double-set trigger, and it was usually as simple as driving out the retaining pin, positioning the new trigger mechanism, and replacing the pin.

The Winchester Model 70 had a trigger of its own design, which was extremely good. It could be adjusted for pull weight and creep, with the positions locked in place by two small nuts. In recent years, gunsmith Paul Dressel has made a Model 70-style trigger for fitting on Mauser actions, and one could do much worse. The Model 70 as now manufactured has a trigger designed by Browning for its bolt rifles in 2006.

* * *

The Mauser 98 action was made in at least two military sizes, the standard and the intermediate, and in different configurations as to the size of the receiver ring (large ring, small ring). The Mexican Mauser, which was actually manufactured in Mexico, was a hybrid and could be counted as a third military variation. The sporting actions from Oberndorf were made in standard length as well as small (*kurz*) and large (magnum). This brief summary does not even

Oberndorf Mauser sporting rifle, dating from the 1920s.

scratch the surface of the variations that are possible within the actions manufactured over the course of one hundred years in a dozen countries, by scores of makers. As well, there are variations that were the preserve of individual gunsmiths.

It is, for example, possible to take a standard military action, cut it in two, remove metal from the center, weld the two parts back together, and make what amounts to an *ersatz kurz*. This was fairly common in the 1960s, when genuine *kurz* actions were scarce and expensive but military surplus actions were a dime a dozen. It is obviously a job for a highly skilled gunsmith, but the end price was not exorbitant. I have even heard of gunsmiths taking two identical actions, cutting them both, switching front and back, and ending up with a *kurz* and a magnum. *Voilà.* This desire

for small actions on which to build the wildly popular .222 Remington (in the '50s) and .22-250 (in the '60s) probably was the impetus for Zastava to make its mini-Mark X action. These were sold through Brownells for many years. Incidentally, the machinery on which the Zastava actions were made came originally from Mauser, handed over to Serbia (Yugoslavia) as war reparations. The shortcomings of the Mark X, such as occasional over-zealous polishing that removed too much metal from one side or the other, were a result of poor workmanship, not bad tooling.

One military action that enjoyed particular attention was the Czech-made G33/40, manufactured at Brno from 1940 to 1942. The G33/40 was intended for mountain troops and similar units requiring lighter, more compact rifles. It has a 19-inch barrel instead of the K98's 24-inch, and a small receiver ring. The action is judiciously milled out here and there to reduce weight further. The result is the best military mountain rifle of its time. A gunsmith wanting to build a light mountain hunting rifle could start with a G33/40 action, which are superb quality overall, and be well on his way. This was the fate of many G33/40s.

One of the enduring regrets of my gun-trading life is my failure to buy, when I had the

One of the most highly prized of military Mausers, a G33/40 manufactured at Brno in Czechoslovakia in 1942. This Czech variation was adopted by the German Army for mountain troops. It has a small action ring and a lightened action, as well as a shorter barrel.

chance, a G33/40 in beautiful condition. It was 1965, I was sixteen, and I had $30 in my pocket. My quarry was a semi-sporterized Enfield P-17, but the seller (who was a family friend, serious gun collector, and occasional gun dealer) suggested the G33/40 was a better rifle for the same money. I took the Enfield instead because I had brainwashed myself with months of reading, as I scraped together the necessary thirty bucks, into believing the .30-06 was a better cartridge. My only consolation is that, had I taken the G33/40 that day, I would certainly not have it now, when such a rifle commands about $5,000. Instead, it would have been traded off along with most of the others to finance one or another trip to Africa in the 1970s. And then I would *really* have regrets.

Not many G33/40s were manufactured. Estimates run to about 130,000. The G33/40 was based on an earlier Czech Mauser (vz. 33). After the German takeover of Czechoslovakia in 1939, the vz. 33 was modified for issue to mountain troops. How many survived the war and came to America is anyone's guess. Not many, for sure, relatively speaking. Of those, many were broken down for parts and the actions used for custom rifles. Hence the high price today among military collectors for an all-original G33/40 in good condition.

Around 2010, Granite Mountain turned its attention to making a G33/40 clone for the custom-rifle trade. Granite Mountain actions are among the best Mauser 98s available for custom makers, but they are not cheap. You are looking at about the same price for the action as for a pristine G33/40 military, but then you don't have the added expense of replacing the bolt handle, shroud, safety, bottom metal, and trigger. Nor will your conscience prick you for mutilating a rare collector's item.

Some other military Mausers were also especially prized for custom rifles. In 1912, Mauser produced a run of 98 rifles chambered for the 7x57 cartridge, and built on a slightly shorter action that is now called either the "intermediate" or the Model 1912. This action is midway in length between the *kurz* and the standard, but has a large receiver ring. It is an excellent action for cartridges like the .308 Winchester.

* * *

For a measure of just how versatile the Mauser 98 action can be, we need look no further than Germany in the 1920s, and the gunmaking firm of August Schuler. The early '20s in Germany were pretty rough, politically and economically. With rampant inflation destroying the value of the mark, and Communists and right-wing *Freikorps* battling it out in the streets, it was a time of considerable hardship. It was especially hard on small businesses.

Most German gunmakers either worked on their own or had two or three men in a small shop. They built what rifles they could on whatever actions they could obtain, and scrambled for export markets. It was during this time that many shoddy and questionable rifles were exported to the US from Germany. Most were built on ex-military actions.

One export market German gunmakers wanted to crack was Africa. After 1918, the British gun trade that had traditionally supplied rifles to colonists and professional hunters was as badly hit by the war, and postwar economic woes, as were the German companies. Worse, firms like John Rigby and Westley Richards specialized in costly double rifles, for which there were few buyers, or built expensive bolt actions on German Mausers and Austrian Mannlichers. Altogether, it seemed like an opportune time for German gunmakers to sell rifles in Kenya, Tanganyika, and the Rhodesias.

August Schuler was a small gunmaking firm in the town of Suhl. The details are sketchy, but it appears that sometime around 1924, Schuler got the idea of building a genuine elephant rifle using the many military 98 actions that were floating around. At that time, the biggest magazine rifle cartridges available were the .416 Rigby, the .425 Westley Richards, and the .404 Jeffery—all powerful rifles, to be sure, but Schuler wanted something that was both bigger and less expensive. They decided on .500 caliber, to compete with the .500 Nitro Express, then calculated the absolute largest cartridge that could fit the standard 98 action. The result was the 12.5x70mm Schuler or, as it came to be known in England, the .500 Jeffery. By nitro-express standards, it is a short, fat cartridge with a minimal neck; it has a rebated rim that fits the standard 98 bolt face.

Obviously, such a stout beast could not fit into the Mauser magazine in a staggered column, so Schuler designed a whole new magazine structure. It held two cartridges in line which, with one in the chamber, gave a three-shot capacity. Instead of the standard follower with

a ridge along one side, the new follower cradled the cartridge in the center, perfectly in line for feeding into the chamber. Since cartridges in line could not be held in the place by the guide rails, Schuler borrowed a feature from the Mannlicher-Schönauer, and fitted a spring-loaded detent into the right rail. It was depressed as the cartridges were loaded, then sprang out to hold them in place.

The ballistics of the 12.5x70 Schuler are nothing if not impressive: a 535-grain bullet at

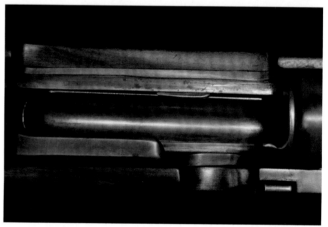

The Schuler rifle for the 12.5x70 had an extended magazine that accommodated two cartridges in line. The standard follower was replaced by a cradle, and the cartridge was held in place by a spring-loaded detent, similar to the system used on the Mannlicher-Schönauer rotary magazine.

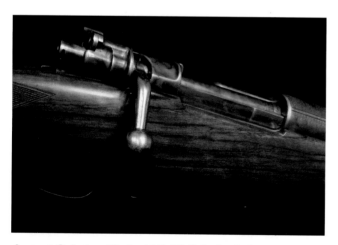

August Schuler rifle in 12.5x70 Schuler (.500 Jeffery) built on a military Mauser 98 action in the 1920s.

a muzzle velocity of 2,400 fps, delivering muzzle energy of 6,800 ft. lbs. Imagine, if you will, unleashing that from a typical German sporting rifle of that time, with a thin comb, a lot of drop, and a narrow buttplate. I have only handled one such Schuler rifle, and while it felt good in the hands, I can only imagine what it would feel like to shoot. Alas, I did not have the opportunity to find out. Drat.

In England, W. J. Jeffery seized onto the 12.5x70mm Schuler, renamed it the .500 Jeffery for the London trade and, in paper ballistics at least, ruled the magazine-rifle world until Roy Weatherby came along with his .460 Weatherby in 1958. Against all the odds, the .500 Jeffery is enjoying something of a renaissance, with at least two factory rifles chambered for it (Blaser R8 and CZ) and Norma providing excellent factory ammunition in their "African PH" line.

To the best of my knowledge, that is as far as anyone has gone with a Mauser 98 action. At the opposite end, any number of variations have been made chambered for the .22 rimfire. There was even a smattering of shotguns made on it, by rebarreling, having one cartridge down and one in the chamber, and depending on just the third (safety) lug to lock the bolt.

I mention all this to give an idea of just how versatile and adaptable the Mauser 98 action can be, and the potential for using it as the basis not only for some spectacular custom rifles, but also some absolutely beautiful—by our definition—hunting rifles.

THE ANONYMOUS BEAUTY

The rifle that illustrates best for me exactly what a custom Mauser can be is one that is still a mystery in many ways, but not in looks, feel, or performance. In those areas, it is an absolute gem. I have no idea who built it, or when, or who the original purchaser was. I don't know who made the barrel or the stock, although I have suspicions regarding the latter.

The rifle caught my eye because it is chambered for one of my all-time favorite cartridges, the .250-3000, and for many years I had hungered for one in a bolt action. In 2004, I even attempted to have a custom Dakota Arms rifle built for it. I ordered the rifle at the Safari Club convention, bought a stock blank at the custom gunmakers' guild show, and shipped it out to Sturgis. On the order, I specified that it was to be a slim, trim deer rifle, built on their small action with a 22-inch barrel, and with *fleur-de-lis* checkering. That summer, I drove out to pick it up. What I found was not what I'd ordered—not by a long, long way. The forend was an oversized beavertail twice as broad as it was deep—a typical varmint-rifle shape and size—and the checkering pattern was hideous. The stock had almost no comb at all. Where the forend was oversized, the buttstock was unnaturally skinny and completely out of proportion. Dakota's explanation was that the stockmaker, seeing the caliber, assumed I wanted a combination rifle for big game and varmints. He either didn't bother to read the order or chose to ignore it, figuring he knew what I needed better than I did. The rifle stayed in Sturgis.

A decade later, I came across my mystery Mauser .250-3000. The asking price was strikingly low for a custom rifle, and I snapped it up. When it arrived, I was pleasantly surprised, and have continued to be pleasantly surprised by the rifle ever since.

It is built on a Mauser "intermediate" action, the 1912 military model that is slightly shorter than the standard. The 24-inch barrel has a 1:10 rifling twist. The stock is an exceedingly pleasing piece of walnut, more or less American classic in lines, but with a graceful *Schnäbel*. The cheekpiece

The .250-3000, built by an anonymous riflemaker on a Mauser "intermediate" action. The stock is a modified American classic style, with a graceful Schnäbel.

is American, with the forward line flowing into the pistol grip, rather than the pancake shape of older European rifles. This type of cheekpiece is credited to an American artist, W. Herbert Dunton. In 1929, he ordered a rifle from Alvin Linden, and specified this cheekpiece. Reluctant at first, Linden soon saw the artistic merits of it, and it became his standard (and that of the American custom rifle trade) henceforth. The pistol grip has a steel cap, the butt a knurled steel buttplate. The checkering is a generous point pattern, wrapping around the forend, which is round in cross-section, affording a solid but comfortable

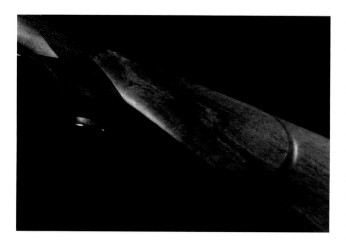

This style of cheekpiece, very graceful and flowing, is credited to Alvin Linden and a client, artist W. Herbert Dunton. It became Linden's standard cheekpiece and has been widely copied throughout the custom-rifle trade.

grip. The comb is undercut on the right side to make room for the base of the thumb.

If I had to guess, I would say the rifle was put together in the 1970s, and that the stock came from Reinhart Fajen. It looks very much like a Fajen style from that period. Those were semi-finished stocks, with inletting, finishing, and checkering left to the gunmaker. It is particularly pleasing to the eye; although the color and grain are not elaborate by today's standards, I have never seen a stock where the grain pattern complements the stock shape so well. It all flows gracefully together. By an odd coincidence (or the intervention of the guardian angel of gunmaking) the grain and color are remarkably similar to the blank I bought for the ill-fated Dakota custom rifle described above.

When the rifle arrived, it had a Timney trigger with the standard sliding side safety that blocks the trigger, but nothing else. Of course, it was a two-position safety, so the bolt could never be locked shut. From Brownells, I obtained a replacement bolt shroud with a Model 70-style three-position safety, along with one of Paul Dressel's Model 70-style triggers for the Mauser 98. When the rifle returned from the gunsmith, it was outfitted to perfection.

Overall, the rifle gives every indication of having been put together by a rifle fanatic who thought everything out carefully. It has a front sight on a ramp with a hood—which gives any rifle a finished, balanced look—but there is no open sight on the barrel. Instead, it has one of the old one-piece Redfield bases with an integral aperture sight that flips up. It can be adjusted for both windage and elevation. This limits the scope-mount options to Redfield split rings (now made by Leupold) but that is no hardship. Redfield/Leupold mounts are among the best available. I developed a load firing a 100-grain Nosler Ballistic Tip at 2,950 fps, and the rifle cheerfully puts them into five-shot, one-inch groups, time after time.

As of today, I have hunted with it only once: an expedition to the Chinati Mountains of west Texas in search of aoudad. On arrival, I was cautioned that such a rifle was far too light, and that I should carry my back-up rifle instead (a Schultz & Larsen .358 Norma). Aoudad, they said, left no blood trail when wounded, and were impossible to track over the rugged Chinatis. As I found out, the Chinati Mountains are not terribly high (7,000 feet) at their peak, but they are steep and as treacherous as any slopes I have ever encountered. It is like climbing on ball bearings and broken glass, interspersed with cactus and thorns, with every step potentially your last. After climbing up and down one mountain in the morning, I got a shot in the afternoon, uphill at a steep angle and 285 yards away. The .250-3000 settled in and shot the big ram through the heart.

I took one bad tumble and landed on the rifle stock, but the ragged scars were soothed with some linseed oil, and are now hardly visible. Roy

The rifle is fitted with a Redfield base, incorporating a hinged aperture sight. The riflescope is a Zeiss Terra 3X 3-9x42.

Chapman Andrews would have been proud—to say nothing of Charles Newton. If you see me out hunting when I'm ninety, it will probably be with that rifle.

* * *

Custom .450 Ackley, built on an FN Supreme action by gunmaker Siegfried Trillus in 1991.

CHAPTER XIII

THE FN MAUSER

In 1889, the Belgian Army adopted the Mauser Model 1889. That same year, a consortium of Belgian gunmakers founded a company to produce it. The company was given the name *Fabrique Nationale d'Armes de Guerre*—FN, for short—and it was set up in the town of Herstal, near Liège. Two years later, Germany's great gunmaking conglomerate, Ludwig Löwe & Co., acquired 50 percent of the stock, and added FN to its wide-ranging stable of gunmaking companies that included the Mauser-Werke and, eventually, Luger.

Today, 130 years later, FN is still in Herstal, still making rifles, and is Europe's largest exporter of military weapons. Tell someone—*anyone*—that a gun is made by FN, and it is a certain guarantee of quality.

The town of Liège is the historical center of Belgium's ancient gunmaking trade, and Belgians have been master gunmakers for centuries. In the years to come, FN was at the center of so many seemingly disparate events in the world of gunmaking that you begin to think there must have been some divine plan. The government contract completed, the FN factory was rather at loose ends when, in 1897, American inventor John M. Browning approached it about manufacturing the semiauto pistol that later came to be known as the Model 1900. Five years later, he came back with a design for a semiauto shotgun that Winchester had rejected. FN snapped it up, and Browning personally placed an order for ten

thousand guns. This ensured immediate commercial success. Browning's ten thousand shotguns were imported by Schoverling, Daly, and Gales, and they sold out within a year.

John M. Browning maintained a close relationship with FN until his death in 1926. It then continued with his son, Val Browning, and with the Browning Arms Company of Utah.

For those who believe in omens and the like, here is an ironic series of events: In 1914, Gavrilo Princip assassinated the Austrian Archduke Franz Ferdinand using a Browning 1900 .32 ACP pistol. Five weeks later, Germany invaded Belgium, and the FN production line, where the gun was produced, was shut down for the first of only two times in its history. The Germans also burned down the ancient (and irreplaceable) library at Louvain. The second time the production line shut down was in 1940, when Germany invaded again. Poetic justice, perhaps, in its own tragic way.

My first encounter with FN occurred when, as a child, I surreptitiously dug out a pistol that my father kept under some sweaters in a bottom drawer, and found engraved on the side *Fabrique Nationale d'Armes de Guerre, Herstal, Belgium*. It was a Browning Model 1926, made under duress for the Germans during the war, complete with *Waffenamt*. My father acquired it during his time with the Canadian Army in Europe. Then, when I enlisted in the Canadian Army Reserve at the age of sixteen, I was handed an FN C1 rifle (the famous FN-FAL). Finally, as a gun-struck teenager who spent hours reading about guns when I should have been studying algebra, I discovered the FN name in the beautiful Browning catalogues, makers of the Superposed, the Auto-5, and the Browning Hi-Power pistol.

As one of the far-flung tentacles of Ludwig Löwe's Mauser-making empire, FN continued to make the K98 for years after the rifle's military role ended. After the armistice in 1918, when the Treaty of Versailles prohibited Germany from making certain military armaments, FN became an important supplier of Mauser 98s to countries such as Brazil, Yugoslavia, and Lithuania.

The plant at Herstal was back in civilian operation shortly after the second war ended in 1945, and one of its earliest products was the K98 action. These were initially K98 clones, but were gradually given civilian dress as FN made modifications—some for the better, some not. Between 1945 and 1965, the FN Mauser progressed through a number of models. These were sold in the white to gunsmiths for building custom rifles, and supplied in bulk to various rifle companies to produce their own rifles. Roy Weatherby used FN Mausers to build his earliest California rifles, before he designed the Mark V.

Browning Arms had its own line of FN-made, Mauser-actioned rifles through the 1960s, called simply the "Browning High Power." They were built on the final iteration of the FN Mauser, called the Supreme. It was the last in a long series of commercial Mausers from FN. Frank de Haas wrote that he first saw FN actions for sale in the 1941 Stoeger catalogue. The action was called the "Peerless," and he immediately ordered one, but received a refund because supplies were cut off when Germany invaded Belgium in May, 1940. When hostilities ended in 1945, FN resumed production of Mauser actions in a rather confusing

variety that seemingly evolved faster than they could rename them. As a result, features that are supposedly unique to one model may be found on earlier or later ones.

Officially, the post-war Mausers were the Series 300 and 400, sometimes called the Deluxe and, finally, the Supreme. The Supreme was the favorite civilian 98 on which to build a custom rifle, if you couldn't afford an Oberndorf and didn't want a military one. No one ever criticized the basic quality of FN Mausers, although some disliked some of the features. For example, the Supreme was marketed with a streamlined, polished bolt shroud without the original wing safety. Instead, it was supplied with a single-stage trigger with an integral safety. As well, on the Browning High Power rifles, the trigger guard and floor plate were made of some indeterminate alloy and given a polished black finish with chintzy gold filigree. Most gunmakers obtained steel bottom metal to replace it, and gunmaker Ted Blackburn later became the source for the highest quality bottom metal for that purpose.

After the war, Firearms International (FI) became a major importer, and offered a rifle called the Musketeer built on the FN action.

Blackburn bottom metal, now made by Swift Bullets in Quinter, Kansas.

Later, Harrington & Richardson marketed a bolt-action rifle using the FN, as did High Standard, Colt, Marlin, and a number of proprietary names like Montgomery Ward's Western Field. The FN Supreme, it seemed, was everywhere. Even the other-worldly Winslow rifles, which out-did the Weatherby look by a substantial margin, were built on FN Supremes.

FN pioneered a number of features on its actions aside from the bolt shroud. It dispensed with the thumb slot on the left side, which stiffened the action (an aid to accuracy), and in 1955 produced a single-shot version with no magazine cut-out. This made it stiffer still, and was intended for benchrest rifles. The FN bolt handle was swept back in a graceful arc, and the bolt knob was flat and knurled on the underside. Some professed to dislike it, but I thought it was the essence of style.

On the Supreme, FN changed the bolt stop and release, replacing the traditional Mauser box with a spring-loaded lever. Again, some criticize it as monkeying with Paul Mauser's masterpiece, but it is both unobtrusive and rather elegant, and in my experience seems to work just as well. Earlier models had a floorplate release inside the trigger guard, but it was not the distinctive Oberndorf grooved button. Instead, it was a rather workmanlike affair that some gunsmiths went to great pains to replace or correct.

Not surprisingly, the quality of the rifles built on FN actions varied widely. There is no all-encompassing rule about them except to say that the basic actions were as good as Mauser actions get. I have never heard any criticisms of the FNs similar to those leveled against the Yugoslav Mark X (Zastava), for example, which were often sloppily finished. In the opinion of Frank de Haas, gunsmith, contributing editor to *The American Rifleman,* and author of *Bolt Action Rifles*: "FN actions are made to the usual exacting FN quality, a quality so outstanding no one should question it."

The Browning High Power rifles are, to my eye, a curious combination of beautiful quality and questionable taste. As a teenager, of course, I thought they were wonderful. Later, I came to dislike both the alloy bottom metal and the two-position trigger-block safety. More than that, however, while the Brownings were stocked in nice walnut, their dimensions were less than graceful. The forend was a couple of inches too long, the buttstock a little too broad. There was neither an ebony forend tip nor a pistol-grip cap—decidedly low-rent in the '60s. I later came to appreciate forends *au naturale,* but not the pistol grip. Still, it had good hand-checkering in generous patterns. There were two higher grades, the Medallion and Olympian, and they were truly lovely examples of the gunmaker's art—albeit with some '60s' touches, now deservedly out of fashion. On the positive side, there was their lovely walnut, rosewood forend tips and grip caps, and varying degrees of superb Belgian engraving. On the negative side were the white-line spacers, skip-line checkering, ventilated recoil pads, and a high-gloss wood finish similar to Weatherby's. Some years later, I owned a Browning Medallion grade .222 Remington Magnum, built on a short Sako action. In 1979, during a moment of derangement, I traded it for a snowmobile, which died in a snowbank before the winter was over. Not a happy memory.

One over-riding complaint about the Browning High Power was its weight. Although it was listed as being as light as 6¼ pounds, depending on barrel length and caliber, I have one (extensively remodeled, but essentially the original rifle) in .30-06 which, while comfortable to shoot, is not going on any hunting trips where I have to climb anything more substantial than an anthill. Incidentally, that particular rifle is built on the FN Supreme action, but does not have the flattened, knurled bolt knob—one more example of how some features migrate from one model to another, seemingly at will.

When FN finally discontinued the Supreme in 1975, it was one of the sadder days in the rifle business. Without that competition, however, the way was open for others to resurrect the K98 commercial action, including Granite Mountain in Arizona and, most recently, the Mauser company itself. There were others, of course—many others. Some were good, some not so good. For years, the Yugoslav Mark X filled the gap left by the Supreme, with both standard and *kurz* actions available from Brownells. As the price of original Oberndorf actions climbed relentlessly through the 1990s and beyond 2000, prices for FN Supremes in good condition slipstreamed along behind, although the bottom-metal question became critical as Ted Blackburn's delivery times stretched ever-longer, eventually reaching, according to legend, ten years! That's a long time to wait for an essential

part on which to start building a custom rifle. Blackburn's business was purchased by Swift Bullets around 2012, and bottom metal is now being produced at their factory in Quinter, Kansas. And very good bottom metal it is, too. That's what I put on the Browning .30-06 described above, to replace the gold-filagreed alloy.

There are two particular rifles built on FN actions included in this book. Both are custom made. One I had built, the other I acquired in one of those lucky accidents.

The first is a .450 Ackley, built on an FN Supreme action. It has a checkered history, to say the least, and I only know the later chapters. This is at least its third iteration as a custom rifle. It could not have begun life as a Browning High Power, because it has no serial number. FN sold actions in the white with no number, allowing the gunsmith to choose his own. Eventually I had "TW 450" engraved on the trigger guard, and it has satisfied several generations of customs officers.

When I acquired the action, in a trade for a Browning 20-gauge SxS, it was the basis of a

Blackburn bottom metal, made by Swift, fitted and finished on a Browning High Power.

Custom-built .450 Ackley, by Siegfried Trillus, on an FN Supreme action, wearing Swarovski Habicht 1.5X riflescope. The rifle is fitted with a claw mount, which is instantly detachable. Without the scope, the rifle becomes a stalking rifle supreme, pointing naturally and instantly at anything that might be coming.

.375 H&H rifle put together by a rifle-loving acquaintance who fancied himself a gunsmith, but wasn't. His plan for the Browning shotgun was to convert it, in some way, into a double rifle, which should give you some idea. This acquaintance had fashioned the .375's stock himself, including a mediocre checkering job. He had also replaced the original bottom metal, whatever it had been, with a trigger guard and floorplate off a Whitworth, a medium-quality line of Mauser-actioned rifles imported from England. On my return from Africa in 1990, having hunted Cape buffalo in Tanzania and Botswana, I had some notions about what constituted my ideal buffalo rifle. I carted the questionable .375 H&H off to my old German gunmaking friend, Siegfried Trillus, and commissioned him to turn it into a .450 Ackley.

Siegfried was a true German gunmaker of the old school who could do practically anything required of either a rifle or shotgun. Many years earlier, he had cut down a black walnut tree,

sawn it into blanks, and painstakingly dried and seasoned the blanks himself. We picked one out, and he began carving it into a suitable stock for a hard-kicking dangerous-game rifle. He ordered a barrel from Douglas and a set of claw mounts from Germany. Swarovski had a 1.5X Habicht scope with a 26mm straight steel tube, decidedly old-fashioned even in 1990, but perfect for my purpose.

Being German, Siegfried liked his scopes high. I do not. We had a meeting of the minds over that, but eventually he got the lowest rings he could that would allow everything to work properly. Because a claw mount is released at the rear and tipped up and forward to remove, an objective bell creates a problem, but with the straight tube of that Swarovski, we could mount it very low.

The scope mount itself presented a few difficulties. The action was already drilled and tapped for scope mounts, but Siegfried did not believe that four screws were sufficient to hold everything

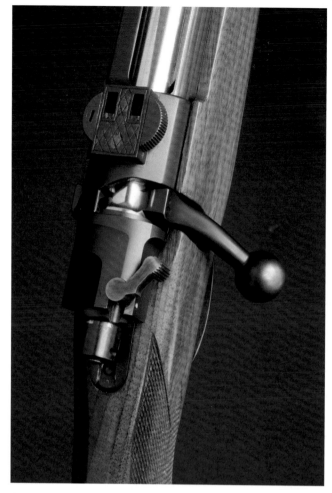

The .450 Ackley has a custom bolt-shroud with three-position wing safety. The bases for the claw mount are both screwed and silver-soldered to the action.

The open sights also came from Germany. The rear sight is a single standing blade on a ramp with a broad "V." This required refining in two ways. One, the elevation is adjusted by sliding the blade up or down its sloping dovetailed base. Under the .450's recoil, it had a tendency to come loose and take up residence in the nearest patch of long grass. This was corrected with an auxiliary locking screw in addition to the original. The second problem was the sharp points on the sight blade. They could (and did) carve up a safari shirt, so those were rounded off with a file.

The barrel is 22 inches long, and in a misguided moment I took it to Mag-Na-Port in Michigan and had them cut a very slight integral muzzle brake. This consists of four short slots on the upper side of the barrel. It does nothing to tame straight-back recoil, but it suppresses muzzle jump considerably, while the increase in muzzle blast is minimal. If I had it to do again, I wouldn't, but that's life.

Unfortunately, Siegfried died shortly after the rifle was completed, and never got to hear about its many trips to Africa. He also never got to hear about some of the rifle's adventures that can be laid directly at my door. One involved an imprudent handload, followed by a second, even more imprudent, handload. The second shot slammed the floorplate open, tendrils of smoke curled from the action, and the Swarovski's cross-wires came loose and recoiled into little fish hooks. I didn't know it at the time, but I had also set back the locking lugs ever so slightly, creating a headspace problem that was later corrected by turning the barrel one rotation and rechambering. The barrel is now 21¾ inches long.

The problem of the floorplate slamming open only occurred when I fired a really inadvisable load, but we felt it should be dealt with. It was solved by sculpting the button inside

together under the recoil of a .450. Accordingly, he supported the screws by silver-soldering the bases to the receiver. Mentioning this to gunsmiths, it is frequently met with horrified looks and blurted objections about the heat drawing the temper and softening the action. Siegfried shrugged this off. "If you know how to use a heat sink," he told me, "there is no problem at all." Obviously, some of the critics did not have that level of knowledge and skill. Tellingly, my rifle wears the same bases, mounted in the same way (a combination of screws and solder) as the old Mauser-Werke did in Germany.

A unique, highly customized method of preventing the floorplate release from springing open in an unscheduled manner.

and believes my .450 Ackley to be the finest rifle Siegfried ever made.

Having said all that, what does the rifle look and feel like in action?

Fully loaded but without scope and sling, as one would want in thick brush with a buffalo's rasping breath a few feet away, it is 8 lbs. 10 oz. Add the scope and sling, and it weighs in at a hair over ten pounds. The best way I can describe its handling is that it comes to the shoulder, with barrel perfectly aligned, like a London bird gun. In fashioning the stock, Siegfried built in a little cast off. The butt is proportioned to allow a generous recoil pad. The pistol grip is slim by modern standards, as is the forend, which in cross-section is a horizontal oval, tapering gently from the floorplate out to the tip. With Siegfried's wrap-around checkering, it affords a secure grip without having to hang on like grim death. In the years since, I have tried to get other stockmakers to copy the design, but they won't. They prefer a vertical oval with flat sides, so they can demonstrate their virtuosity with a checkering tool.

Siegfried had the tremendous advantage, as a riflemaker, that he was also a serious hunter. Every year, he took two weeks and headed for northern Ontario to hunt moose. He also hunted deer in the fall, black bear in the spring, groundhogs whenever he found them, and was an avid target shooter. He loved shotguns, but rifles were his religion. He knew how a big-game rifle should feel, and he also knew how to make them feel that way. The same is true of Edwin von Atzigen. In a riflemaker, it is critical that he not only know how a rifle should feel, but how to get it there. This is the element that is missing in so much riflemaking today.

Shortly after the war, English gunwriter G. T. (Gough Thomas) Garwood looked at the English gun trade, then in considerable disarray, and

the trigger guard to be very unobtrusive, while fitting a removable pin through the guard to lock it in place. Since Siegfried's death, two other gunmakers have worked on the rifle. One is Edwin von Atzigen, a Canadian of Swiss extraction who is one of the best gunmakers I have ever met. The other was a somewhat difficult London-trained gunmaker. The latter fitted the retaining pin and engraved the serial number, but bolt-action rifles are not his forté. Von Atzigen, being Swiss, was born with a bolt action in his hand. He was also a close friend of Siegfried Trillus, knows his work inside out,

The .450 Ackley in its natural element. Tanzania, 2006.

lamented the fact that too many shotguns were being produced that lacked the exquisite balance and handling of those made between the wars, and before 1914. The fact that shooters would happily accept such guns filled him with misgivings. He shrewdly foresaw that client demand was what drove the best gunmakers, and if clients did not demand good balance and handling (which is difficult to achieve), then gunmakers would not bother to provide them. Since the only way to appreciate wonderful balance and handling is to heft and carry and shoot such a gun, for an hour or a day, too many clients simply did not know what a gun could (and should) feel like. The same is true of riflemaking today, even among custom riflemakers. Fortunately for me, Trillus and von Atzigen did know.

To borrow from Gough Thomas again, my .450 scores extremely high on the eumatic scale. One of the previous owners of the action found a way to make it as smooth as silk—smoother than any other Mauser 98 I've ever handled. According to the guy I obtained it from, he made the action smooth by pouring Ajax cleanser (a very mild abrasive) into the bolt channel, and then working the bolt back and forth as he watched television, evening after evening. I merely report what I was told. Also very eumatic is the claw mount: Wrap your hand around the ocular bell, pull back the catch with thumb and forefinger, lift, and the scope is released purely by feel. It comes away held firmly in the hand, and all without needing to look down even once. When you have an urgent need to take the scope off such a rifle,

The author in Tanzania in 2006, with the second of two Cape buffalo killed in a matter of minutes on a Great Rift mountainside. The trackers are, from left, Lekina Sandeti, Abedi Shimba, and Momella Torongoi. Lekina and Momella are both Masai, while Abedi was a Bushman. All of us were immensely grateful the buffalo went down where they stood, and did not disappear into the thick undergrowth.

Al Biesen .270 Winchester, built on an FN Deluxe action. It has been extensively remodeled, with a custom bolt shroud and three-position safety made by Biesen himself, and fitted with a Canjar trigger.

looking down is usually a luxury you can't afford. The scope can be replaced by feel, too, simply by positioning the forward claws with thumb and finger, then pushing down on the ocular bell. It snaps into place.

This is one of those rifles that are a pleasure to pick up, hold in your hands, work the bolt, take off the scope, and put it back on. It is eumatic and ergonomic to an almost unbelievable degree.

Since 1992, it has been to Africa several times and accounted for everything from gemsbok, zebras, and a greater kudu, to two Cape buffalo, the pair of them disposed of in a matter of minutes on a mountainside in Tanzania. I have used other big rifles in the meantime, for one reason and another, but every time I do, I find myself comparing them to Siegfried Trillus's masterpiece, and every time they finish second best.

* * *

The second FN-based rifle was built by Al Biesen (the "genius of Spokane," as Jack O'Connor described him) on an FN Deluxe action. Although the rifle was completed around 1985, the action is considerably older. It preceded the Supreme and was probably made in the 1950s. The Biesen family has no firm records of his work, so most of the details about the rifle we can only surmise.

Biesen was a highly skilled metal worker as well as a stockmaker, and he emphasized "hunting" rifles, as opposed to showpieces to hang on a wall. It is impossible to say, today, how much he absorbed from O'Connor, and how much O'Connor learned from him. Their relationship began in the late 1940s, after the death of Alvin Linden, when Biesen approached O'Connor and asked him to try some of his work. It endured until O'Connor's death in 1978. During that time, Biesen completed about twenty separate jobs for

Al Biesen was one of the few custom riflemakers to engrave his name on his masterpieces. He always used the old-fashioned "WN" abbreviation for Washington.

him, from restocking shotguns to building complete rifles.

As an early and devoted admirer of Jack O'Connor, it was only natural that I came to revere Biesen's name. I longed to own one of his rifles, but never thought it would come to pass. And, along the way, a strange thing happened. As a writer, it became my habit to attend hunting shows, like the Safari Club convention in Reno. I also started visiting the American Custom Gunmakers Guild show, which for many years was held in Reno at the same time. I got to know some of the gunmakers there, both stockmakers and metal guys. I would ask about Biesen, and was usually given an answer like "Really nice guy, but . . ." It seems they did not feel that Al Biesen, riflemaker to the stars, was in their league in terms of painstaking, meticulous, nigh-perfect work. I can say now, although I could not then, that a Biesen rifle feels and handles like a hunting rifle, while theirs (most of them, anyway) felt and handled like something meant to be looked at, not fired, and certainly not hunted with.

Tom Turpin is the recognized expert on custom bolt-action rifles, at least as far as writers go. It's his specialty, and he has written three books

Biesen was a master stockmaker. Although not of precise "American classic" styling, it is graceful and harmonious. The cheekpiece blends into the grip, and the recessed checkering is exquisitely done. Yet this is an unapologetic hunting rifle, not a showpiece.

on the subject. Asked about Biesen, his response was that Al Biesen was skilled enough to produce a rifle that would stand in any company, including the finest the Guild members could turn out. Instead, he had chosen to avoid making show pieces in favor of hunting rifles—rifles to be used, carried, shot, and carried some more. To function flawlessly, to be both ergonomic and eumatic, and handle like an English game gun insofar as that is possible with a bolt-action rifle.

I acquired mine through chance. It was 2016, Mauser-actioned sporting rifles were going through a period of disfavor, and prices were low. It fell into the hands of a gun dealer who did not know what **AL BIESEN GUNMAKER SPOKANE WN** meant to a rifle lover. He thought it was just one more customized Mauser, and priced it accordingly. As soon as I saw the name, I knew I had to have it.

The rifle is a .270 Winchester with a 22-inch barrel. Fitted with a 3-9X Swarovski scope, it weighs 8 lbs. 2 oz. Loaded with six rounds of ammunition (five down, one in the chamber) and wearing a leather sling, it tips the scale at 8 lbs. 13 oz. That is light enough to carry comfortably, but with enough heft for solid shooting. The action is probably an FN Deluxe. Some of its fea-

tures, however, are found on the later Supreme, and others are not. As well, it has had rather extensive modifications. Gone is the Mauser bolt shroud with over-the-top wing safety, replaced by a shroud of Biesen's own making, incorporating the Model-70 style wing that moves forward and back. The FN bottom metal appears to have come from a Supreme, but the floorplate release has been converted to the Oberndorf style.

The rifle is wearing a checkered steel grip cap of Biesen's own making, but instead of a steel buttplate, it has a thin recoil pad. This would be disdained by the purists of the gunmakers' guild, but I personally prefer it. Hunting rifles need to be stood up at times on all kinds of surfaces, and the surest way to send your rifle banging to the ground is to stand it up on a slick surface. As well, in climbing, it's inevitable that the butt will make contact with the ground, even if it is inadvertent. A recoil pad can take this without whimpering, but not a beautifully crafted, checkered steel plate. If nothing else, the damage will break your heart and make you more interested in protecting your rifle than hunting. A stockmaker once told Jack O'Connor that putting a recoil pad on a custom rifle was like seeing a man in evening dress, wearing rubber boots. Perhaps,

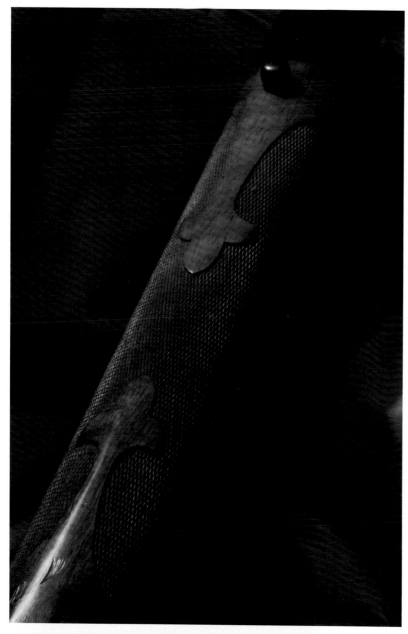

Biesen's recessed fleur-de-lis *checkering was almost a trademark.*

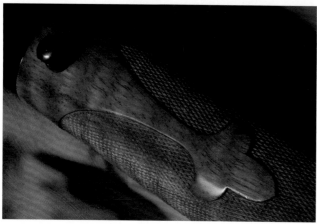

but a recoil pad is functionally superior by a vast margin.

Similarly, the Biesen rifle has glass bedding around the action—anathema to the purists. Whether this was his decision, or done at the request of the client, is impossible to say. Either way, it is functional, beneficial, and no one can see it anyway. The stock is not quite correct for modern tastes, having a very modest Monte Carlo comb. No matter whose decision that was, it works like a dream.

Every person who has picked up my Biesen has had the same reaction: "Unbelievable. I've never felt a rifle like this." It feels, they say, *alive*—slim and light in the hands because it does not have the bulky dimensions of so many modern stocks, either in the pistol grip or the forend. The pistol grip has a circumference of 4 3/8 inches, while the forend, also slim, is a modest pear shape in cross section. The checkering is Al Biesen's signature *fleur-de-lis*, recessed slightly so the lilies stand out.

The rifle is fitted with a Canjar, one of the great names in triggers from back then. It is crisp and the pull weight seems lighter than it actually is—exactly the qualities we want in a trigger but so seldom get.

The barrel is a Douglas, chambered by Biesen so precisely that when a 130-grain Nosler Partition is seated to exact SAAMI overall cartridge length (3.34 inches), the ogive of the bullet just brushes the lands. It shoots almost any .270 factory or handload very well, and some of them *extremely* well. The hunting load I developed, using Sierra 130-grain GameKings, will group five shots inside an inch consistently. It never strings shots, and is very predictable. When the velocity changes, it moves the group exactly where you expect it to move.

This rifle is a masterpiece of functionality as well as form and aesthetics. There is nothing on it that does not serve a purpose, except perhaps the forend tip. Nor does it lack anything you might need. It has no iron sights, but these are hardly necessary on a .270, even as a back-up.

When I bought the rifle, it was fitted with an older Leupold scope in Redfield Jr. rings, but whether that outfit was originally fitted by Biesen is impossible to say. I replaced it all with a Swarovski Z3 3-9x36 in S&K mounts with a customized rear base. All the parts look happy with each other.

* * *

Granite Mountain magnum action, .505 Gibbs.

CHAPTER XIV

THE MAGNUM MAUSER

In 1898, John Rigby & Co. of London became Mauser's English agent and the sole distributor of Mauser 98 rifles, actions, and barreled actions throughout the British Empire. Almost immediately, Rigby asked the Mauser-Werke to produce a slightly longer action, to accommodate the .400/.350 Rigby, one of the company's double-rifle cartridges. Mauser complied, and around 1900 delivered an action that was .400 inches longer than standard. To accommodate the rimmed .400/.350, it had a slanted magazine box.

From this modest beginning grew the Magnum Mauser action of lore and legend. Before long, Rigby was importing these for sale to other gunmakers, who chambered suitable big cartridges for them, such as W. J. Jeffery's .404 in 1909. Mauser itself also made finished rifles using the action, among them the .404 and the .280 Ross. In 1910, Rigby introduced its most famous cartridge, the .416 Rigby, and ever since it has been the cartridge most associated with the magnum action. The other major development in this regard was the introduction, in 1911, of the huge .505 Gibbs.

No one knows for certain exactly how many magnum actions were produced, but relatively speaking, it was not many. It is estimated that over the forty-seven-year period between the introduction of the Mauser 98, and the shutdown of commercial manufacture at Mauser in 1946, a grand total of about 125,000 sporting rifles were made. That includes both finished rifles and actions of all sizes.

From the beginning, Oberndorf magnum actions were expensive and hard to get. Combined with the romance and allure of such cartridges as the .416 Rigby and .505 Gibbs, they became a benchmark for desirability, and this translated into high prices. Magnum Mauser actions were never cheap, selling for $500 in the white when you could buy a very decent American-made rifle, complete, for $100.

As wars started and ended, economic woes came and went, and production at the Mauser-Werke ebbed and flowed, obtaining a magnum action at any price presented difficulties. It was not surprising, then, that the magnum Mauser was the action that other civilian manufacturers (as opposed to military suppliers, like FN) tried to duplicate. In the 1960s, the most notable of these was the French Brevex, which was both hard to get and difficult to work with. In the United States, Fred Wells, the Prescott, Arizona gunsmith who was America's reigning Mauser expert, produced some magnum actions virtually by hand. Wells, in turn, inspired Mike Roden, another Prescott-dwelling Mauser admirer, to found Granite Mountain Arms with the avowed intention of producing absolute, true-to-original-form Mauser 98 actions in all the original sporting configurations—standard, *kurz*, square-bridge, round-top, and magnum. Through the 1990s, Granite Mountain actions became the standard against which all other Mausers were measured. They were (and are) superbly made and priced accordingly.

This magnum Mauser action was made by Fred Wells of Prescott, Arizona.

In Germany, a few companies also produced Mauser actions, including Prechtl, which supplies actions to high-end custom shops like Hartmann & Weiss. Prechtl also supplied the actions for the prototype "Original Mauser" 98s from the Mauser company around 2010.

The most famous British cartridge of all, the .375 H&H, introduced in 1912, does not require a magnum action. With a bit of cutting and filing, it fits nicely in the standard-length Mauser. When FN began producing its so-called magnum line for Browning in the 1960s, its "magnum" actions were standard actions that had been opened up. However, when Mauser (the modern company) seriously returned to the 98 in 2015, the first rifles were built on square-bridge magnum actions, and the two initial chamberings were .416 Rigby and .375 H&H. An interesting sidelight is that the most recent 98s were created by Mauser at the behest of John Rigby & Co., now returned to London after fifteen years in an American wilderness of fraud and theft. The new John Rigby & Co. is owned by the same company that owns Mauser. They have come full circle, a mirror image of the saga of Winchester, Browning, and FN.

* * *

The rifle shown at the beginning of this chapter is a Granite Mountain .505 Gibbs, built in 2009, custom-stocked and checkered. It has a 22-inch barrel and no provision for a scope. Instead, it has iron sights on an integral quarter-rib and a barrel-band front sight, with a standard bead and folding moon sight. Unloaded with no sling, it weighs 10 1/2 pounds. Throw in a sling and three of the massive .505 cartridges, and it tops eleven pounds easily.

Magnum Mauser, in .375 H&H, made by Mauser in Germany.

There is only 1.5 pounds difference between this rifle and my .450 Ackley, but the difference in handling qualities is remarkable. The pistol grip and forend of the .505 are both considerably larger in circumference, and consequently more difficult to grip. In turn, it makes the rifle hard to handle.

There is little that can be done about this with such a large cartridge. Obviously, you need the magnum Mauser action, and the barrel will be thicker, heavier, and require a forend that is commensurately larger. In turn, so as not to look out of proportion, the pistol grip will also be thicker. And, inevitably, there is always the question of strength to withstand the .505's punishing recoil.

When I had this rifle made, I wanted one standing leaf for the rear sight, and no folding ones. My plan was to sight-in the rifle so that the bullet crossed the line of sight for the first time at 20 yards. It would then be sighted in for whatever distance the bullet crossed the line of sight coming back down—80 to 100 yards, most

likely. A .505 is an elephant gun first and foremost, and elephants are not hunted at long range. Therefore, a rifle sighted dead on at twenty yards would be the most useful, but you would still have usable trajectory out to one hundred yards or so. Beyond that range is beyond the .505's practical limit. Because of this plan, I wanted no folding leaves on the rear sight. Leaves that are folded down can pop up under recoil, especially this kind of recoil, and get in the way. I wanted no chance of that. The folding moon sight presented the same potential problem, but I raised no objections, thinking I would probably use the moon most of the time anyway.

I spent an afternoon with the rifle, firing one shot after another at a 20-yard target while a gunsmith filed a notch into the standing rear blade. When it was planting its bullets one on top of the other in the bull, he stopped filing and I stopped shooting. My shoulder was grateful, since I had done exactly the same thing, earlier in the day, with another .505 Gibbs built on one

Custom .505 Gibbs, built on their magnum action by Granite Mountain Arms. Hemingway's fictional professional, Robert Wilson, called his .505 Gibbs "this damned cannon." One can see why.

of Fred Wells's magnum Mauser actions. As a day of shooting goes, it was certainly an experience. It is quite remarkable how you can bear down and not jerk the trigger when you know that, if you get a flyer, you will just have to repeat the shot anyway.

The ammunition we used was Norma's "African PH" loaded with the 600-grain Woodleigh Protected Point soft-nosed bullet. It had always seemed to me that George Gibbs missed a trick in designing his mammoth cartridge to shoot a 525-grain bullet—which is light by .500-caliber standards—when a 600-grain would equal and even out-do the .500 Nitro Express with its 570-grain. To my knowledge, no one ever complained about the 525's stopping power, so I may have been over-analyzing and over-correcting. I've been known to do that. Still, 600 grains seemed a better weight. It's a terrific bullet, and both bullets and loaded ammunition are readily available.

* * *

Dangerous-game rifles constitute a whole separate area of discussion when it comes to hunting rifles. The disparate requirements and effects of recoil, weight, and power largely preclude the kind of handling that is possible with a Mannlicher-Schönauer 1903 or a Winchester 92. Practically speaking, rifles for dangerous game can be divided into two groups, one starting with the .375 H&H and ranging up to the .470 NE, and the other beginning with the .500 NE and continuing up to the .600 NE. We won't even include such monsters as the .700 H&H, or the old 4- and 8-bores. Those require rifles so heavy they are not really practical for any kind of hunting.

As I have mentioned, it is possible to build a .500 NE in a double rifle that is light enough to carry and still pleasant to shoot. The same is

true of bolt-rifle cartridges like the .458 Lott and .450 Ackley. Beyond that, when you get into the .500 Jeffery and .505 Gibbs, the rifles become both heavy and cumbersome. In the days of professional ivory hunting in Africa, hunters might have had a .577 or .600 NE for the worst contingencies, but they were carried by gunbearers while the hunter himself carried something lighter, like a .450.

Unless you are possessed of bodybuilder strength, it is not possible to carry a sixteen- or eighteen-pound rifle through rough country, hour after hour, and still have the strength to handle it quickly when you need to.

In bolt rifles, the two big cartridges that get the most attention are the .500 Jeffery and the .505 Gibbs. Factory rifles are available for both, and Norma offers both calibers in its African PH line of ammunition. There have been attempts to make even more powerful magazine-rifle cartridges. Usually these are .577 caliber, based on something like the .50 Browning machine gun case. Most of these seem to me to be merely stunts, gunmakers trying to momentarily claim the crown for "most powerful," as if that's worth anything. Wildcatters who have created some of these quickly find they will run into all kinds of ballistic obstacles, such as getting a powder slow enough to work, and which, in that great a volume, can actually be ignited by a conventional primer.

About a decade ago, I was granted the privilege of trying out a .585 GMA, which is an oversized number developed by Granite Mountain for chambering in their magnum action. It used a .577 bullet, and the case was as long as a banana. There had been repeated ignition problems with it during development. I took solid hold, braced myself, pulled the trigger, and "click." I lowered the rifle and was turning my head to say something when the rifle finally went off. It was the longest hangfire I've ever experienced. The rifle leapt skyward with me hanging on as it came over my head in an arc and ended up pointing at the rapidly parting crowd behind me. Fortunately, I didn't lose my grip so the $15,000 rifle did not end up in the gravel.

As these kinds of problems mount up, the reliability of the rifle suffers. In a rifle for dangerous game, reliability is everything. No matter how much power you have, no matter how accurate it is, no matter how heavy the bullet, if the rifle does not feed, fire, eject, feed, and fire again, shot after shot without a shadow of doubt, then you should trade it off and get something that does.

The British had by far the most experience with dangerous game all over the world. They developed rifles and cartridges for the purpose, and found that there was a practical upper limit beyond which the problems mounted up so fast that rifles quickly became useless. We talk about the .600 NE with bated breath, but it was both a late-comer and something of a curiosity. Introduced by W. J. Jeffery around 1900, only around one hundred rifles were made in total, including both doubles and single-shots. It was just too big and too heavy.

The .577 Nitro Express, on the other hand, was made in considerable numbers and used by many elephant hunters. Rifles are heavy but not totally unmanageable, recoil is tolerable in small doses, and anything a .577 NE can't do, probably can't be done. It was no one's everyday rifle, except perhaps Jimmy Sutherland, who had a pair of them. Old-time professional hunter Tony Henley told me that he once had the use of one of Sutherland's .577s for a season, and found it gave incredible penetration and stopping power. For his last years of hunting, however, Tony carried a H&H .500/.465 and considered it more than adequate for Cape buffalo and elephant.

Since interest in the big .500s for bolt rifles was rekindled, they have become available in various rifles. CZ offers both in its magnum bolt action, and Blaser even chambers its R8 straight-pull rifle for the .500 Jeffery. Former Zimbabwe PH Don Heath, when he was with Norma, told me a few years ago that .500 Jeffery ammunition outsold .505 Gibbs by a ratio of six to one. There is certainly more interest in the .500 Jeffery, probably because on paper it is the more powerful of the two and, being smaller, does not need as large an action.

No matter how I try, however, I cannot understand why anyone would buy a CZ magnum rifle in .500 Jeffery in preference to the Gibbs. You have to carry the extra weight anyway, so why not get the unassailable advantages of the .505? Personally, I prefer the Gibbs for its roomy case, lower pressures, and long neck, which grips heavy bullets under recoil better than the stubby neck of the .500. It does not have a rebated rim, with any of the real and theoretical problems that presents, so it should have both more reliable feeding and surer extraction with the Mauser extractor. And if the Gibbs requires a bigger, heavier action, and hence a heavier rifle, that is all to the good. For those so inclined, by the way, the Gibbs can be handloaded to out-perform the Jeffery, though I don't believe that is a rational activity for any sane person.

The Granite Mountain .505 Gibbs shown here represents the upper limit of hunting rifles, by our definition, in weight, size, and power. If I were going elephant hunting, I would retain a gunbearer to carry the .505 while I carried my .450 Ackley. Those professional elephant hunters of old knew what they were doing.

* * *

Schultz & Larsen Model 65DL, .358 Norma.

CHAPTER XV

A NORDIC SYMPHONY: SCHULTZ & LARSEN, NORMA ÅMOTFORS, AND PHILIP B. SHARPE

Philip B. Sharpe is one of the more interesting characters in the history of American shooting—interesting, but puzzling. He made major contributions in the fields of cartridge design and ballistics, and the two books he left behind were major works. *The Rifle in America* and *Complete Guide to Handloading* are two references that belong on the bookshelves of anyone with an interest in rifles.

Sharpe is credited with being one of the fathers of the .357 Magnum. Success has many fathers, it's true, and failure is indeed an orphan, but in Sharpe's case, his involvement with the .357 Magnum is documented. He was a personal friend of Daniel B. Wesson, who is generally regarded as the corporate figure behind the .357, and their correspondence during the 1930s was extensive. The .357 Magnum was introduced in 1935. Two years later, Sharpe published his first book, *Complete Guide to Handloading —A Treatise on Handloading for Pleasure, Economy and Utility.* This was more than a handloading manual; it was a history of gunpowder, primers, brass, military ammunition, and virtually every other snippet of arcane information that Sharpe had gathered during a lifetime of squirreling away every scrap of data available.

Yet, here's the puzzling part: Sharpe did very little big-game hunting, yet he was considered an expert on big-game rifles and cartridges. The only reference I can find to him hunting anything larger than a woodchuck is an article that

appeared in the 1952 *Gun Digest* titled "I Hunted Illegal Deer." It was about the Pennsylvania deer season in 1949. Sharpe collected a buck early and spent the rest of the week helping the game wardens in finding illegal kills. It evolved into an article about whitetail management in general. There may be more about Sharpe's hunting experience in *The American Rifleman*, for which he wrote extensively, but if so it's news to me.

Philip Burdette Sharpe was born in Portland, Maine, on May 16, 1903. Little is known about his early life, except he later said he was interested in firearms from an early age. He also stated that he had spent his life "in the service of the American shooter," and that probably sums it up. Sharpe was only thirty-two years old when the .357 Magnum appeared, and by that time he had built up an impressive pile of correspondence with gun companies, makers of reloading tools, and other "gunbugs" such as Ned Roberts, Elmer Keith, and Daniel B. Wesson.

When Sharpe was still a boy, Sir Charles Ross was in full stride, Charles Newton was getting underway, and Harry M. Pope was established as the "old master" of rifles and target shooting in America. The correspondence in Sharpe's papers (now archived in the Adams County Historical Society in Adams County, Pennsylvania) dates from 1918, when Sharpe was just fifteen years old. Obviously, guns of all kinds became a passion for him at an early age, and shaped his entire life. In this way, Sharpe is very much like contemporaries such as Jack O'Connor. Unlike O'Connor, however, Sharpe's focus was on rifles, cartridges, and ballistics rather than hunting. He knew both Charles Newton and Harry Pope personally. *Complete Guide to Handloading* was dedicated to Pope ("The Old Master") and the frontispiece is a photograph of Sharpe, resplendent in outsized sun helmet and aviator frames, conversing with Pope at Camp Perry.

Camp Perry and the world of match rifles was really Phil Sharpe's element, with a strong emphasis on military rifles and cartridges. Just one year after *Complete Guide* was published, Sharpe followed it with a massive tome (there is no other appropriate term) called *The Rifle in America*. If nothing else, these two volumes are evidence of Sharpe's workaholic nature, and represent a lifetime's accumulation of knowledge and information—a formidable accomplishment when you consider that he was then only in his mid-thirties. Both works went through several editions and many reprintings, with the last ones coming in 1953 (*Complete Guide to Handloading*, Third Edition, Second Revision with Supplement) and 1958 (*The Rifle in America*, Fourth Edition).

The US entered the Second World War on December 7, 1941, and a year later Sharpe was commissioned as a captain in the ordnance department of the army. For such a dedicated rifleman, this assignment was heaven on earth. He went to Europe as part of a team investigating German ballistics development, with the authority to poke his nose into anything that seemed interesting. During his time in Europe, he came to know many influential people in the German ammunition world, as well as the French, Danes, and Norwegians. A few years later, these contacts stood him in good stead when he undertook his last major project: development of the ultimate long-range cartridge and hunting rifle.

* * *

Philip Sharpe was outspokenly contemptuous of wildcat cartridges which, he wrote, "are born daily and die weekly." If he was to design a cartridge, it would be "a factory number." He wanted to see his name on a factory headstamp.

In 1947, newly discharged from the army, he began work on the cartridge that came to be known as the 7x61 Sharpe & Hart. That same year, he moved to Fairfield, Pennsylvania, where he purchased a house and small farm, and created his "gunbug's paradise." It included workshops, a shooting range, and a complete Potter chronograph system, as well as equipment for testing chamber pressures. The pressure-testing apparatus alone, with pressure barrels, cost $2,500, he wrote. A life member of the National Rifle Association (NRA), he was a member of its technical division from 1950 to 1955, and was a regular contributor to the *Rifleman*.

Sharpe tells the story of the development of the 7x61 S&H in the last chapter of the supplement to the final edition of *The Rifle in America*. It is a long and convoluted tale with an ending that was semi-happy at best. The 7x61 Sharpe & Hart was only a modest and fleeting success, as were Sharpe's efforts to introduce Americans to a new style of bolt-action rifle. In spite of my boyhood infatuation with both rifle and cartridge (based solely on the photos and description in *Gun Digest*) and having finally acquired one after almost fifty years of panting and drooling, it is not included in this book because, with considerable regret, it's just not one of the "great" hunting rifles of the century.

The rifle that *is* included in this book is a later development by two European companies, Norma Åmotfors (as it then was) and Schultz & Larsen, but it developed from Sharpe's work and would never have come about were it not for that.

There is really no way of telling that story without some detailed background on Philip B. Sharpe.

Sharpe created a company to go with his gunbug's paradise, called The Philip B. Sharpe Ballistics Laboratories. As he tells it, while in Europe during the war, investigating French ballistics developments in the French gunmaking centre of Saint-Étienne, he came across an early experimental French infantry cartridge dating from 1907. It was probably intended primarily as a machine gun cartridge, and never went any further because smokeless powders of the day were inadequate. In fact, of course, the Germans had the powders to make it go, as did the British (for the .280 Ross) and du Pont, in America, just a few years later. That, however, did the French no good, and the cartridge was shelved.

This French cartridge gave Sharpe the idea for a 7mm hunting round that would build on the work of everything that went before, and be available to American shooters in factory form with ammunition, brass, dies, and all the necessary paraphernalia. In partnership with his friend Richard Hart of California, Sharpe went to work developing the cartridge. He found that he could create basic brass by trimming the belt from .300 H&H brass on a lathe, shortening it, and then running it through six (*six!*) forming dies. Because this brass was rarely concentric, however, there was a high wastage rate. One day, Dick Hart suggested they simply leave the belt on, and Sharpe agreed.

Meanwhile, a friend from Sharpe's time in Europe, Amund Enger of the Swedish-Norwegian ammunition company, Norma Åmotfors, visited Sharpe in Pennsylvania and became interested in the new cartridge. He offered to manufacture brass with the 7x61 S&H headstamp, and when a few thousand rounds arrived from Sweden "work proceeded more quickly."

Sharpe later wrote that development of the cartridge took five years and cost $10,000 in out-of-pocket expenses. Exactly how this could be true is puzzling, until you consider that an acquaintance of Sharpe many years later described how he would conduct extensive testing to prove something, and then conduct the same tests all over again to prove exactly the same point all over again. This eats up time and money. Exactly what his partner, Dick Hart (Sharpe & Hart Associates) thought of this, we don't know.

Meanwhile, Amund Enger approached his friend, Niels Larsen, of Denmark's Schultz & Larsen, about producing a hunting rifle for the new cartridge. As a company, Schultz & Larsen dates from 1904, when it began as a gunsmith's shop in the town of Otterup. At first, it produced rifle barrels, and later target rifles and free pistols. Sharpe himself was introduced to Larsen after the war, when he spent a brief period as US Army liaison officer, involved in research work by the Danish Madsen company, of machine gun fame. Phil Sharpe was nothing if not well connected.

Schultz & Larsen produced two prototype rifles using a bolt action of its own design. One went to Sharpe, the other to Amund Enger. He tested it, moose hunting in Sweden, and pronounced it to be "outstanding." There then followed a three-way partnership among Norma Åmotfors of Sweden, Schultz & Larsen of Denmark, and Sharpe & Hart Associates in the US, with Phil Sharpe and Richard Hart the American importers for rifles and ammunition.

Before the rifles were actually produced, according to Sharpe, "thousands" of custom rifles had been built for his new cartridge, and "hundreds of thousands" were in use by the mid-1950s. Presumably, by hundreds of thousands, he is referring to cartridges, not rifles, because there is absolutely no way that anything remotely approaching that number of custom rifles was made. But, to hear him tell it, his cartridge was already a huge success, sweeping the shooting world, before a factory rifle was ever chambered for it. Reports from the game fields, he wrote, were arriving in such numbers they had no way of filing them, so they simply threw them away.

The first Schultz & Larsen rifle was the Model 54J ('J' for *Jaeger*, or hunter, to differentiate it from the Model 54 target rifle). This led to some confusion with dealers ordering target rifles when they really wanted hunting rifles. Sharpe soon persuaded S&L to refine their design, and come out with the Model 60, which was later replaced by the Model 65 and 65DL.

The basic Schultz & Larsen bolt action was quite different from the Mauser 98 in several ways. Sharpe the rifle expert attempted to convince his readers that it was actually superior to the Mauser 98, but history has shown this to be a dubious claim. The Model 54 had four locking lugs in a rear lock-up arrangement. This allowed a lower bolt lift, which accommodated low scope mounting. As well, since no lug raceways were required, the receiver was stiffer and stronger, and with no lug recesses required either, the barrel could be screwed into the receiver another quarter-inch for additional stability. Altogether, it would be, in theory, stronger, safer, and more accurate than a Mauser 98. Sharpe dismissed the idea that the bolt could compress under high pressure, allowing cartridge cases to expand unduly, and wrote that after the firing of "thousands of rounds," nothing resembling that had ever occurred.

In spite of Sharpe's claims, this became an area of considerable conjecture among shooting writers, with some insisting it was a problem and others dismissing it completely. In 1969, long after Sharpe's death and with the Schultz & Larsen

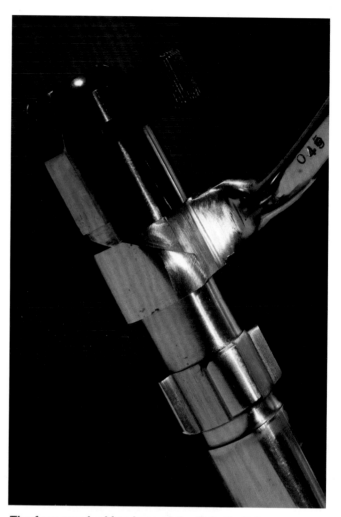

The four rear locking lugs of the Schultz & Larsen provide a very strong, and also very smooth, action.

rifles now being imported by Fessler, offered in a dozen different calibers, a test rifle was sent to the H. P. White Laboratory to settle the matter once and for all. The rifle was the recently introduced Model 68DL, in .30-06. White was unassailably objective, its only allegiance being to the truth. It reported on the results of two tests, one with the .30-06 case filled to the brim with IMR 3031 and generating measured chamber pressure of 120,000 pounds per square inch (psi). When this failed to cause a problem, the laboratory switched to a full load of IMR 4198 and pressure of 129,000 psi. While the bolt was so stiff that forcing it open bent the bolt handle, no other damage was found. The cartridge case wanted to flow into any available crack, but since these were so few it really had nowhere to go. "The action maintained its minimum headspace," the lab reported.

This would seem to put the matter to rest, but there is a hidden caveat. The lab reported no *permanent* increase in headspace. But what about compressing the bolt temporarily, and allowing undue case stretching? My own experience, with a Model 65DL in 7x61 S&H, is that with

The last iteration of the Schultz & Larsen rifles of the 1960s was the Model 68DL. Tested by the H. P. White Laboratory to pressures of 129,000 psi, no problem was found beyond an exceedingly stiff bolt lift.

full-power, high-pressure loads, this is exactly what can happen. The result is not an increase in headspace in the rifle, but in cartridge cases that will not rechamber easily even after the fullest of full-length resizing. With some of these cases, it's merely difficult to close the bolt, while others refuse to chamber altogether. The solution is to screw the sizing die in to the point where the handle of the press stops, then force the handle down and push the case in beyond maximum. This sounds impossible, and does your dies and press no good, but it does work. Another solution, of course, is to use more sensible loads, and that is the one I finally adopted. I don't like stiff bolts, either opening or closing.

Another major difference between the Schultz & Larsen and other bolt actions is that, instead of being open along the top of the receiver between bridge and ring, the receiver is one long shroud with an oval opening on the right for an ejection port. This feature added to stiffness, and hence potential accuracy. Such shrouds, either integral or bolt-on, later became a standard feature on a wide variety of custom benchrest actions. Schultz & Larsen also offered a single-shot version of the action for building target and benchrest rifles.

In the Model 60, S&L built into their bolts a mechanism for very quick and easy takedown. The shroud has a small pin on the left side. With the safety in the middle position, the bolt is withdrawn, the pin moved along its slot, and the shroud turned clockwise 30 degrees. The shroud, spring, and striker mechanism, as a unit, is then pulled out of the body of the bolt. This is not wildly different than the Mauser 98, except in ease and convenience. Complete takedown is accomplished by compressing the firing mechanism with the nose of the striker on a block of wood, again similar to the 98. This is a very worthwhile feature in any rifle likely to be used in bad or very cold weather. The takedown method changed slightly with later models, with the safety left in the "fire" position as the bolt was dismantled and reassembled.

* * *

Throughout his works, Philip Sharpe never missed an opportunity to criticize wildcatters for their extravagant claims for their creations, so it's ironic that his 7x61 S&H foundered, among other reasons, because he then did exactly the same thing. Its advertised ballistics are indelibly branded in my memory: a 160-grain bullet at 3,100 fps. The cartridge never—*never*—delivered this performance, although anyone who has hunted with any of the 7mm magnums will agree that it would have been fantastic. Instead, it was fantasy.

In the 1950s, chronographs were few, far between, and expensive, and readers of shooting magazines tended to believe what they were told. Since that was also the heyday of the pursuit of higher and higher velocities, they were confronted monthly with claims for cartridges that were never proven. The only plausible explanation for Sharpe's claims is that the velocity was measured by Norma in the usual (at that time) 28- or 30-inch pressure barrel, just as Norma's 6.5x55 ammunition was tested in the old military 28-inch Mauser Model 96 barrel, but delivered nothing like that velocity in the usual 22- or 24-inch sporting barrel. Regardless of how it came about, the 7x61 S&H bullet normally departed the muzzle at around 2,950 fps—a far cry from 3,100 fps.

An odd thing, too, is that Sharpe said development took five years and cost him $10,000. Coincidentally, Ned Roberts claimed that development of the .257 Roberts cartridge in the 1930s cost $10,000. Like Sharpe, Roberts was given to

testing and re-testing, but really: ten thousand Depression-era dollars? The .257 Roberts (and its forerunner, the .25 Roberts) is merely the 7x57 necked down. Roberts apparently fiddled endlessly with the shoulder angle and neck length, and you can certainly run up expenses having rifles endlessly rebarreled, but even so, that barely dents my disbelief.

In Sharpe's case, the 7x61 S&H cartridge which he finally adopted resembles, physically, nothing so much as the .275 Belted Magnum (H&H), introduced in 1911. Ballistically, it duplicates the .280 Ross (1908). To my teenage eyes, the 7x61 S&H was about the sexiest cartridge in the world, with its belted case, slight taper, and sharp shoulder. Truth to tell, my heart still beats a little faster when I look at one. In spite of not living up to its ballistic billing, however, it could

The 7x61 Sharpe & Hart (left) resembles the much earlier .275 H&H, albeit in a slightly smaller case. The puzzle is, where did Phil Sharpe spend $10,000 in its development?

have and should have been a success. There was nothing whatever wrong with the performance it did deliver, and it was used extensively by hunters in Canada, where it became very popular in Alberta, British Columbia, and the Yukon.

When the Schultz & Larsen rifle sprang upon the scene in America, it was styled after the Weatherby, and priced accordingly. Not surprisingly, its main competition was the high-priced Weatherby, and so anyone in love with velocity, faced with a choice between the 7x61 S&H and the Weatherby in 7mm Weatherby Magnum, would naturally choose the Weatherby because of its higher velocity. Also, Sharpe was not the only cartridge developer working with the 7mm. There were wildcat competitors like the .280 Dubiel, developed by John Dubiel by necking down and blowing out the .300 H&H. Even with the powders of the day, the .280 Dubiel shaded the 7x61 by a substantial margin.

These were just some of the headwinds faced by Sharpe and his baby when, in 1957, he suffered his first heart attack. His work slowed drastically at that point. Four years later, on the morning of January 24, 1961, he suffered a second heart attack and died that afternoon.

To all intents and purposes, the 7x61 died with him. A year later, Remington hammered the final nail in the coffin when it introduced both the Model 700 rifle and the wildly successful 7mm Remington Magnum. The Model 700 was cheaper by far than the Schultz & Larsen, the 7mm Remington Magnum delivered demonstrably better performance than the 7x61 S&H, and both rifle and ammunition were American made. Was the Remington round as sexy as the 7x61? Not to my eye, then or now. You never completely grow out of a teenage love affair.

* * *

In 2007, I fulfilled my lifelong dream and acquired a Schultz & Larsen Model 65DL in 7x61 Sharpe & Hart. The rifle was in Canada, and I handed it over to Edwin von Atzigen, my Swiss-Canadian gunmaking and gun-restoring wizard. He refinished the stock in oil, installed a new recoil pad, mounted a scope, and I took the rifle on a backpack hunting trip in the mountains of the Yukon. I had a grizzly tag, but saw nothing, shot nothing, and carried that rifle up and down mountains for eight days. Later that year, I took it to Africa and hunted bushbuck in the riverine bush of the Limpopo. Over the next few years, I shot the rifle quite a bit. Norma still made brass for the 7x61, although by that time it had undergone a strange metamorphosis.

Philip Sharpe was, if not obsessed, then at least unduly preoccupied with case strength. The dimensions he specified for the 7x61 had a thicker base, web, and case walls than Norma subsequently believed necessary. In the 1970s, after Sharpe's death and with sales of the 7x61 lagging, they undertook to redesign the cartridge internally. It would have the same external dimensions, and be loaded to the same maximum pressures, but with an additional four or five grains of capacity, it could squeeze out one hundred or more additional feet per second. The redesigned case was designated the Super 7x61. Norma did not finally abandon the 7x61 until around 2010, and there is no loading data provided for it in the Norma handloading manual published in 2013.

Although almost forgotten today, the 7x61 Sharpe & Hart is a very fine cartridge. Lyman loading manual #45, which appeared in 1970, notes that "The 7x61mm proved to be one of the most efficient cartridges we tested. Accuracy was good and velocities were extremely uniform. Compared to other magnum cases, this cartridge

Schultz & Larsen Model 65DL in 7x61 Sharpe & Hart, refurbished and renovated by Edwin von Atzigen into a very elegant rifle. The riflescope is a Swarovski Habicht 3-10x42. The rifle will usually match my Kenny Jarrett custom-made .257 Weatherby.

produced very high velocities with minimum amounts of powder." Using the original S&H case, a 150-grain bullet, and IMR 4350, Lyman was able to get velocities over 3,100 fps from a 24-inch barrel, and more than 3,000 fps with a 165-grain. That may not match Sharpe's original claims, or even quite measure up to the 7mm Remington Magnum, but it shades the .280 Remington by a good margin.

As for accuracy, my Schultz & Larsen Model 65DL in 7x61 S&H—a factory rifle in every technical sense—will shoot right along with my Kenny Jarrett .257 Weatherby at 300 yards. Sometimes the Jarrett wins, sometimes the Schultz & Larsen. One day, I threw a Weatherby Mark V safari-grade custom .270 Weatherby into the fray, and it came out third in every contest. No one can ever say Schultz & Larsen did not know how to make an accurate rifle. What's more, they were able to build in match-level accuracy without compromising the rifle's hunting qualities.

* * *

Their involvement with Philip Sharpe drew both Schultz & Larsen and Norma Åmotfors into the North American market, and after his death both attempted to stay. Coincidentally, perhaps, both were already involved through a mutual connection

with Roy Weatherby in California. Norma began producing ammunition in the Weatherby magnums in 1953, while Schultz & Larsen provided actions for the first Weatherbys built for the massive .378 Weatherby. Roy Weatherby stopped using Schultz & Larsen actions when he introduced his Mark V in 1958, but Norma continues to produce Weatherby ammunition to this day.

Norma was founded in 1902 by the three Enger brothers of Norway. Looking for a place to establish a manufacturing company to produce the new smokeless ammunition, Lars Enger traveled by train from Norway into Sweden, eventually finding what he was looking for in the small town of Åmotfors. The result was the company "Norma Åmotfors," and so it remained for many years. It's the only munitions company named after an opera. Lars Enger was a great opera fan, and loved Vincenzo Bellini's *Norma*. At a loss for a company name, it became Norma. Well, why not?

Sweden is a great hunting country, a nation of riflemen just as much as the US used to be. This is true of all the Scandinavian countries, which also produce serious target shooters. Both hunting and match rifles have been manufactured in Sweden, Denmark, and Finland, and Norma is the region's hometown ammunition company. Unlike others which specialize in either hunting or match ammunition and bullets, Norma devotes considerable effort to both. Until the early 1950s, the Norma name was almost unknown in North America, but the efforts of Roy Weatherby and Phil Sharpe changed that. Knowing the Americans were the key to prosperity in the years to come, with Europe rebuilding after the war, cracking the American market became a priority for Norma.

Part of Norma's drive into the American market was its "Gunbug's Guide" of handloading data, first published in 1957. In 1959, it introduced the .358 Norma Magnum, and followed it a year later with the .308 Norma Magnum. Both cartridges used exactly the same short belted case as the .458 Winchester, and the .264 and .338

Original promotional material for the .358 Norma. It lives up to its billing in every way.

Winchester Magnums. The final member of that family was the 7mm Remington, which came a little later.

Norma's .358 and .308 magnums were added to Schultz & Larsen's lineup in the Model 65DL. The .308 Norma was also offered in the Browning High Power, made in Belgium on the FN Supreme action, and while Browning listed the .358 Norma as well, it seems none were ever produced. Husqvarna, the Swedish riflemaker, produced some Mauser-actioned .358 Norma rifles, and in the early 1970s the Carl Gustav bolt action from Sweden was listed in .358 Norma. Alas, no American manufacturer ever chambered it. If one had, its history would have been substantially different. As it was, the cartridge was released "to the trade" as the British say, with Norma supplying brass, loading data, and even chambering reamers for gunsmiths. Many custom rifles were built in .358 Norma, but a cartridge cannot thrive on custom chamberings alone.

The .358 Norma factory load was a 250-grain bullet at 2,790 fps. It was designed by Nils Kvale, a well-known ballistician, and was intended to duplicate the performance of the old .35 Newton. It was—and is—an excellent big-game cartridge. It will largely duplicate the performance of both the smaller .338 Winchester Magnum, which arrived on the scene a year earlier, and the larger .375 H&H, and it offers some advantages over both. When it was introduced, there were many more .358-caliber bullets available than either .338 or .375, and that is still pretty much the case. This makes the .358 Norma more versatile than either of the others. It can be loaded down with lighter bullets far more easily than can the .375, and loaded up with heavier bullets easier than the .338. The .338 Winchester Magnum was able to supplant the .375 H&H in the hearts of Alaska bear guides because both rifles and

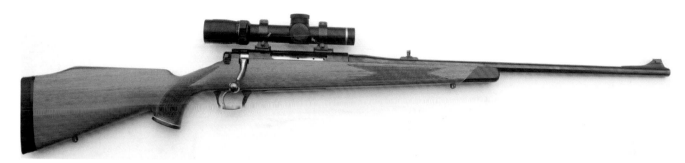

Schultz & Larsen Model 65DL, in .358 Norma, wearing a Leupold VX-7 1.5-6x24 in quick-detachable Talley mounts.

ammunition were cheaper, and there is no reason the .358 could not have done the same had suitable rifles been available. As it was, oddly enough, the .358 Norma in the original Schultz & Larsen rifles developed a substantial following in Canada's Yukon Territory, next door to Alaska, and home to both big grizzlies and the giant Alaska-Yukon moose.

* * *

Schultz & Larsen produced a succession of sporting rifles for the American market, initially under

The .358 Norma was made for the mountains of Alaska and the Yukon.

the guidance of Phil Sharpe. The Model 54J was oversized, ungainly, and homely bordering on ugly. Its in-line magazine gave it a deep belly combined with a sharply up-sloping forend. It had a shotgun-style trigger guard which looks lovely on a Purdey, but not on most rifles (the Mannlicher-Schönauer being a notable exception). Sharpe persuaded them to switch to a staggered-column box magazine, which provided the same capacity without the belly, as well as to emulate the emerging California look that distinguished the Weatherby rifles from the more conservative Winchesters and Brownings. This was no problem for Schultz & Larsen, since they had been combining with Sako to produce early Weatherby rifles and knew the look very well. According to Sharpe, the 54J was available in several calibers other than 7x61 S&H. The last batch was built in late 1956, and arrived in America in early 1957.

The next Schultz & Larsen was the Model 60 which, despite the nomenclature, was unveiled in early 1958. Sharpe describes the differences between the 54J and 60 in considerable detail. A major change was the safety. In the 54J, it had two positions only, and when it was "on" it locked the sear, trigger, and bolt. The Model 60 safety was a three-position wing, similar to the Winchester Model 70, with a central position in which the sear and trigger were locked but the bolt could be cycled to unload. Both the receiver and bolt were slightly longer than in the 54J, to improve feeding. It was initially available only in 7x61 S&H and, provided sales held up, "would stay that way."

In spite of Sharpe's description of the Model 60, according to which it was nigh perfect, it was followed quickly by the Model 65 and then the 65DL. In the 1962 Gun Digest, the Model 65 is listed as a "Sharpe & Hart" rifle, not a Schultz & Larsen. Also, it is offered in both 7x61 S&H and the "new" .358 Norma Magnum.

In the spring of 1963, the Model 65 was replaced by the 65DL, and testing was reported by Ken Waters in the 1964 Gun Digest. It was in its newest chambering, .308 Norma Magnum. "The rifle itself is a beauty," Waters wrote, "with all the smooth working, perfect functioning and superb fitting and finishing that bespeak careful, skilled craftsmanship."

As listed in the "Foreign Rifles" section of the 1965 Gun Digest, the 65DL was a racy number with a Weatherby-style stock, available in 7x61 S&H, .308 Norma, and .358 Norma. It is listed at $245 compared with a Weatherby Mark V at $285. A standard Winchester Model 70 was $139.95. Big difference.

One major difference between the 65 and 65DL was the safety. On the 65, it was a forward-and-back three-position wing, like the early Winchester Model 70; on the 65DL, it became an up-and-down wing, similar to the Buehler used in Mauser 98 conversions. Again, it was—supposedly!—three-position, with a middle position that allowed the bolt to be opened while the trigger and sear were locked. It's hard to be certain what the thinking was, but in the earlier version it was possible to accidentally move the safety while carrying the rifle on the shoulder (I have done that with Dakota rifles) while the newer version tucked the wing up under the scope where it was more protected and less prone to accidental movement.

But now here is a very odd thing: I have two Model 65DLs—one in 7x61 S&H, the other in .358 Norma. The .358 has a three-position safety, while the 7x61 S&H, outwardly identical in every way, is only two-position. When the bolts are dismantled, there are visible differences in the shape of the wing inside the shroud. Nor are they dismantled as Sharpe describes, in detail, for the Model 60. The .358 Norma has an earlier serial number (107xx vs. 110xx). Was this a deliberate difference between the two calibers? Did Schultz & Larsen change the design in mid-stream for all 65DLs because of some difficulty with three-position safeties?

Trying to get to the bottom of this, I contacted two friends who also own Model 65DLs, both in .308 Norma. Both have serial numbers *earlier* than my .358, yet both have two-position safeties. How does one explain that? I cannot.

It would appear the company never resolved its problem with safeties, their shape, and their function. This is not to suggest the rifles are not safe, or the safety catches themselves do not do their job, simply that S&L never finalized a foolproof design that functioned to their own satisfaction. Apparently, they gave up on three-position safeties sometime during the 65DL production run, then switched to a forward-rocking, two-position design in the 68DL.

Along the way, there were Schultz & Larsen models listed as M61 and M62, but mostly these interim designs were target rifles. Since many were centerfires intended for 300-meter matches and the like, there is considerable confusion about them.

The last Schultz & Larsen rifle to be offered to Americans was the Model 68DL, similar to the 65DL except for the safety and the floorplate release. The floorplate release became a button similar to the Model 70 and the Weatherby Mark V. It was offered in a wide variety of cartridges in addition to the original three. The new ones included the 7mm Remington Magnum, the cartridge which more than any other consigned the 7x61 S&H to oblivion. It was listed for the last time in the 1972 *Gun Digest*, at $485, or $585 in .458 Winchester—serious money when a comparable Weatherby Mark V then listed for only $339.95. If the Schultz & Larsen was a tough

sell before, it was doubly so now. The 1971 dollar devaluation and the inflation that followed wrought havoc with all European firearms, and the Schultz & Larsen rifles disappeared from the American scene. Contrary to popular belief, Schultz & Larsen itself did not disappear—at least, not forever. The company did shut down for a while, its five rifling machines were purchased by an American company, and one of them even ended up in the shop of Classic Barrel and Gunworks (Danny Pedersen, Prop.) in Prescott, Arizona. Today, a reconstituted Schulz & Larsen company is in business in Europe, but its rifles bear little resemblance to the old ones, and they are not imported to the US.

An interesting sidelight comes from the 2013 edition of the Norma reloading handbook. In it, there is a photo of an employee in the 1970s holding what appears to be a Schultz & Larsen 65DL. It is identified as "The Norma Rifle," was chambered in the three original cartridges (7x61, .308 N., .358 N.) and, according to the book, was designed by Schultz & Larsen for Norma, which then marketed it in Europe. No mention whatever of Phil Sharpe.

* * *

My experience with my 7x61 S&H 65DL led me into a rather ill-advised splurge for Schultz & Larsen rifles, including a .308 Norma and a 68DL in 7mm Remington Magnum, but I parted with those two soon after. Hunting in the Yukon in 2008, I developed a yearning for one in .358 Norma, but alas, rifles in that chambering are hard to come by. Their owners generally refuse to part with them. Then, around 2012, one came along, offered for sale by an Alaskan hunter who wanted to move on (not up) to a lever-action rifle in one of the short .50s. Why he felt this would be in any way superior to the .358 Norma beats me, but I wasn't about to argue. The rifle was equipped with both iron sights and a Schmidt & Bender scope in a detachable mount. I bought the rifle, sold the scope, and ended up with a lovely Model 65DL in .358 Norma for about $600. As bargains go, you can't beat that.

This is the rifle whose photo appears at the head of this chapter and which earned its way into this book on sheer merit.

Three generations of gun writers have sung the praises of the .358 Norma, all to no avail. That hardly makes it unique. Other great cartridges have been commercial also-rans, ignored by both manufacturers and the public. The fact, however, that the .358 Norma still has adherents, and that loading data is still published in current loading manuals, tells you a lot. There may not be many .358 Norma devotees, relatively speaking, but they are faithful. I am told that those who live in the Yukon are only now giving up their .358 Norma rifles in favor of newer ones because brass is hard to get and they can buy cheap, weather-proof rifles in chamberings like the .325 Federal.

My one and only experience killing big game with the .358 Norma was a custom Mauser 98 with which I hunted nilgai in Texas in 1989. The nilgai, or blue bull, is a big animal, with a reputation of being hard to put down. Mine dropped in his tracks at about ninety yards when the 250-grain Trophy Bonded Bear Claw went in behind his shoulder and struck the opposite shoulder from the inside. Our guide said it was the only time he'd seen such a thing—but then, how often do they say that? The next day, my hunting pal, using an 8mm Remington Magnum, put three bullets (also Bear Claws) into a nilgai and we never found him.

Unfortunately, Norma's original load of a 250-grain semi-spitzer soft-nosed bullet was simply not very good. It was too frangible, especially when it hit an animal at close range. After my nilgai was dead, and in the interests of science, I put one factory round into it, along with several other handloaded bullets of different types. The 250-grain Norma bullet was recovered in small shards, and not many of those. In the years since, Norma bullets have improved dramatically, and more recent .358 Norma ammunition performs very well. Nosler makes both a 225-grain and 250-grain Partition, which are fantastic bullets for any .358-caliber rifle except the .35 Remington. Woodleigh makes .358s in weights up to 310 grains; at the other end, Speer makes a 180-grain flat-nosed bullet which, loaded in the .358 Norma, makes it the equal of the .30-06 for longer ranges on lighter game.

Another virtue of the .358 Norma is that you can load cast and jacketed bullets intended for the .357 Magnum, using powders like SR-4759, for light practice loads that allow you to shoot thirty or forty rounds at steel plates without needing new bridgework. For that matter, though, it should be noted that the .358 Norma, even in its heavy loads, seems to have relatively mild recoil. There is a good variety of old bullet moulds for .358-caliber bullets, including quite heavy ones, which allows another practice dimension as well as possibilities for hunting smaller game. Or, you can concoct light-game loads using 200-grain round-nosed bullets intended for the .35 Remington.

The old Schultz & Larsen stocks closely resembled Weatherby's California-style from the same period. Those were somewhat outlandish in appearance, but ergonomically excellent; this may not be fashionable to say, but it's true, and it applies equally to the Schultz & Larsens. They were somewhat toned down compared to the Weatherby, but had the same virtues: The triangular forend is slim and easily gripped by the lead hand, while the wrist is slim. The Monte Carlo comb positions the eye right in line with a low-mounted scope. Generally, the walnut grain is pleasing but not extravagant. The forend tip and grip cap are of rosewood, like the Weatherby, and replete with white-line spacers, but I have found that when you get rid of the ventilated pad and its white line, the remaining ones on forend and grip cap are not all that displeasing. In fact, they're almost endearing, reminding one of a less purist era.

One has to feel sorry for the Europeans in that age, when Europe's economy was barely back on its feet after the Second World War, and its armaments industries were either crippled or struggling to get back to sporting-rifle production. The post-war American appetite for rifles and shotguns was almost insatiable—a market begging to be filled—and the Belgians, Danes, Austrians, and Germans did their damnedest to fill it. It seems their importers told them Americans wanted the Weatherby look, and they did their best, probably with their tongues clenched firmly between their teeth. Some were mildly successful, others less so. Some artifacts from that era that appear on the market look like tarnished courtesans in the twilight of their careers. It makes one regret they did not apply their undoubted quality of workmanship to something more tasteful. The thing is, the tasteful European stuff was criticized at the time as being old-fashioned, and it mostly didn't sell all that well either.

One area in which manufacturers like Steyr-Mannlicher and Schultz & Larsen were never criticized was their engineering and quality of metal work. If anything, the Schultz & Larsen with its four rear locking lugs and cylindrical bolt is even smoother than the legendary Mannlicher-Schönauer. It has three gas-escape ports in the bolt (a feature later adopted by Weatherby on the Mark V) as well as a solid shroud to protect

against punctured primers and escaping gases. There is a cocking indicator you can both see and feel. The trigger pulls on my two Schultz & Larsen rifles are as crisp as you would expect from one of the world's foremost makers of target rifles.

The Schultz & Larsen is roundly criticized for its ejection port in the otherwise solid cylinder of its receiver. It is, they howl, impossible to load the magazine because you cannot get your thumb through the opening to press the cartridges down. This is very true, except for one thing: *It was never intended to be loaded that way.* If you want a round in the chamber and a

The S&L 65DL action is cylindrical. The ejection port is there for one reason—to eject cases. The magazine is loaded from the bottom, with the floorplate open.

full mag, you drop a round through the loading port, close the bolt, apply the safety, then turn the rifle over, open the floorplate, and drop in three more rounds. It matters not whether they go in left-right-left, or right-left-right, just so long as they're staggered. The follower is ambidextrous and will accommodate either. The floorplate, follower, and spring are designed in such a way that they guide themselves into position, and all you have to do is snap it shut. Try doing that with a Mauser 98, and good luck to you.

My .358 Norma weighs 8 lbs. 4 oz., naked—unloaded, devoid of scope or sling—and a touch over ten pounds dressed to kill. Like most bolt actions of its class, remove the scope and suddenly the rifle feels completely different. Lighter, handier, more agile, more alive. Even with its 24-inch barrel, it has that indefinable something that you want in a rifle that might save your life in the thick brush. Its iron sights are very basic, just a folding rear leaf combined with a bead on a ramp with no shroud. The rifle did not come from the factory this way, being one of the very first factory rifles intended for a scope and equipped with no iron sights at all. Someone who owned it before me obviously knew his stuff.

To hark back to references earlier in this book, it is notable that the men involved in designing and building the Schultz & Larsen rifles were all big-game hunters. They knew from experience how to build an accurate target rifle, but they also knew what was needed in a hunting rifle, and how to combine the two. It is unfortunate that events conspired against them, limiting both its acceptance in the American market, and precipitating its premature departure.

* * *

Philip B. Sharpe was only fifty-seven years old when he died, young even for that era of heavy smoking, hard drinking, and late nights. But there is no denying that he packed a lot into those fifty-seven years, and he left an enviable legacy. Aside from his two books, which are historically invaluable, there is the .357 Magnum, one of the great cartridge success stories of any age. The 7x61 S&H may be almost forgotten today, but there is a strong case to be made that, had he not promoted the Big Seven to the American shooting world as vigorously as he did, the 7mm Remington Magnum might never have seen the light of day. At the very least, he hurried it along. He also helped to bring both Norma and Schultz & Larsen to America, and today Norma (now a subsidiary of RUAG, the giant European munitions, aerospace, and defense conglomerate) is a fixture in the American market. For those of us with obscure European calibers, Norma is a vital source of brass, and its "African PH" line of ammunition was, and is, a godsend for aficionados of big cartridges like the .500 Jeffery and .505 Gibbs.

Sharpe's goal with the 7x61 S&H cartridge and the successive Schultz & Larsen rifles was to create the ultimate big-game hunting rifle. By any measure, no matter how sympathetic, he never succeeded in that. In fact, the whole venture could be termed a failure—just another stepping stone to modern rifles, such as the Ross and the Newton.

In the .358 Norma such as I have, however, Schultz & Larsen created something very close to the ideal moose and grizzly combination. With its 24-inch barrel, three-position safety, detachable scope, and very ergonomic stock, there is very little about it I would want to change. It's no wonder the moose hunters of the Yukon clung to theirs as long as they did. And who do they have to thank? Philip B. Sharpe.

The German claw mount, properly fastened and with the scope low, comes as close to perfection as any.

CHAPTER XVI

SCOPES AND MOUNTS

The invention and perfecting of the telescopic sight was truly one of the great advances in riflery, but it was not without cost. Scopes add to the weight of a rifle, they increase bulk and make it more awkward to carry, and they slow down reaction time when a quick shot is needed. Older scopes fogged up in rain and cold, and any scope can go off zero with no warning or indication that anything is wrong until you miss an easy shot.

For riflemakers, scopes added the problem of how and where to mount them, as well as how to make the rifle's mechanism function around them. Some rifles never could be adapted very well—the Winchester 94 is probably the best-known example—while others presented chronic difficulties in one respect or another.

Although scopes were used on long-range rifles as far back as the Civil War, and by Lt. Col. David Davidson in India thirty years before that, it was a century before they came into mainstream use. Early scopes were long, heavy, and relatively fragile. Generally, they were seen only as complementing open sights, not as the main sighting equipment. European rifles before 1914 favored detachable scope mounts that allowed the hunter to carry the scope in a case, and install it on the rifle only when it was needed, or as circumstances warranted. For everyday use, the rifle had iron sights.

In America, it took even longer for the hunting riflescope to make its appearance, and when it did, it was usually German- or Austrian-made.

It was not until the bolt action displaced the lever rifle as the favorite for hunting that scopes really became popular.

Because of the way scopes were used in Europe, gunsmiths developed detachable mounts, with the claw mount being the most common. Claw mounts come in many shapes, sizes, and configurations, and from the beginning were a custom feature that did not lend itself to mass production. Essentially, there are two sets of claws, one on each scope ring, and they snap into recesses in the bases which are attached to the receiver bridge, ring, or even out on the barrel. One set of claws has a spring-loaded latch that snaps into place as they are pushed home.

Claw mounts can be very exact or very sloppy. The steel can be properly hardened or left soft, allowing excessive wear and, eventually, loss of accuracy. The Teutons being Teutons, no compli-

Claw mount on early Mannlicher rifle. The claws, front and back, fit into recesses in the bases. Painfully simple, but extremely good.

cated variation was too outlandish. In addition to having a mount that allowed the scope to be removed, some gunmakers liked to have a mount that also allowed the use of the iron sights without removing the scope. They mounted them very high, with tunnels through the bases through which the shooter could line up the iron sights. This can be traced to an innate distrust of glass.

The Pachmayr Lo-Swing mount, on a Mannlicher-Schönauer Model 1956.

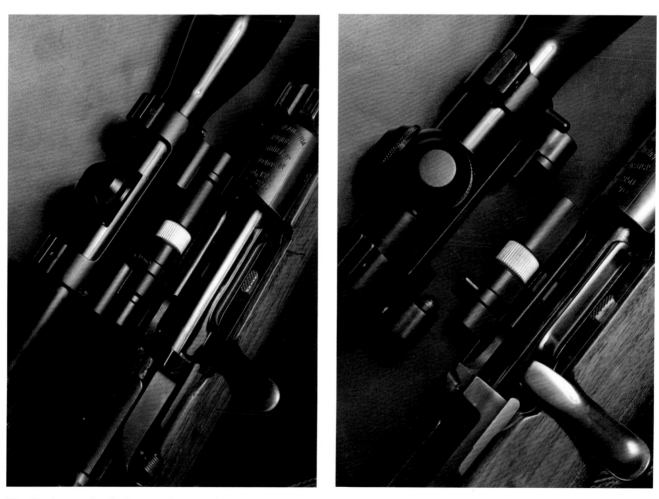

The Pachmayr Lo-Swing can be rotated out of the way to allow the use of iron sights, or removed completely. This Mannlicher-Schönauer Model 1950 was originally fitted with a claw mount (the front base is visible). Either the scope and rings were lost somewhere along the line or the owner wanted to use a more modern scope.

Most of us, when we think "glass," subconsciously think "break." Because glass is an integral part of a scope, hunters were afraid it would shatter, crack, fog up, or otherwise malfunction, and insisted on a back-up system. American hunters had similar fears, although they did not go to the same lengths to allow for any eventuality. It is no accident that some of the custom side mounts made in the USA, such as the Jaeger and the Pachmayr Lo-Swing, were designed by German gunsmiths.

This is not intended to be a history of rifle-scopes and scope mounts, only to show how scopes can improve or detract from a good hunting rifle. What we have to remember is that when we put a scope on a rifle, we are essentially taking two mechanisms and bolting them together. It can be done in such a way that it's either a net gain or a net loss, depending on whether the two mechanisms complement each other. Some rifle and scope combinations I've seen resemble a farm tractor with a Rolls-Royce Merlin bolted onto its chassis, not only rendering it useless for its original purpose, but for any purpose whatsoever aside from being a curiosity.

In the modern age of riflescopes that are wondrous optical instruments, the practice of "over-scoping" is almost epidemic, but it's not a new phenomenon. In the 1960s, hunters would decide to scope their trusty Winchester 94, in the admirable but admittedly limited .30-30, and contrive some mount that would let them put a big 3-9X variable scope on it. No .30-30 ever made benefits demonstrably from having a nine-power scope. By adding it, they made their rifles heavier, awkward, and much more difficult to carry. At three-power, they may have gained a sighting advantage within the .30-30's practical range, but that's where it ended.

There is a tendency among teenage boys and newcomers to the shooting game which has been noted by several generations of gun writers. It bears repeating for the simple reason that the phenomenon keeps resurfacing with every new influx of shooters. This tendency is a desire to allow for every eventuality by providing the maximum in versatility in rifle, sighting equipment, and even caliber. Complicated gizmos appeal to those who have done little hunting but are fond of planning, in theory, the perfect rifle. For those who have climbed mountains, hunkered down in long grass, and gone into the bush after a wounded animal, the qualities that appeal are simplicity and reliability.

Let's look at a hypothetical case of one of these rifles as imagined by a gun-struck teenager. Actually, it is not entirely hypothetical, since about thirty years ago I received a seven-page, typewritten letter from a boy outlining his thoughts on the matter, and I realized to my horror that they reflected my own attitude when I was his age. Since the possible variations and permutations are almost endless, down to and including interchangeable barrels, bolts, and magazines, for the purposes of this lesson in horror stories we will just stick to the sighting equipment. Here goes.

The rifle, a .300-.338 Thunderstruck Super-Ultra Magnum, will have the usual open sights, but the front sight will have a folding "moon" sight for dangerous game in low light. There will be a standing leaf on the barrel, with four folding leaves for ranges from fifty to five hundred yards. We will add a detachable aperture sight on the receiver which, when not in use, will be stored in a tiny compartment accessed through the pistol grip cap. The scope will be fitted in a detachable mount, but the rings will have tunnels bored through so we can use the iron sights without removing the scope. Since the scope can be removed, however, it allows us to get three different scopes with suitable rings. We can then choose which scope to mount depending on what and where we are hunting.

Sound feasible? Actually, it's a nightmare.

It would be interesting to know, of all the guys with detachable mounts and iron sights, exactly how many have actually sighted in the iron sights with the same ammunition for which the scope is set. If I had to guess, I would say it would be 10 percent or less—possibly *much* less. I believe this because, more than once, I have found myself leaving for a trip with a scope-sighted rifle and carefully handloaded ammunition, only to realize that I have not taken the scope off and checked where that ammunition prints with the iron sights. It's one of those things that always gets left to the last minute, if you think about it at all, and generally never gets done. In the case of a dangerous-game rifle, which is where iron sights are most likely to be used in today's world, this is a frightening thought.

Even something as seemingly simple as making sure your variable scope prints to the same point of impact, regardless of power setting, seems to find itself on the "forgotten" list. This is not as much of a problem today as it was with the first variables, but it still happens and should still be checked. At the very least, knowing that your scope is dead on at all settings will increase your confidence, and reduce the chances of an attack of jitters when a big bull steps out of the bushes.

A few years ago, I was on a hunt for driven big game in Germany, as the guest of Zeiss, the optics giant. There were about forty of us altogether, from a dozen countries, and all very experienced big-game hunters. We were provided with new Sauer 404 rifles in .30-06, fitted with the latest 30mm, 2.8-20x56 scopes. As an experiment, at the end of the hunt when the rifles were being gathered up to return to the factory, I did an informal check of all the power settings on those scopes. With one exception, they were set from 2.8X to 4X; the exception was one set at 5X. I made a point of asking the two most successful hunters there, who were from Norway and Denmark, what power settings they had used. Both shrugged and said, "Something low. I don't know exactly."

That is a big, heavy scope. Optically magnificent, of course, but for the hunting we were doing it was unnecessary. In fact, it added so much weight to those Sauer rifles with their sexy but awkward thumbhole carbon-fiber stocks, that they were not easy to handle in the small, closed-in stands. In driven hunting, the key is to be ready to shoot at any second, and often at a fast-moving target. Those scopes, made for very deliberate long-range shooting, were actually a

A German EAW side mount on a Mannlicher-Schönauer Model 1956. The scope is detachable, and sits very high to allow space for the bolt to clear. The unique cheekpiece of the Model 1956 allows the eye to slide up or down comfortably to accommodate either the scope or open sights.

liability. At the time, I thought to myself that, if I were outfitting this crowd, I would give them light .308 Winchesters with a 2-7X or 1.5-6X, one-inch scope. That pretty much describes the favorite hunting rifle of my friend Jørund Lien, from Norway. We have hunted together in Sweden, Poland, and Germany, and he is one of the best hunters I've ever seen. He does a lot of driven shooting, as well as stalking in the Norwegian Alps, and uses a light, short-barreled .308 Winchester fitted with a low-power variable.

There are two factors at work in what I perceive as this epidemic of over-scoping. One is lack of experience on the part of many shooters, who believe that more and bigger is always better; the other is the relentless dick-measuring contest that takes place constantly on rifle ranges. When you get a new rifle, the first place anyone will see it is at the range when you go to sight it in. Inevitably, someone will pull out a rifle with a bigger scope on it, to show that he has something better. It's not better, of course, but you always find yourself trying to justify investing in something smaller, lighter, and lower-powered than the lunar telescope he has mounted on his super-magnum, complete with bipod, sniper sling with eighteen different straps and buckles, and a cartridge case taped to the buttstock. He may think he's the second coming of Carlos Hathcock, but usually such an outfit just shows nothing more than inexperience.

* * *

Choosing an inappropriate scope to put on a rifle can turn it instantly from an ergonomically sound, graceful, and deadly instrument for hunting, into an awkward beast with sighting equipment that actually makes it less likely that you will be able to hit anything.

The Marlin 336 provides an excellent example. In its original form, the 336 is a fine stalking rifle, similar to the Winchester 94. It carries easily, balanced in one hand where it's instantly available if a deer bursts out of the bushes. One advantage of the 336 over the 94 is that, with its side ejection, a scope can be mounted low over the receiver. Once you do that, however, the rifle no longer carries so easily in the hand. It doesn't matter what size the scope is, it interferes with that natural "trail" carry. The answer for many is to fit the rifle with a sling, so it can be carried on the shoulder, and that is where it will ride forevermore. And when a deer bursts out of the bushes? You don't have a chance at a shot because your rifle is hanging on your shoulder instead of in your hands, where it should be.

In recent years, riflescopes have unquestionably become optically superior to what they used to be. Today, it is a rare scope that leaks or fogs up, regardless of conditions. The glass is better, the coatings are excellent, reticle adjustments are positive and stay where they're put. Most scope tubes are made of aluminum or some other alloy, which reduces weight without unduly reducing strength. The really top scopemakers, like Swarovski and Zeiss, have coatings that cause lenses to shed water so they never need to be wiped dry. To me, that is vastly more useful on a hunting rifle than an extra 1 percent light transmission. Variables have expanded their range of powers; where in the old days we had a three-to-one ratio (2-7X, 3-9X), scopemakers began pursuing greater ranges. As of today (and who knows what it will be tomorrow?) the greatest range is eight to one, meaning a scope can be a 1-8X, 2-16X, 3-24X, and so on. Finally, scope tube diameters are larger. Today, 30mm tubes are common. Most of us assume that means greater light transmission for better low-light visibility,

This detachable mount by Joe Smithson is on a custom .375 H&H rifle, with a Zeiss 30mm scope. It is beautifully made—one of the most elegant of scope mounts.

but they are also required for those high power ratios mentioned above. Another advance is the illuminated reticle, usually in the form of a red glowing dot or cross at the center of the aim point, and a 30mm tube affords more room for the electronics required for that.

Now for the disadvantages. Scopes with 30mm tubes and large objective lenses are heavier and bulkier. Adding an illuminated reticle means there is a mechanism that can malfunction, with a battery that can go dead when you need it most. High power ranges are a questionable asset. How many times would you need to have both a 2X

and 16X available on the same rifle? If you only need 2X, or maybe as much as 6x, you are carrying all that extra weight and bulk to give you something you'll never use, and it will make the rifle slower to handle. You also run the risk— and this is no small thing—of having the power setting at 16X when you need to make a quick shot on a moving target at a few yards. Good luck.

Another factor to be considered is eye relief. As power ranges expand, ocular bells get longer. Manufacturers insist that eye relief is more than ample, but sometimes you'll find you can't mount the scope far enough forward to make use of that eye relief and have your head and eye in a natural, comfortable position on the stock. To keep your eye away from that long ocular bell, you have to contort your neck to get your cheek down on the stock, far enough back.

Years ago, I espoused the idea of paying a lot of money for the best scope (buying one good one instead of three cheaper ones), and getting a wide enough power range that the scope could be switched around from rifle to rifle, depending on which one I wanted to use that day. It didn't take me long to grow out of that. Every good hunting rifle needs its own scope, tailored to its particular uses, mounted and left in place. The idea of switching scopes around may be good in theory, but it ain't very good in practice.

With the recent fascination with all things military, and especially all things sniper-related, scopes have gone off the deep end in terms of size and power. Now, instead of 30mm tubes, we have scopes with 36mm tubes. For example, the Zeiss Victory 4.8-35X has a 36mm tube and a 60mm objective lens, illuminated reticle, weighs over two pounds (thirty-four ounces) and sells for around $4,000. For $4,000, you could buy four excellent—and I mean first-rate, top-notch, and A-number-one—hunting scopes, and still have money left over. There is no genuine hunting rifle I can imagine that would require that Zeiss Victory. And no, it would not double as a spotting scope. Potential targets should be viewed with a binocular. It is a little jarring to find you've been scoping out an unknown movement in the distance with your finger near the trigger, only to learn it's someone out walking with his dog.

Along with this headlong rush to the unergo-nomic, there has been a cascade of wild designs in reticles. We have always had complicated reticles, going back to the 1960s when we saw the first "rangefinder" reticles with multiple crosswires.

Today's creations bear about as much relation to those reticles as an F18 does to a Sopwith Camel. There are reticles available now that literally fill the entire field of view when you look through the scope. The military began this trend with the mil-dot system (which few civilians really understand, and no civilian needs) but scopemakers and reticle designers have left all semblance of common sense behind in their rush to make these as complicated and confusing as possible.

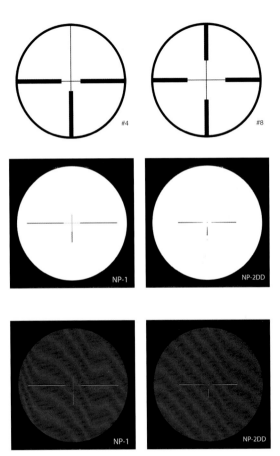

A selection of reticle designs, old and new: The German #4 reticle has a crosshair and three posts, the #8 a crosshair and four posts. The #8 is a forerunner of the Leupold duplex reticle, now copied by virtually everyone. Nightforce has engineered some innovative and very good reticle designs, incorporating the principles of the simple crosshair or duplex with illuminated reticles.

Needless to say, they have made such scopes less usable for hunting, rather than more.

For my money, the best reticle ever designed for a hunting scope is Leupold's duplex, now copied by virtually everyone. A duplex is a simple crosshair with the horizontal and vertical wires thin in the center, thicker on the outer ends. The duplex may have been made popular in America by Leupold, but it was in use in Europe much earlier. A remarkably similar reticle is shown in the 1914 Charles Lancaster catalogue. Add an illumination feature that lights up the thin, center wires and you have an almost perfect arrangement. Reticle preferences are as personal as blondes versus brunettes. One principle does apply, however: When you need to make a quick shot, the reticle should help you, not hinder you.

In the days when it was still a big name in high-quality hunting optics, Bausch & Lomb introduced the first great variable, the Balvar 8. It had one of the simplest but most ingenious reticles ever devised. In those early days, the reticle was always in the first focal plane, which meant it grew larger and smaller as the magnification varied. B&L solved that problem with a reticle that was like a simple crosshair. Instead of thin wires, however, it consisted of four extremely narrow black triangles, thicker at the outer edges and dwindling to nothing at the center. As power changed, the reticle stayed exactly the same in the center. It was an optical illusion, but who cares? For a while, other scopemakers offered this reticle as an option, but it seems to have disappeared. Since most reticles now are in the second focal plane and never change size anyway, it's not necessary.

The above is true of hunting scopes. In tactical or target scopes, however, where reticles are increasingly used for additional purposes such as gauging distance, the trend is now back toward reticles in the first focal plane. This leaves the relative measurement the same regardless of magnification. Thirty years ago, the "in" thing was second focal plane; now the "in" thing is back to first focal plane. On a hunting scope, however, the reticle in the second plane is vastly superior.

Some military reticles, intended for snipers, allow you to shoot at different ranges, using different intersections of lines, or allow for wind by moving to auxiliary vertical lines to the left or right of center. These are all very well for sniping situations where the shooter has a lot of time to calculate, settle in, decide on which intersection to use, and then take all the time he needs to squeeze off the shot. They are a decided disadvantage when you are trying to pick out a moving bull elk on the edge of a clearing, in failing light with snow falling. One highly visible reticle, in the center, thank you very much and I'll decide whether I need to hold a little high or a little low. That's the reality of hunting.

Another disadvantage of larger scopes is that, not only do they need to be higher over the rifle's action to allow room for the large objective lens, placing them higher gives their weight more leverage to work on the scope mounts under recoil. Higher and heavier scopes present difficulties. Combine this with heavier recoil, and you can really have problems. And no, a muzzle brake is not the answer. All a muzzle brake does is turn two recoil impulses into three. You may not feel it that way, but your scope mounts certainly do.

Before moving on, we should take a look at what the future might hold for riflescopes. In 2004, an electronics manufacturer showed up at the SHOT (Shooting, Hunting and Outdoor Trade) Show, with a new scope they expected would sweep the world. It was not a riflescope in the conventional sense, although it vaguely resembled one. Actually, what it looked like was the original range-finding riflescope introduced by Swarovski in 1995, and abandoned soon after. It was a long, square tube. Instead of looking through it, it was a video camera that produced its image on what we would call the ocular lens, which in turn was rectangular like a television. And that's what you were looking at: a small TV screen. This contraption allowed the user to design his own reticle and program it in, or have different reticles for different situations. It allowed you to film your shot (and kill) when you took aim and pulled the trigger. It could download information from a satellite. The price at the time was around $3,500, which was outlandish for a riflescope in 2004. In the display booth, two non-hunting, video-and-computer geeks stood by to explain its workings to the passers-by.

That particular invention seemed to disappear—at least, I never saw it again, thank God. But the idea of a riflescope that can talk to a satellite, downloading information like weather conditions, atmospheric pressure, or even ballistics data that will automatically program the scope, is not far-fetched in the least. The European scope manufacturers are at war with themselves, producing such gizmos on the one hand, but preaching ethical hunting practices on the other. They argue that they do not encourage shooting at extreme ranges, even while producing scopes that encourage you to try it. They also argue that, if people must shoot at those ranges, with a rangefinder and high-power scope they have a better chance of a clean kill. I would argue that, the world being what it is, such equipment only increases the chance of wounding the animal, rather than missing it cleanly. Take your choice as to which argument you buy.

This is as good a place as any to look at exactly how much sniper technology and techniques can be applied to hunting rifles. The short answer is: they cannot. Today's snipers are ultra-specialists,

trained in all manner of military skills, tuned to a high pitch. They work in teams, with one man on the trigger and one (or more) in supporting roles, calculating trajectories, measuring distances, judging wind, and so on.

The major difference between a sniper and a big-game hunter is that the sniper really doesn't care if his shot kills his target, cleanly or otherwise. A live enemy with a ghastly wound will do nicely, and fulfills the psychological aims of sniping just fine. It not only removes a combatant, it gives the enemy logistical problems looking after the victim. Plus, it's bad for their morale.

A big-game hunter with even the most cursory grasp of ethics, however, wants to make a clean, quick, painless kill with one shot, if possible. Even a meat hunter who doesn't care whether it's a buck or a doe wants a clean kill, so the meat will be good.

There are shooting schools that teach hunting courses based on everything from street-fighting techniques to SWAT teams bashing in doors, and claim that this is good training for hunting animals like Cape buffalo. They use ARs with tactical slings, holding the rifle straight up and down in front, and moving in approved military

Detachable mount on a new "Original Mauser" Magnum 98, introduced in 2015. This is a variation on the Redfield/Leupold dovetail mount.

Detachable mount on the new "Original Mauser" 98, introduced in 2017 , simpler and more compact than the one offered two years earlier (previous page).

fashion. There are also those, mostly veterans of wars but without much hunting experience, who claim that "having hunting armed men," they are ready to take on lions or elephants. Piece of cake.

Aside from the obvious difference between an AR in .223 and a bolt-action .505 Gibbs, military tactics and hunting dangerous game, or going into the bush after a wounded animal, bear as much similarity to each other as the above-mentioned sniping and big-game hunting. Wind and scent are vital in big-game hunting, but are inconsequential in tactical situations. This is straying somewhat from the subject of this chapter, which is optics, but in hunting almost everything is interrelated. Tactical scopes and tactical rifles go together.

Before leaving the subject of hunting scopes, it is worth noting that anyone contemplating a hunt on horseback needs to pay attention to what will, or will not, fit in the standard saddle scabbard. Most of the scabbards provided by outfitters will not accommodate much more than a one-inch-tube, 3-9X scope, if that. However, even if you have a custom scabbard made to fit an oversized scope, most wranglers are likely to look at it askance. There is a limit to what you can comfortably fit on a horse, under his saddle leathers, and

still have him tolerate you, much less like you. Your horse's opinion may not matter to you now, but it will when he sees you coming and starts rolling his eyes and stomping. The alternative of slinging your oversized rifle on your back and riding that way may seem like a good idea at the base of the mountain on an open trail. It will be less appealing (and considerably more hazardous) when you get into the inevitable brushy tangles that occur along any trail, in any mountains.

* * *

If forced to choose one scope mount that has proven to be the best, under the widest range of situations and circumstances, it would be the standard Leupold split ring. Originally designed by Redfield (and commonly called Redfield rings and bases), it was adopted by Leupold and quickly squeezed out all of its own earlier designs, including the Adjusto mount and several others.

The Redfield/Leupold has a dovetail on the front ring, with locking screws on the rear base that allow windage adjustments if needed. There are all kinds of variations, including the "double-dovetail" that employs this immensely strong feature both front and back. The single dovetail allows the scope to be installed in the rings and moved on and off without disturbing them, while the double-dovetail requires the lower parts of the rings to be installed and aligned, and the scope installed afterwards. The double-dovetail is intended for hard-kicking rifles or to secure extra-heavy scopes.

Conetrol mounts are very good, but extremely finicky to install. The ring looks like one smooth, seamless piece of steel if installed correctly. I like Conetrol mounts very much, and had them on one or two rifles. A similar approach is the S&K mount, in which the rings really are one piece of steel. They are flexible and bend enough to be fitted on the scope tube, then pulled snug. They are locked into place with a set screw on each side of the base that tightens the ring like a clamp. They look elegant, and are guaranteed to bend in and out through three hundred or so installations without weakening. They allow installation of the scope low over the action, and have absolutely no projections to get in the way.

At the other end of the elegance scale is the Weaver mount. They are strong, cheap, easy to install, and downright ugly. That pretty much exhausts both their good and bad points.

Another manifestation of our current phase of military adoration is the increasing use of the Picatinny rail, a device designed at Picatinny Arsenal many years ago. It resembles the Weaver mount, except that instead of having two bases, it is one long base with multiple grooves its entire length. The Weaver ring locks onto its base by a cross screw that fits into that groove, preventing any unscheduled movement forward or back. With multiples grooves, the scope (or any other device you care to attach, like a flashlight) can be adjusted just by loosening the lock screws and

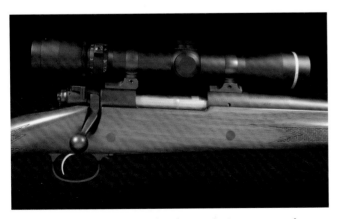

S&K mounts have no projections whatsoever, and can be as low and unobtrusive as the scope and bolt handle will allow. For elegance, they are unbeatable. The rifle is a Montana Rifle Co. ASR, in 7x57; the scope is a Leupold VX-III 1.75-6x32.

repositioning it. Picatinny rails come in different lengths, and many tactical rifles are festooned with so many of them you'd think it was a fashion statement, like wearing camo to the beer store. I have nothing against a Picatinny rail on a military rifle, but I object to them on a hunting rifle, not just on the grounds of looks or utility, but because I have taken too much skin off too many knuckles, brushing them against the sharp corners of Picatinny rails. The standard Picatinny rail resembles a saw blade. There is no reason I can see why these sharp corners could not be beveled off and rendered less life-threatening, but no one seems to do it.

In the early heyday of custom rifles, Conetrol or Buehler mounts were used if something more upscale than the Redfield or Leupold was desired. In the 1990s, these began to be displaced by Talley mounts, to the point where Talleys became *de rigueur* on any rifle aspiring to elite status. Talleys are detachable mounts, with a lever on each ring that locks it into place, or allows the scope to be removed. Dave Talley's spluttering denials notwithstanding, his mounts are both tricky to install, and possible to install in such a way that the scope is held tight to only one of the bases. I know this, because I've done it.

As a detachable mount on a dangerous-game rifle, I dislike them because removing the scope requires three separate movements (loosen one ring, loosen the other, rock scope off bases), whereas a properly fitted claw mount is so eumatic as to defy belief. You can do it entirely by feel, keeping your eye on the opening in the brush where you expect the buffalo to appear. With a claw, there is nothing to fall off, and nothing that needs tightening after removing the scope to keep it from falling off, unlike the Talley. On top of which, with their cross screws to connect the two halves of the rings on the

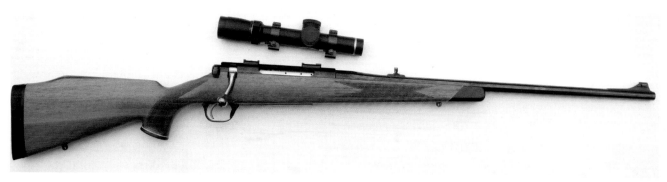

Talley mounts on a Schultz & Larsen Model 65DL, in .358 Norma.

top, Talleys are anything but elegant. How they became so popular is beyond me, unless it's the fact that having a claw mount installed today is hideously expensive, as well as requiring gun-smithing skills that seem to be disappearing.

There are other alternatives if a detachable mount is desired. Phil Pilkington, years ago, designed a system to convert the standard Redfield or Leupold. The left lock screw on the rear base is replaced by a lever that locks over the ring, but when rotated 180 degrees presents a flat surface, allowing the scope to be rotated out to the left and lifted out of the front dovetail. I had one of these on a .416 Weatherby and it worked fine. As long as the right lock screw is pinned so it can't move and throw the windage off, the scope returns to zero.

In the early 1990s, Leupold got back into the detachable-mount game with their QD mounts. The rings had little posts that fit into the bases, and were locked or released by a small lever. Actually, by a *too* small lever. They were certainly short and unobtrusive, but under recoil they would tighten down (good, in theory) to the point where they could not be removed with simple thumb and finger pressure (bad, in practice). You needed either pliers or a little wrench, neither of which I normally carry hunting. I found this out the hard way, high on Mount Longido in the Rift Valley, hunting Cape buffalo. The rifle was a .458 Winchester belonging to a friend, and one shot was

all it took to weld those levers in place. When the wounded buffalo came out after us, the scope was still clamped firmly in place, and I found myself shooting at anything black through the scope. The last shot was fired from the hip, at which point the scope had ceased to matter. Having come out of it alive, I decided not to tempt fate, and have never used Leupold QD mounts since.

European makers of scope mounts, such as EAW, Bock, and Recknagel, have come up with many different designs over the years. They still love detachable mounts, and have new designs for those as well as making countless variations on the venerable claw.

Much as I admire the claw, it has limitations. For example, in an earlier chapter I looked at my favorite dangerous-game rifle, which has a Swarovski 1.5X, on a 26mm straight steel tube, in claw mounts. Because it lifts from the rear, you are limited as to the size of the objective lens, with a straight tube really working best. Where there is a large objective but a smaller ocular bell, mounts have been made that release and rock upwards from the front. Others place the ring around the objective lens, which solves one problem but then forces the gunsmith either to mount the scope too far back, or with the front base out on the barrel.

Of all the different detachable systems I have seen, including at least two dozen variations on the claw, the one that gets my vote as the most eumatic, intuitive, and easy to use is the above-mentioned claw on my .450 Ackley. Not only can it be removed with one motion of one hand without looking down, you can replace it the same way by holding the scope with your finger beside the front claw, feeling for the base, and then snapping into place. This is possible with no other scope mount, to the best of my knowledge, and certainly, with no other detachable mount is the scope faster to remove or replace.

In case you are wondering, the expense with claw mounts is in fitting the bases. They are not merely screwed to the bridge and ring. Mine are both screwed and silver soldered. This soldering makes them practically part of the action, but it requires great skill and knowledge of how to use a heat sink, if you are to avoid compromising the hardness of the action. My old German gunmaker, Siegfried Trillus, could do this, and scoffed at those who said it was impossible. Would that Siegfried were still around, and that I could afford the cost of installing claws on a couple of other rifles at about $2,000 apiece.

Another drawback of claw mounts that really should be mentioned is that they pretty much limit you to having one particular scope on a rifle. However, if it is the right scope, I can live with that.

* * *

At various times, scope makers have included lens covers with their scopes, and after-market manufacturers have produced different types of covers, mostly to keep raindrops off lenses, but also to protect the scope from knocks and bangs.

In the 1980s, someone came up with the bright idea that if these covers were made of clear plastic, then you could see to shoot with the covers on. This sounds great, unless you have your scope mounted low with minimal clearance for the bolt handle, and the cover prevents the bolt from opening. That can be exciting after your first shot at a brown bear in pouring rain. One German scope maker who refused to do this explained that the plastic would prevent the shooter from enjoying the full benefits of his superb lenses. I suggested that heavy rain on the lenses would do the same thing, and with transparent covers you'd at least have a chance. He counter-argued that, if the rain was that heavy, then the drops would prevent you seeing through the plastic cover, no? With the development of water-repellant coatings, the problem is solved, at least regarding water. Scope covers

Swarovski 1.5x20 Habicht Nova scope in claw mounts on a .450 Ackley. The scope can be removed easily, without looking, and replaced almost as easily.

also keep out dirt and prevent scratches. They are worthwhile having on even when it isn't raining, so the see-through feature does have its merits.

Then there are the little spring-loaded flaps that fit on the scope front and back. They certainly provide a degree of protection, but it takes two motions to flip them up and I detest the look of them.

All of this is getting very arcane and nit-picky. My point is that some of these accoutrements, which may seem like a dynamite idea in the store, can seriously impair the usability of your rifle under certain conditions, and often in ways you never suspect until it actually comes to pass. A scope cover that prevents the bolt opening and closing is one example, and how many of us would take the time to practice with the cover on to find this out ahead of time? Or releasing those spring-mounted flaps within the (very sharp) hearing of a whitetail, to see how he reacts to the sound of that gentle twang?

* * *

In an article titled "The Ideal Big-Game Rifle," which appeared in the *Outdoor Life Guns & Shooting Yearbook* in 1985, writer and big-game guide Bob Hagel observed that "A scope of no more than 4X, and as short and light as possible, is the best all-around big-game scope available. If you can't see a big-game animal well enough to hit it with a good 4X hunting scope, that animal is sure as hell too far away for you to be shooting at it."

A great deal has changed in the world of optics in the third of a century since Hagel wrote that, but I agreed with it then and I agree with it now. This is not to say that I don't outfit many rifles with scopes of more than 4X, but the reason is that it is getting damned difficult to find a high-quality scope with those simple specs. The best-quality scopes available today are

A modern package—the Ruger Model 77 Hawkeye FTW Hunter, in 6.5 Creedmoor, fitted with a Swarovski Z8i 1-8x24.

variables, with fixed-power models largely made using yesterday's technology and costing as little as possible. There are exceptions, of course, but why move heaven and earth to find a high-quality fixed 4X when you can buy a perfectly good Leupold Vari-X III 2.5-8 for less money?

Most such scopes that I have fitted on my rifles are set at maximum for sighting in (the better to see the target, my dear), then moved to 4X or 5X for hunting. I do have a Leupold fixed 3X that I ordered from their custom shop to go on a .256 Winchester Magnum rifle, but I was being deliberately retro. Leupold also makes a neat little fixed 2X that is a straight one-inch tube, is eight inches long, and weighs about six ounces. It is so inexpensive, a serious rifleman should buy two or three, just to have around. In their catalog, Leupold says the scope was made at the insistence of its employees in Oregon, serious hunters all, who appreciate the virtues of such glass.

In various places, I have written that, were I condemned to use nothing but Leupold scopes for the rest of my hunting life, I would not feel disadvantaged. There is not much you need to do in hunting that cannot be done by one or another Leupold scopes. Their forté is the one-inch tube, and the hard fact is that for 90 percent of the hunting done by 90 percent of the big-game hunters in the world, a one-inch-tube scope is not only good enough, it is better than most.

They are universally lighter than a comparable 30mm tube scope, can be mounted lower, and are generally more compact and less clumsy. They give nothing away in terms of durability, being shock-, water-, fog-, and everything-else-proof. They may lag behind in light transmission, but this is less important for most American hunting than it is in Europe.

Swarovski, Zeiss, and Schmidt & Bender all make one-inch models. If you can find one, the Kahles one-inch scopes that were sold in the US for a while are superb, both in terms of optics and durability.

The current fashion, even among the average deer hunter, is a 30mm tube and high power—the higher the better. In a deer camp in Kansas a while back, there was a group from Ohio that included a couple of young kids. One went around to every table at dinner, telling all who would listen that his father had a rifle that could kill a deer out to a thousand yards. Never mind the fact that we were hunting from stands, and it was the wooded hills of east Kansas where there was not even a view longer than four hundred yards, he was ready, by golly! The guy I was with shot a buck at one hundred yards, while I shot a buck and a doe at 140 and 110 yards respectively. Only one hunter had a chance at more than three hundred yards, and he missed. What does that tell you?

The best buck, as I recall, was decked by a hunter in his seventies who was there with his fifty-year-old son. He was armed with a Savage 99 in .308 Winchester that had obviously been around, but was well looked after. It was topped with a Redfield 3-9X that had been on it since he bought it in the 1960s. The whole outfit added up to a slim, trim, practical hunting rifle. When the aforementioned kid came around to our table to tell us about his dad's super-rifle, the old gentleman listened politely, nodded, and said, "Well, good luck to him." It's nice to spend time with courteous people.

And an ultra-traditional package: the Mannlicher-Schönauer 6.5x54 M-S, in the "African" model produced by both Mauser and Steyr in the 1920s. At one time, this rifle was fitted with a claw mount, since replaced by a Leupold "Adjusto" mount and a Leupold FX-II 2.5x20 scope. The rifle has an old-fashioned, elegant look to it, and is a very efficient hunting rifle out to 250 yards—easy to shoot, accurate, and smooth as glass.

A variety of rifle slings, old and new, European and American. Some are more decorative than others, but all fulfill the most basic requirement of making it easier to carry the rifle while not getting in the way.

CHAPTER **XVII**

BITS, PIECES, AND ACCOUTREMENTS

As the old line goes, what sets mankind apart from the animals is his (or her) ability to accessorize. With hunters, nowhere is this more true than with rifles. Even cars, traditionally our other great love, seem almost neglected by comparison.

A man buying a new rifle is not allowed out of the store until he has spent as much again on a cleaning rod, jags, brushes, patches, solvents, scope, mounts, scope cover, lens cleaning kit, ammunition, cartridge pouch, sling, and bipod. Some of these items are certainly essential, and others are at least useful. Unfortunately, several not only are not worth the money, they can seriously compromise the ergonomics and utility of the rifle on which you just dropped a grand or two.

Thirty years ago, hunting pronghorns in eastern Montana, a group of us gathered around a target board to check our zeroes. I was chatting with our guide, who pointed out a couple of hunters armed with shiny new rifles, fitted with outlandish cobra-style slings complete with initials tooled in the leather and a five-round cartridge pouch.

"You watch," John said. "I guarantee you, those guys are going to miss any buck we put them on."

We then stood by as they fired round after round, trying to sight in rifles that should have been sighted in before they left home, but were not. Their misses had nothing directly to do with those slings, admittedly, but the fact that they

had them, had not sighted in properly, and were generally behaving like complete novices, are all connected. Nothing marks you out as a rookie like a garish and completely impractical sling.

Please do not misunderstand. I am a huge fan of rifle slings. I long ago lost count of how many I have. As a teenager, I tried assiduously to learn how to shoot with one the way the top marksmen did, and I practiced getting into a sitting position to shoot with a sling like Jack O'Connor in the photos. My first bolt action, an Enfield P-17, came equipped with the complex military sling of its day, one and a half inches wide, with more holes than a sieve, and near-impossible to adjust exactly the way you wanted it.

Those slings were not just made for carrying the rifle. They were also a shooting aid. Soldiers between the wars were taught to shoot from various positions, with the sling looped firmly to their arm. There were leather keepers, and when your arm was through the loop, the keeper was tightened down to keep it in place above the bicep. You then contorted yourself into position to shoot, and the sling provided a very tight (it seemed *too* tight) tension on the forend, steadying the muzzle. Undoubtedly, this did work in the standard military shooting positions—mainly the prone and the solid sitting position. The purpose of all the pairs of holes in the sling was to allow any recruit, regardless of size and arm length, to adjust his sling to his own measurements. Subsequently, whenever he needed to lengthen

237

Slings don't come much more basic than this military-issue web sling on a Lee-Enfield No. 1 Mk. III. Unlike the American Springfield sling, it was intended only for carrying the rifle, never as a shooting aid.

the sling to shooting size, he simply pulled down on the outside strap, and he was ready to go.

There were complicated instructions for adjusting these slings to fit you, and they were provided with double brass hooks for the holes. Once adjusted properly, these hooks were squeezed tight with pliers, and the sling was set for you and you alone. I never did get the sling on my P-17 exactly right. Finally, I gave up and simply used the "hasty sling" position, wherein you push your arm between sling and rifle, loop the sling around, and then push your hand up against the swivel while grasping the forend. It might not have worked as well as the formal method, but it worked well enough and was immensely faster. There is even a "hasty hasty" position, in which you grasp the forend while the sling is looped behind your elbow. It may be better than nothing, but not by much.

The Springfield-style military sling is almost useless as a shooting aid for most hunting purposes. It is simply too slow and cumbersome to get into. The hasty sling works pretty well, but preferably with a narrower sling than the military one.

On a hunting rifle, the opportunity to shoot with the aid of a sling does not seem to be nearly as frequent for me as it was for O'Connor, but then my shooting opportunities are not as frequent, period.

In America, the wide leather sling as found on the Springfield 1903A3 evolved for hunting purposes into a narrower version of the same thing, and then to the simplified Whelen sling, developed by the eminently practical and knowledgeable Col. Townsend Whelen. Through the 1960s, George Lawrence Leather in Oregon sold a half-dozen varieties of sling, including the original military pattern, the Whelen, a traditional buckled strap, and one or two others. Gradually, the 1¼-inch sling was displaced by the one-inch.

In Europe, slings are rarely if ever used as shooting aids in hunting. The traditional sling for a European is a strap of fixed length that allows the rifle to hang off the shoulder, horizontal at about waist height, so the muzzle can swing in an arc, terrifying everyone around. These slings are usually quite narrow—three-quarters of an inch at most—and the sling swivels on European rifles reflect this. Some, like those on the Mannlicher-Schönauer, are not easy to replace, and so you are locked into whatever sling you can find to fit.

In the 1950s, John Bianchi registered the name "Cobra" as a trademark for his slings, which were wider at the shoulder in order to spread the weight of the rifle over a greater area. This is a fine example of selling something for which there is no real need, since short of a .50-caliber machine gun, no hunting rifle is *that* heavy. The name "Cobra" belonged to Bianchi, but not the credit for inventing it. They had been around for years, in one form or another, from different makers, including George Lawrence.

Sometime in the 1980s, the modest Lawrence cobra-style sling (a bit wider at the shoulder, but not too much) was transformed into a variety of monstrosities that even today I am at a loss to explain. They went from a wide point of 1½ inches all the way to three inches or more. Instead of being a simple, thin strap, they were lined with suede or felt, and were often padded as well. They became so wide they could hardly be carried on the shoulder at all. Instead of nestling between the muscles where they could be carried comfortably, leaving hands free if necessary, the wide strap always wanted to slip off. Slings became a vehicle of self-expression, complete with tooled leather in multi-colored patches, the owner's initials, or the maker of the rifle, embossed for all to see. Cartridge loops were added, along with little pouches to carry cleaning kits, shooting glasses, and other paraphernalia. These monstrosities flopped around, getting in the way, and doing everything except the two things for which a sling is made: carrying the rifle comfortably and looping around the arm to steady the shot.

This is not to say that shooting slings ceased to exist. On the contrary, ingenious designers began a search for the "perfect" shooting sling, and this led to a succession of offerings, each making extravagant claims, and each in turn fading into the distance. One sling from around 1985, called the Viper, was a complicated arrangement in which one part of the strap fitted around the body and another around the arm, and the rifle hung down over the chest. When a shot presented itself, the hunter could grasp the rifle, swing it into position, and the strap would

already be tightly on his arm steadying the muzzle. In theory this was fine, as far as it went. But if you were wearing a backpack, or carrying a binocular, or any of a half-dozen other possibilities, it just didn't work. And there was no way the Viper could work at all, except that exact way.

Another, called the Ching sling after its designer, was a modification of a later military sniper design. Again, it worked for some people under some conditions, but not for me. Still another design had a split strap, one for each shoulder like the carrying straps on a backpack, that allowed the rifle to hang straight down the back. This supposedly made it easier to climb, with both hands free. And if you were carrying a backpack as well? Uh oh. Back to the drawing board.

Here is my formula for the ideal sling on a big-game rifle: It should be made of leather, wide enough not to cut into the shoulder, yet narrow enough to stay in place on your shoulder when you need your hands for something else. It should lengthen with a simple pull for carrying, or shorten with a similar pull so it's quiet and not flopping around when you're slinking through the woods. It should be quick to lengthen, in case you do want to loop it around your arm in the "hasty sling" shooting position, which is admittedly not as good as the formal "shooting sling" position, but considerably better than nothing.

Most slings today are fitted out with detachable sling swivels, and I applaud that, provided they are the more modern locking swivels that won't come undone on their own and cause your rifle to fall off your shoulder and plunge into the valley far below. I worry about things like that.

The absolute very best sling I have ever encountered is the Brownells Latigo sling, made from the finest leather available—soft, pliable, quiet, and well-behaved. At last count, I owned

Brownells Latigo sling on a custom Mauser rifle. In the author's opinion, the Brownells Latigo is the best, most useful, and most practical rifle sling on the market today.

four of them. Brownells has been selling these since the 1940s or '50s. My own oldest one dates back to the 1980s, and is still in perfect shape. Each is set to a different length, and I match them to whatever rifle I'm using at the time. Outwardly, they resemble the old Whelen design, and are 7/8ths of an inch wide. They get soaking wet, then dry out, then wet again, and still they remain soft and pliable; they are quiet in the brush; they can be lengthened or shortened in a heartbeat. If I want, I can take the sling off the rifle in the bush and tuck it in a pocket—a good feature on a dangerous-game rifle. The Latigo is adjustable for length, but frankly, it's easier to own several, set each to a different length, then cut off the excess leather. May Brownells never stop selling them!

By contrast, walk into any gunshop today and chances are you will see nothing except gaudy, exaggerated Cobra-style slings, or synthetic slings with thick, wide, sliding pads. The more complicated and elaborate, it seems, the better. Generally speaking, however, the more elaborate a sling becomes, the less useful it is. There is a lot to be said for braided binder twine. Seriously.

There are also slings made for tactical use on rifles like the AR-15, and some have tried to adapt those to standard hunting rifles. There are shooting schools that even try to convince hunters to carry their rifles in front, pointed at the ground SWAT-team style, lashed to their body by a multi-strap sling. I do not, and never have, bought into that system, if for no other reason than it ignores the fact that in hunting, especially in the woods or mountains, you are almost always forced to shoot from an unexpected, improvised position. Never in hunting have I shot from a doorway, from a window in a turret, crouched against a wall on a sidewalk, or around the corner of a building. Funny thing, that.

Hunting in Africa, you will almost always, at some point, use shooting sticks. For this, a sling that is big and floppy just gets in the way. As for attaching cartridge pouches, sheath knives, sunglasses, and smart phones, all they do is add weight and make the sling awkward. They also complicate your life. For example, if you have your spare cartridges in loops on your sling, and you remove the sling and leave it in the safari car while you go into the bush after a buffalo, what then? Same with a knife. Cartridges belong in a pouch on your belt, as does your knife; sunglasses should be left at home, and as for smart phones . . .

A sling is a sling, not a backpack.

* * *

Another piece of equipment that has really gained popularity over the last thirty years is the detachable bipod. Having used a few—or attempted to use them—I've found that I am far better off improvising a rifle rest with the backpack that I *always* carry and am *never* without.

Bipods work best on level ground, shooting from prone, with a clear view in front of you. They are neither quick nor easy to adjust, and it is nigh impossible to get one at the exact height you need, especially when you have a moving target that could disappear in a few seconds. A bipod that is not the correct height is more a liability than an asset, forcing you either to strain upwards to see through the scope, or hunker down into an uncomfortable position. Either one defeats the purpose, which is to get a more stable hold. On a mountainside, or uneven ground, or in a rocky area, they just do not work very well.

A hunter who can improvise a rest with a tree, a rock, a fallen log, a backpack, or even a convenient shrub, is better off than with a bipod. Add to this the fact that a bipod is noisy and clanking, adds weight to the rifle, and gets in the way when you're not using it, all adds up to a major liability for the average hunter. We should add that they are generally noisy to open into position, being made of metal and springs that bang, sproing, and clank. They do, however, look vaguely military, which is seductive to the uninitiated. As an added disadvantage, with a bipod attached to the front sling swivel where they normally ride, they are in the way if you decide you need to dispense with their assistance and shoot from a sitting position, or use an improvised rest.

Bipods are common on sniper rifles, and for certain types of long-range military or target work, there is nothing to compare with them for stability except a couple of sandbags. Unfortunately, sandbags are even less convenient to lug around than a bipod. Shooting schools that train in the use of bipods commonly have the left hand (for a right-handed shooter) holding the sling where it attaches to the buttstock, squeezing it to move the butt up or down. This is fine, shooting at a steel plate six hundred yards away from a flat, prepared shooting position. Casting back over fifty-some years of big-game hunting, on four (or is it five?) continents, on plains, in

the mountains, in river valleys, I cannot recall a single instance where it would have even been possible, never mind practical, to assume such a shooting position with a real, live game animal.

* * *

Another of the truly dubious developments in hunting rifles is the muzzle brake. The original purpose of the muzzle brake was to reduce recoil by redirecting gases emerging from the muzzle. At first, it seemed like the answer to many different prayers. This reckoned without two laws of physics—one formal, the other informal.

The formal law is that energy can be neither created nor destroyed. The informal one is that, in ballistics, there is no free lunch.

Recoil is a result of energy, and a muzzle brake redirects that energy. The most immediately noticeable effect of this redirected energy is vastly increased muzzle blast. A less noticeable effect is increased stress on scope mounts, which in turn can be aggravated by a heavy riflescope. Finally, there is the question of the rifle's zero. If the muzzle brake is detachable, as they soon

Muzzle brake arrangement from a Ruger Model 77 Hawkeye FTW Hunter. The muzzle brake can be removed and replaced by either a short cap that simply protects the threads, or a longer one that duplicates the balance with the brake in place.

came to be, the difference in zero with and with-out the brake can be extreme—reportedly as much as eighteen inches at one hundred yards.

My first experience with a muzzle brake was on a .416 Weatherby. The brake could be removed and replaced with a steel cap to protect the threads. With the brake in place, the already long barrel (twenty-four inches, as I recall) became almost three inches longer. That is an awkward length for a dangerous-game rifle. Hunting Cape buffalo in Tanzania, and later in Botswana, it quickly became apparent that the .416's horren-dous muzzle blast was having an effect not only on me (the shooter) but on those around: pro-fessional hunter Robin Hurt, my colleague, Finn Aagard, and the trackers. We all experienced a ringing in the ears after even one shot—the sure sign of a slight but irreversible hearing loss.

Through the 1990s, as muzzle brakes came into common use, trackers and other safari staff began to go seriously deaf. This can be a fatal affliction if your profession requires acute hearing, such as tracking wounded buffalo. By 2000, many safari companies were prohibiting the use of muz-zle brakes by their clients, and insisting they be removed. This raised the second problem, which was a change in zero. I also experienced this, in Botswana during the second part of that 1990 safari. Because of the muzzle blast, I took the brake off, but did not re-check the zero. Hunting buffalo, my first shot at about one hundred yards was off. Subsequent shots were at much closer range and it all ended well for us, if not the buffalo. When I got home, I shot a lot of ammunition comparing the zero with and without the brake. There was a good six-inch difference at one hundred yards.

Shooting a rifle like the .416 Weatherby with a muzzle brake, in an enclosed space like a firing line with a roof and walls, the concussion has to be experienced to be believed. Even using both

fitted ear plugs *and* the muff-type hearing pro-tection, the concussion can cause headaches very quickly. It also makes you extremely unpopular with other shooters on the line, partly because of the noise and partly because dust, mouse droppings, and dead spiders rain down from the rafters onto everyone around.

Since my experience with the .416 Weatherby, I have owned several rifles with muzzle brakes. One is a custom .257 Weatherby made by Kenny Jarrett. It is a superbly accurate long-range hunting rifle. I never shoot it with the brake. The muzzle blast from a .257 Weatherby is bad enough without that, and anyway, the recoil is negligible by nitro-express standards.

One company that made muzzle brakes pop-ular in the 1980s was Mag-Na-Port, in Michigan, and after I got home from that 1990 safari I started work on a custom .450 Ackley. I took the barrel down to Mag-Na-Port and had them cut what they called a partial brake. It consists of narrow slits in the barrel itself—obviously not detachable—but instead of taming straight-line recoil, it is intended only to limit muzzle jump. With a big rifle like that, muzzle jump is the most jarring aspect of recoil, and such minimal cuts do not increase muzzle blast unduly. The rifle is still a beast, but it's a friendly beast. If I had it to do again, however, I probably wouldn't.

Gradually, muzzle brakes have worked their way down until today you find them as factory-standard on even such mild cartridges as the 6.5 Creedmoor. This is a popular cartridge for long-range shooting, and sniper schools want minimum of recoil of any type. Also, everyone on the shooting line wears maximum ear protection at all times.

Some manufacturers of muzzle brakes claim they have come up with a revolutionary new technology that reduces recoil while not increas-

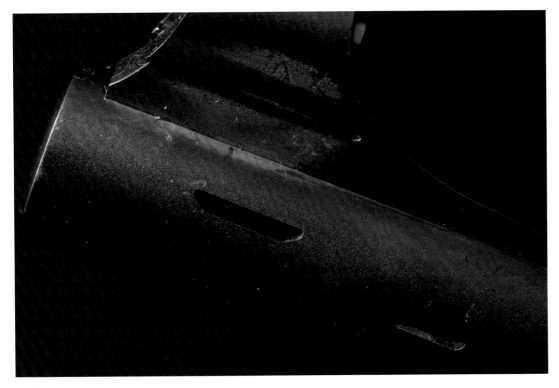

Minimal muzzle brake, cut into the barrel, by Mag-Na-Port. This tames muzzle jump, but neither reduces straight-line recoil nor (allegedly) increases muzzle blast. This was done on a custom .450 Ackley. If the author had it to do again, he wouldn't.

ing muzzle blast, but they never explain how this is possible given the law of physics quoted at the beginning of this section. Where does the redirected energy go, and in what form? This brings us to the law regarding the price of lunch. Shooting a rifle—any rifle—is a zero-sum game. When you unleash the energy in the smokeless powder inside a cartridge case, you set in motion a sequence of events in which many things happen, almost simultaneously. Some of these can be reduced, but only by increasing one or more of the others.

I have seen it recommended, in print, that if you shoot a rifle with a muzzle brake, you should wear hearing protection at all times, even when hunting. You can buy headset ear protection that magnifies sounds around you while blocking the blast at the instant of shooting. So, instead of limiting your hearing, they would actually make it more acute. Great, right? Well, aside from the discomfort and inconvenience of wearing these things in the field, it has been my experience that they magnify the sounds you don't want (like the

wind) at the expense of those you do (like a big buck chewing on a tasty twig). In cold weather, admittedly, they do keep your ears warm, but that is not enough of a benefit to make me wear them.

At the risk of sounding like a Luddite, the best solution of all is either not to use the muzzle brake while hunting or to dispense with it altogether. As with many things in modern life, the more we try to make things easier, the more we complicate them and create whole new problems that did not exist before.

The great boon of the self-contained cartridge was that it allowed hunters to lighten their load considerably, getting rid of powder horns, shot flasks, possibles bags, spare flints, ramrods, and all the other paraphernalia that weighed down big-game hunters of the 1800s. Now, we seem intent on reversing that with a whole host of gadgets, most which are best left on the shelf.

*   *   *

The Ruger Model 77/44.

CHAPTER XVIII

THE MODERN HUNTING RIFLE

No chapter of any book on guns is more fraught with peril than the final one, wherein the author (usually ill-advisedly, and almost always incorrectly) predicts what the future might hold. Some prognosticators on rifles and ballistics have been so wildly off base it makes you wonder what they were smoking. At least one sage from the 1950s predicted future routine velocities of 10,000 fps, and working pressures in the neighborhood of 120,000 psi. Even more sober folk considered 5,000 fps a foregone conclusion. Another writer suggested the primer was obsolete, and in the future all ignition systems would be electrical. Still another touted caseless ammunition as the way of the future.

No one in 1965 predicted a general take-over by synthetic stocks, or a mass migration to AR-15s as one of the dominant sporting rifles. In 1967, the 6.5 Remington Magnum was already fading into obscurity after a brief and inauspicious life. The main knock against it was that it did not deliver the promised velocity. Had anyone suggested that, fifty years later, the hottest rifle cartridge, in terms of sales, would be something

The J. P. Sauer & Sohn Model 404 Synchro XTC has a carbon-fiber stock that promises the greatest strength combined with the lightest weight. It has drawbacks, too, but it's a matter of taste. The comb is adjustable for height.

called the 6.5 Creedmoor, offering slightly *less* in the way of ballistics than the rejected 6.5 Remington, he would have been laughed out of the saloon.

As I am writing this in the fall of 2017, there are several trends clearly visible. One is the increasing prevalence of synthetic stocks. This subject has been covered in chapter XI, but it bears repeating. Today, even the plainest walnut stock is a luxury item, and most of those are pretty ho-hum. In an age of laser-cut checkering and the technological ability to shape a stock properly using mass-production methods, it need not be this way. There are exceptions, and we'll get to them. As for synthetic stocks, to quote my old shooting pal Bruce Cockburn, "The trouble with normal is, it always gets worse." How right you are, Bruce, and in the case of synthetic stocks, doubly so.

For the past decade, there has been a concerted effort on the part of individuals, companies, the National Shooting Sports Foundation (NSSF), and the NRA to legitimize the AR family of semi-military semiauto rifles as "modern sporting rifles." This includes trying to have them recognized, legally in some cases but culturally everywhere, as perfectly fine rifles for hunting. By my aesthetic and technical standards, they don't qualify on a number of grounds. It's not because I don't like semiautos, or object to their military look. It has to do with practical aspects, like excessive weight, poor balance, sharp edges and corners, difficulty in carrying, awkward handling in most hunting situations, noisy operation, and so on. Ergonomic they are not, nor are they smooth, silky, and seductive. In terms of Gough Thomas's eumatics, at best they are barely adequate. I'd as soon enter the Monaco Grand Prix driving a Tiger tank.

Do I think they should be illegal? Absolutely not. If a Dall sheep hunter wants to handicap himself by carrying an AR in some semi-adequate caliber, that's his business. All I fervently wish is that hunters who do use ARs give some serious thought to the ethics of the situation, and fairness to the game. This does not mean an AR gives you an unfair advantage. Quite the opposite. I believe they raise the chances of wounding animals simply because you can't get a usable AR in a serious hunting caliber like .270 Winchester. The 6.5 Grendel is a neat cartridge for playing around, but that's where it ends unless your idea of hunting is potting whitetails under a feeder at seventy-five yards.

If this sounds like relentless doom and gloom, it is not meant to be. Savage Arms, having abandoned such classics as the Savage 99, has turned its economy-priced 110 bolt-action series into an extensive line of highly accurate rifles, with an excellent trigger system. These are priced within range of the average teenager, and nothing like that was around when I was sixteen. Winchester Repeating Arms, having been saved from oblivion and folded under the protective wing of Browning Arms and its parent, FN, is making some of the best rifles in its history, if you can just get past the idea that "Made in Portugal" can be better than "Made in New Haven, Conn." Remington and Marlin, two venerable names, don't seem to be exactly thriving, but that's the ebb and flow of an industrial economy.

Sturm, Ruger & Co., when last we looked, was the largest general firearms company in the US, and strictly on merit. Not bad, from a standing start of zero in the late 1940s, working from a garage. The company was built on Bill Ruger's seemingly infallible instinct for what shooters wanted, and what they would buy even though they might not even know they wanted it, because it did not yet exist. That's a talent you don't acquire at MBA school, or working as

The Blaser R8 straight-pull rifle, with its interchangeable barrels, removable trigger groups, lightning-fast operation, and superb accuracy is the ultimate in versatility in a hunting rifle, available in (at last count) forty-three different cartridges ranging from the .204 Ruger and .222 Remington up to the .338 Lapua and .500 Jeffery.

somebody's corporate lawyer. Since Ruger's death, the company has put a foot wrong here and there, but they have also produced some stuff that is really good. As a company, Sturm, Ruger has the resilience to recover from the odd bad move and, apparently, the good sense to do so.

One really bright area of both innovation and quality is the European connection—Blaser, J. P. Sauer, and Mauser in Germany, Steyr in Austria, and CZ in the Czech Republic. Mauser has just reintroduced the Mauser 98 with "Original Mauser" engraved on the barrel in the old Mauser banner, and it is a superb rifle, if an expensive one. J. P. Sauer's modern turnbolt designs, and Blaser's straight-pull rifles, set a standard of quality that everyone else aspires to.

* * *

What are some specific modern rifles that, in my opinion, qualify as potentially great hunting rifles? There are several, actually, and each of

them just barely missed making the cut for this book.

To start with Ruger, it has a small on-again, off-again line of Model 77 bolt-action derivatives, chambered for such cartridges as the .44 Magnum and .357 Magnum. These are built on a very short action, and employ a detachable rotary magazine. Of the various iterations, the Model 77/44 and 77/357 are the only ones that really qualify as big-game rifles. They are light, handy, agile, and quick to shoot. Feeding and ejection are very smooth and reliable. They are not the fastest to reload, since you have to position the rimmed cartridges carefully to press them down into the spool, but with four or five shots available, this is not a huge issue. Putting a scope on is unnecessary, to my mind, and would considerably reduce their value as stalking or still-hunting rifles, since a scope would only make them awkward to carry. If there were a readily available receiver sight, like the old Lyman 48, to replace or augment the standard

The Ruger Model 77/44, one of a class of rifles based on the venerable Model 77 bolt action, but employing a rotary magazine. The synthetic stock is surprisingly good, and the rifle functions well. It is an excellent stalking rifle for deer and similar game at shorter ranges. Although it is equipped for scope mounting, that would detract from its carrying qualities and quick handling.

open sights, it would improve them, but they work very well with the open sights they come with.

The actions and barrels are of stainless steel, so the bolt always has that feel of galling slightly. It can never be silky slick, but that's purely aesthetics. Functionally, they step up every time, and that's what's really important.

One great point about these rifles is their synthetic stock. It is so good it would almost make a convert of me, were I not so irascible and set in my ways. They have the general shape of American classic. There is "checkering" moulded in, but it's sharp, with large diamonds, and gives a really good grip. The forend and wrist are slim. Walnut stocks are supposedly available on some

This Ruger 77/357 is not only a model of restrained good taste, it is a deadly little deer and pig rifle at shorter ranges.

models, as are (or were) laminates, but they never seem to be in stock, and the .44 Magnum is available with blued steel. With this model, however, one can never tell what's in production and what isn't from one month to the next. For the practical ranges at which one might use a .44 Magnum or .357 Magnum for big-game hunting, this rifle fits right in with others in this book, like the Winchester 92, Savage 99, and even the Mannlicher-Schönauer.

A rotary magazine has been a high-class feature on bolt actions for more than a century, and only fell into disuse because it was expensive and required precision manufacture. Ruger's version is very good, and in some ways better than either the old Schönauer or Savage 99. For one thing, it can be removed while still holding its cartridges, so in theory you could carry a full spare. The rifle's trigger is good, and the three-position safety is even better than the Model 70's.

Another notable Ruger is a new version of the Model 77 Hawkeye, called the FTW Hunter. The one I've used is chambered in 6.5 Creedmoor, is fitted with a synthetic stock and detachable muzzle brake, and is both quick to operate and highly accurate. Unfortunately, it has no iron sights. Why anyone needs a muzzle brake on a pussycat like the 6.5 Creedmoor is beyond me, but the

Ruger Model 77 Hawkeye FTW Hunter, chambered for the 6.5 Creedmoor, and fitted with a Swarovski Z6i 2.5-15x44 P HD scope. Of the new crop of synthetic-stocked stainless rifles, this is the best "hunting" rifle I have seen.

sniper types insist they need every assistance to make those nine-hundred-yard shots. Since I don't attempt nine-hundred-yard shots, unless it's a steel plate and there's nothing at stake, the muzzle brake comes off and stays off. The rifle was configured by Ruger with advice from the staff at the FTW Ranch in Texas, home of a noted rifle-shooting school. The people at FTW certainly know their stuff, and if I was condemned to using just one rifle henceforth, and it was this one, I would not weep for too long. It's certainly a pleasure to shoot, but the 6.5 Creedmoor is not really my idea of a serious big-game cartridge.

How can I write that when one of the early rifles in this book is a Mannlicher-Schönauer Model 1903, in 6.5x54 M-S? That is simply because, if I had to climb an Alp in pursuit of a chamois, I would take the Mannlicher over the Ruger. The Mannlicher is a silky, eumatic pleasure to use, and the Ruger is not. Also, I probably would not attempt a shot with the Mannlicher beyond 250 yards at the absolute most, while everything about the FTW Hunter is designed for ranges far beyond that. And once you get beyond 250 yards, I would like a .270 Winchester, at least.

Winchester, now safely under FN's protective wing, seems to have rediscovered its soul, and I believe the Model 70 now being manufactured is, overall, the best that venerable rifle has ever been. New-production 70s are ergonomic, well made of the best materials, and highly accurate with a superb trigger. Aesthetically, they are examples of restrained elegance in the old, *old* New Haven style. The Super Grade is very nice, but the Featherweight is a gem, especially in calibers like .270 Winchester, if you like to walk a lot, carrying your rifle.

Since 2000, the Mauser brand has been part of Michael Lüke's consortium of companies that includes Blaser and J. P. Sauer & Sohn. After a few hesitant starts, Mauser is once again manufacturing its best-known rifle, the 98, in both standard and magnum actions. The workmanship is beautiful and the quality superb, but the price pretty high for the average hunter. Well, there have always been wonderful hunting rifles I could not afford, so this is nothing new. It is offered in two grades of walnut: beautiful and expensive, and *more* beautiful and *more* expensive.

For their part, Mauser's sister companies in the Lüke stable, J. P. Sauer and Blaser, are pursuing two different paths in bolt actions. The Blaser R8 is a straight-pull design with a unique lock-up system that appears, to my skeptical and suspicious eye, foolproof. It caters to the European love of combination and takedown rifles, and it's possible to switch barrels, magazines, bolts, and riflescopes, thereby turning one basic action into three, four, or ten different rifles. The R8 is certainly a mechanical marvel, but the concept of assembling different parts as the situation requires does not fit my criteria for a great hunting rifle. Too many things to go wrong or get lost, and too many possible configurations that might be anything but great.

J. P. Sauer & Sohn has always been a turn-bolt company, and still is. It's the second-oldest gunmaking company in the world (after Beretta), in business since 1751. Sauer is renowned for its superb metalwork and the smoothness of its bolts. From 1958 until the mid-1970s, Sauer produced the Weatherby Mark V, and those actions were beautifully smooth. Over the past decade, Sauer has offered various turnbolt designs of its own, but it seems to pursue modern, other-worldly patterns more than I personally like. Mechanically, however, in terms of quality materials and workmanship, it's impossible to fault them. They are also extremely accurate, with excellent triggers.

Steyr, ancient home of the Mannlicher-Schönauer, is still in business and still making rifles. They are slick, fast, and chambered for some very powerful cartridges. Like the Sauers, there is absolutely nothing to fault in either materials or workmanship, and Steyr barrels are renowned.

Looking at all of these rifles, it's apparent that rifle companies have learned from some of the mistakes of the past, and are paying attention to the finer details that make a good hunting rifle a great hunting rifle. Not every factory product is the ideal stalking rifle, but then they never were, and at least we have several very fine ones from which to choose.

J. P. Sauer's futuristic Model 404 Synchro XTC, with its rather reptilian carbon-fiber stock, is a little far out, but it shoots like a dream. This one is a .270 Winchester, fitted with a Schmidt & Bender Summit 2.5-10x40 scope.

The old German company Gebruder Merkel, of Suhl, is now owned by Steyr-Mannlicher. This is the new Merkel RX Helix straight-pull rifle. The bolt is completely contained within the solid receiver.

As for prognostications for the future, I believe the primer is here to stay, brass-cased ammunition will be the standard for the foreseeable future, we will never see routine velocities above 4,000 fps, and 60,000 psi was and is about as high as rifle pressures should go. Optics will continue to progress toward the totally unusable, and computers, the internet, satellites, and digital technology will try to play bigger and bigger roles, with the eventual goal of turning hunting into something akin to a video game.

In light of that, it's difficult to be optimistic, but impossible to be totally pessimistic, either. History shows us that things tend to go in cycles. Just when it seemed that the march of ever bigger, ever louder cartridges was unstoppable, shooters rediscovered the joys of amiable rounds like the .300 Blackout, and suddenly the 6.5 Creedmoor was the hottest cartridge extant—a cartridge with a shape like the old wildcat 6.5-250 Savage Improved, and ballistics not much different than the 6.5x55. If ever there was a cartridge of demur demeanor and outsized capabilities, the 6.5x55 is it.

* * *

Big-game rifles have always been shaped by the hunting itself. Hunting in America today is vastly different than it was even fifty years ago, much less one hundred, and is changing all the time. It has always been fashionable for American writers to sneer at the way things are done in Europe, especially if they are done by the upper classes. It doesn't really matter whether the "upper classes" were hereditary princes, like the Prince of Wales or the Archduke Franz Ferdinand, or the commissars of Communist Eastern Europe. Nothing gets you a chorus of approval from American hunters like denigrating the gentry and their "fancy rifles."

Yet here's the odd thing. Hunting in America is becoming more and more like hunting in Scotland, Poland, or the Austrian Alps. As populations increase and country becomes more settled, this is inevitable. Hunting in Europe is the way it is today because, over the centuries, a few wealthy and dedicated individuals or classes have gone to great lengths to preserve habitat, manage game populations, and combat poaching. If it costs a great deal to preserve game—and it does—then logically it will cost a great deal to hunt.

The Archduke was the most dedicated big-game hunter of his day. Reportedly, he killed more than five thousand red stags in his life, but obviously he did not rack up such an astonishing total by stalking, as they do in Scotland, or still-hunting like Theodore van Dyke. In Europe, red stag are hunted two ways: either from a stand, or by driving. Often, shooting from a *hochsitz*, the stags emerge near or even after dark. Rifle weight hardly matters in a stand, and scopes need to be huge to work in low light. But look at how most whitetails are hunted in the US today: from stands, at dawn and dusk. And what scopes are most popular? The big European glass. There are farms and preserves where whitetails are raised like pedigreed beef cattle, with herd sires and offspring limited to this paddock or that, and the chance to shoot one of the offspring marketed like a stud book, with prices to match. And the celebrated "beanfield" hunting of the deep South, made famous in the 1980s by Kenny Jarrett and his rifles? It could as easily be in the sprawling farmlands of Silesia as in South Carolina.

Realistically, as the years go by, there will be more such hunting, not less. As for traditional means, such as the venerated Rocky Mountain pack trip on horseback, that is disappearing fast. With horseback hunting no longer a major market, how many riflemakers are going to pay much attention to what works in a saddle scabbard and what doesn't? That used to be a major consideration. Now, where can you even buy traditional saddle scabbards?

One of the inevitable results of mass production, albeit unintentional, is the transformation of objects from prized possessions, to be handed down from one generation to the next, to mere commodities to be bought, used, then thrown away if they break down or something newer comes along. Whether hunting rifles will ever reach a stage of disposability like cell phones or laptop computers is a question no one can really answer. However, the signs are not promising.

Much so-called "custom" riflemaking today consists of merely bolting together a collection of manufactured parts, like plastic stocks, different barrels, or interchangeable scopes. What happens when a particular part is no longer available? A Holland & Holland double rifle can be kept shooting as long as there is one man with knowledge of metallurgy and skill with a file. But what about the Ruger 77/357 mentioned above? Suppose you lose the detachable magazine, and

can't find a replacement? It combines steel alloy and polymer parts that would be almost impossible to make. A polymer magazine may be virtually unbreakable, but it can still be lost or stolen, and then what do you do? Similarly, I would hate to ask even the most skilled gunmaker to try to make a replacement part for a Blaser R8.

Finally, there is the question of demand. Many observers today point to the habits of teenagers and decry the future of everything from printed magazines to tailor-made suits to fine shotguns. Fortunately for us all, nothing in the world was based on my own preferences as a teenager, most of which I grew out of. Like reading great literature, listening to classical music, and wearing tailored suits, shooting a fine shotgun is something you grow into.

Just as we have to hope that at least a minimal percentage of teenagers will develop a love of reading and appreciation for the feel of a tailored suit, we also have to hope they will develop a sense of hunting ethics, a regard for game animals, and esteem for fine traditional hunting rifles.

* * *

If the Ruger Model 77 Hawkeye FTW Hunter is the mainstream way of the future for hunting rifles, things are not looking too bad.

BIBLIOGRAPHY

Barnes, Frank C. *Cartridges of the World*. The Gun Digest Co., 1965 [and subsequent editions].

Booth, Martin. *Carpet Sahib*. London: Constable & Co., 1986.

Burrard, Major Sir Gerald, Bt., DSO. *Notes on Sporting Rifles*. 2nd ed. London: Edward Arnold & Co., 1925.

Carmichel, Jim. *Jim Carmichel's Book of the Rifle*. Outdoor Life Books, 1985.

——*The Modern Rifle*. The Winchester Press, 1975.

——, ed. *Outdoor Life Guns and Shooting Yearbook*. 1985–1990.

Dallas, Donald. *Alexander Henry, Rifle Maker*. Quiller Press, 2017.

——*The British Sporting Gun and Rifle—The Pursuit of Perfection, 1850-1900*. Quiller Press, 2008.

——*Holland & Holland—The 'Royal' Gunmaker*. Quiller Press, 2003.

——*Purdey, The Definitive History*. Quiller Press, 2000.

Foral, Jim. "The Model 1910 Ross: 'The Best Rifle in the World'." In *Gun Digest*, 56th ed., edited by Ken Ramage. Krause Publications, 2002.

Haas, Frank de. *Bolt Action Rifles*. 2nd rev. ed. DBI Books, 1984.

Kimmel, Jay, ed. *Savage & Stevens Arms, A Collector's History*. Self-published, Corystevens Publishing, 1990.

McBride, Herbert W. *A Rifleman Went to War*. Small-Arms Technical Publishing Co., 1935.

Murray, Douglas P. *The Ninety-Nine, a History of the Savage Model 99 Rifle*. Printed by the author, 1985.

Nesbitt, Mike. "Savage Featherweights." *Guns*, February 1987.

O'Connor, Jack. *The Big-Game Rifle*. New York: Alfred A. Knopf, 1952.

——*The Hunting Rifle*. New York: Winchester Press, 1970.

——*The Rifle Book*. 2nd rev. ed. New York: Alfred A. Knopf, 1973.

——*Sheep and Sheep Hunting*. New York: Winchester Press, 1974.

Olson, Ludwig. "Alvin Linden, Dean of Stockmakers." In *G&S Yearbook*, 1987 [first printed in *Rifle*].

——*Mauser Bolt Rifles*. F. Brownell & Son, Publishers, Inc., 1976 [and subsequent editions].

Petrov, Michael. *Custom Gunmakers of the 20th Century*. 2 vols. Precision Shooting, Inc., 1985–2013.

Phillips, Roger F., Dupuis, François J., and Chadwick, John A. *The Ross Rifle Story*. The Casket Publishing, 1984.

Rose, R. N., ed. *The Field 1853-1953*. London: Michael Joseph, 1953.

Scott, Sir Walter. *The Lady of the Lake*. 1810.

Sharpe, Philip B. *Complete Guide to Handloading*. 3rd ed. Funk & Wagnalls Co., 1953.

——"Halger and His Rifles," In *Gun Digest*, edited by John T. Amber. 7th ed. Gun Digest Company: 1953.

——*Philip B. Sharpe Papers*, Adams County Historical Society, Gettysburg, PA.

——*The Rifle in America*. 4th ed. Funk & Wagnalls Co., 1958.

Simmons, Dick. *Custom Built Rifles*. New York: Bonanza Books, 1955.

Smith, W. H. B. *Mannlicher Rifles and Pistols.* Stackpole, 1947.

Stent, H. V. "Sir Charles Ross: His Controversial Rifles and Cartridges" In *G&S Yearbook*, 1987 [first printed in *Rifle*].

Stroebel, Nick. *Old Gunsights, A Collector's Guide, 1850–1965.* Iola, WI: Krause Publications, 1998.

Taylor, John "Pondoro." *African Rifles and Cartridges.* Stackpole, 1948.

——*Big Game and Big Game Rifles.* London: Herbert Jenkins, 1948.

Turpin, Tom. *Modern Custom Guns.* Iola, WI: Krause Publications, 1997.

Van Dyke, Theodore Strong. *The Still Hunter.* 1882.

Wales, Lawrence. *The Newton Rifle.* 2nd ed. Self-published, 2015.

Walsh, J. H. ("Stonehenge"). "The Sporting Rifle, Match Rifle & Revolver." Vol. 2 of *The Modern Sportsman's Gun & Rifle.* London, 1884.

Wieland, Terry. *Dangerous-Game Rifles.* 2nd rev. ed. Shooting Sportsman Books, 2009.

Wilson, R. L. *Winchester—An American Legend.* Chartwell Books, 1991 & 2004.

INDEX

Note: Page numbers in italics refer to figures.